Brains / Practices / Relativism

BRAINS/ PRACTICES/ RELATIVISM

SOCIAL THEORY AFTER COGNITIVE SCIENCE

STEPHEN TURNER

THE UNIVERSITY OF CHICAGO PRESS / CHICAGO AND LONDON

Stephen Turner is graduate research professor and chair of the Department of Philosophy at the University of South Florida. He has written or edited fourteen books in various areas of the philosophy of social science and the history of social thought, the most recent being *The Cambridge Companion to Weber.* In addition, he has contributed to many reference sources, among them the *Routledge Encyclopedia of Philosophy* and *Cambridge History of Science,* and has published scores of articles.

The University of Chicago Press, Chicago 60637
The University of Chicago Press, Ltd., London
© 2002 by The University of Chicago
All rights reserved. Published 2002
Printed in the United States of America
11 10 09 08 07 06 05 04 03 02   1 2 3 4 5
ISBN: 0-226-81739-3 (cloth)
ISBN: 0-226-81740-7 (paper)

Library of Congress Cataloging-in-Publication Data

Turner, Stephen P., 1951–
  Brains/practices/relativism : social theory after cognitive science / Stephen Turner.
    p. cm.
  Includes bibliographical references and index.
  ISBN 0-226-81739-3 (cloth : alk. paper) — ISBN 0-226-81740-7 (paper : alk. paper)
    1. Practice (Philosophy)   I. Title.

  B831.3 .T86 2002
  301'.01—dc21

                                                        2001037609

For Evan Wills Turner

CONTENTS

ACKNOWLEDGMENTS

"Throwing Out the Tacit Rule Book: Learning and Practices" appears in *The Practice Turn in Contemporary Theory,* edited by Theodore R. Schatzi, Karin Knorr-Cetina, and Eike von Savigny. Copyright 2001 Routledge, London. Reprinted by permission. "Searle's Social Reality" first appeared in *History and Theory* 38, no. 2 (1999): 211–31. "Imitation or the Internalization of Norms: Is Twentieth-Century Social Theory Based on the Wrong Choice?" was first published in *Empathy and Agency,* edited by Hans Herbert Kogler and Karsten R. Steuber, 103–18. Copyright © 1999 by Westview Press, Inc. Reprinted by permission of Westview Press, a member of Perseus Books, L.L.C.

"The Limits of Social Constructionism" was originally published in *The Politics of Constructionism,* edited by Irving Velody and Robin Williams, 109–20. Copyright © 1998 by Sage Publications, Thousand Oaks, California, and London. Reprinted by permission of Sage Publications. "Making Normative Soup out of Nonnormative Bones" was first published in *What Is Sociological Theory? The Philosophical Debates,* edited by Alan Sica, 118–44. Copyright 1998 Blackwell Publishers, Oxford. Reprinted by permission.

"Teaching Subtlety of Thought: The Lessons of 'Contextualism'" appeared in *Argumentation* 15, no. 1 (2001): 77–95. Copyright 2001 by Kluwer Academic Publishers B.V. Reprinted by permission. "Practice in Real Time" is reprinted from *Studies in the History and Philosophy of Science* 30, no. 1 (1999): 149–56. Copyright 1999, with permission of Elsevier Science. "The Significance of Shils" first appeared in *Sociological Theory* 17, no. 2:125–45. Copyright 1999, The American Sociological Association. Reprinted by permission.

INTRODUCTION /
SOCIAL THEORY AFTER COGNITIVE SCIENCE /

My purpose in collecting these essays is to pursue what I believe to be the central challenge for social theory today: a revised understanding of a great many of our core concepts in light of the lessons and implications of cognitive science, especially connectionism. Connectionism, as Paul Churchland explains, assumes "that humans are multilayered neural networks that learn, under the continuing pressure of experience, by the gradual modifications of the strengths or 'weights' of their myriad synaptic connections." The key implication of this for my purposes is that these gradual modifications mean that every mind is the product of a distinctive and individual learning history (Churchland 2000, 151). This point is very important for social theory, for reasons that will become clear in several of the chapters in this volume. The individualizing character of learning histories is a brute fact about brains that agrees with a minority tradition in social theory, and conflicts—or so I will argue—with the dominant one. Thus social theory after cognitive neuroscience will be different from social theory before it. These "social theoretical" considerations also have, I believe, a great deal of bearing on more traditionally "philosophical" matters, because they undermine the social theory that is concealed within philosophical positions.

My concern will not be with the technical details of cognitive science, though I will assume the rough truth of a certain relationship between connectionism and social theory: that connectionism is the best model for what social theory traditionally called "habit," and that there are no sufficiently plausible competitors to connectionist/habit models for explaining the "tacit" parts of culture. As it happens, this is one of the areas of cognitive science that is the most deeply grounded in studies of physical processes in the brain (cf. Jog et al. 1999). In the broadest terms, the problem that concerns me is that social theory, including its most "advanced" postmodern forms, employs or depends on the models of mental life, mostly handed down through various routes, from late nineteenth-century neo-Kantianism and involving the idea of "shared premises" that do not correspond to—and indeed conflict with—the models that presently figure in cognitive neuroscience. In these essays I concentrate on topics that lie either within or close to the intersection of philosophy and social theory, and concern the idea of culture, or practice, or worldviews, understood as collective objects. Part of what I have to say here continues the argument I presented in *The Social Theory of Practices* (1994) against what I called collective object solutions to the problem of what culture is. In that book I was careful not to wed these arguments to any particular position in cognitive science. Much of cognitive science is after all programmatic, disputed, and evolving. It would have wrongly dated the argument to link it to its most natural allies, such as connectionism, on which it did not logically depend. In this present volume I have been circumspect as well, but the papers included here run the argument the other way around, by considering the implications of cognitive science and particularly connectionism for various basic models and usages in the social sciences, such as the rules model, and by exploring implications of abandoning some of the familiar conceptual furniture of social theory. I do not pretend that this argument is complete; indeed, I suspect that in the long run a much more radical revision of such basic concepts as rationality and normativity is likely to be the inevitable outcome of our improvements in modeling the cognitive realm. But this is a beginning.

Connectionism might be wrong or might have very limited application; so might my characterization of the effect of the inputs that produce the habits that make up *habitus*. So let me be very explicit about the underlying rationale of the essays in this book. Much of what is argued in this volume is based on what might be thought of as a working hypothesis with the following elements:

1. Non-universal mental contents, and much of the universal ones, are probably acquired through learning.
2. The kinds of learning that vary "socially" are connectionist habituation.
3. Some of this—language "rules" and perhaps a few other things, such as gestures and conversational structures—may stem from a vast quantity of more or less consistent input; consequently, the acquisitions of one person are more or less the same, at least as outwardly manifested, as the acquisitions of other people. It may be convenient to represent these acquisitions as rules, but they aren't, at the mental level.
4. Much of what makes up social life for the individual involves skills and

expectations based on inputs that do not obliterate differences between the mental contents of individuals. Representing these things as rule-like is not only false, at the mental level, but seriously misleading about the nature of social life.

5. Some inputs are explicit sayings, symbols, metaphors, images, gestures, performances, accessible through the ordinary senses of people. Some occur through structured feedback resulting from rituals, disciplinings, trainings, and education. These all can be thought of as "shared" in a prosaic sense. But as Margaret Mead's phrase "significant symbols" suggests, something in the way of individual mental content—"skills at interpreting," so to speak—is needed to convert what is explicit and shared, or collective, into personal mental content, lived experience, and so on.

6. Other inputs are nonexplicit: either they are "wild" rather than disciplined or trained, or they are the tacit or habitual accompaniments to training, ritual, and discipline. They may consist, for example, in expectations about the behavior and responses one acquires in interaction with others.

7. These nonexplicit acquisitions may be very important to social life. Indeed, all intentional thinking, and this includes emotional responses as well as conscious problem solving, depends on the operation of mechanisms acquired by habituation. But it is a mistake to "collectivize" them as "shared tacit knowledge" or practice in the sense of a collective object possessed by members of a group. There is no way for such a hypothesized object to be acquired by the individuals in whom it is supposed to operate.

Of these basic ideas, it should be noted that the connectionism of the argument is not critical to it, in the sense that a symbolic, processing, "rule"-oriented Turing-Chomsky model of cognitive processes that recognizes the differentiating consequences of experience would also fit the argument. And indeed, in chapter 3 I give some reasons for thinking that another universalizing cognitive science account, in this case of knowledge of other minds, the "theory theory," also conflicts with the standard Geertzian model of culture. But there is a link to connectionism: if the relevant processes are connectionist in character, and the present understanding of these processes is largely correct, it would be difficult to square with the neo-Kantian "shared premises" inheritance of much social theory; thus the inheritance has to be given up. The concern of the book is to elaborate this thought.

WHY IT MATTERS: THEORETICAL OBJECTS IN SOCIAL SCIENCE AFTER COGNITIVE SCIENCE

Why should it matter to social science or social theory that, say, a study of rats running mazes shows that "large numbers of units in the sensorimotor striatum were newly recruited to respond to some aspect of the task, most of the units came to have multievent response profiles, and the entire pattern of re-sponsivity of the active striatal neurons changed" (Jog et al. 1999, 1746)? What is the methodological issue here? Can we just treat these as interesting but ir-relevant findings from a different field? On the surface, of course, there is no relevance. But if this is an accurate account, at the neuronal level, of what a habit is, it can be relevant. Social theory uses the concept of habit, and con-cepts such as practice and culture that depend on the concept of habit. If ac-quiring a culture consists in reorganizing neuronal patterns, it may very well be that some concepts of culture turn out to fit badly with what we have come to understand about these brain processes, and others fit better.

Attitude is a concept that has already been rethought in these terms, and the history of the concept indicates the kind of issue that is likely to arise with other scientific concepts. Indeed, for some odd reasons rooted in the specific history of the concept itself, it is especially relevant to our purposes here. By 1935 Gordon Allport could identify a vast number of different usages, based on the notion of "a neuropsychic state of readiness for mental and physical ac-tivity" ([1935] 1967, 799). Attitudes were contrasted with states of conscious-ness, and became important in the struggle against introspectionism as an ex-ample of an experimentally detectable phenomenon at least partly beyond the reach of consciousness.

In social theory, the concept had emerged in connection with the problem of the relation between the individual and society. In his methodological note to *The Polish Peasant in Europe and America* (1918–20), W. I. Thomas formu-lated the concept in terms of the problem of the causal relations between val-ues, the objective or publicly accepted reasons for action, and attitudes, which are subjective, private, or individual. He gives the example of the truthfulness of legal testimony. Truth telling in court is a public value. But the attitude of the Polish peasant is that judicial proceedings are combat, in which solidarity with one's family is foremost, and this attitude leads him to lie. "People tell the truth in court," consequently, is a bad behavioral theory. A good theory would need to account for the values and the attitudes that produce behavior in ac-cord with the value as well as behavior opposed to it. The missing element in commonsense generalizations, which use a reason to explain an action, is the attitude—which, Thomas argues, is to be found only in the individual (Thomas and Znaniecki 1918–20, 61).[1] The decisive fact about attitudes is that although they are partly caused by values, by which it is important to note

1. Thomas concluded that a true science would perhaps best proceed by discarding com-monsense generalizations in favor of attitude explanations, or more precisely in terms of a three-element model which included value, individual attitude, and the act, plus the causal relations of values interacting with other values, and attitudes with other attitudes, as well as of values infl-uencing attitudes and attitudes influencing values. Thomas contrasted his views with Durkheim's idea of a collective consciousness, treating Durkheim as attempting to reduce explanation of so-cial facts to what Thomas calls "values" (Thomas and Znaniecki 1918–20, 44 n. 1).

that Thomas means explicitly uttered things such as the law, each individual reacts differently to this cause.

The recording, study, and testing and measuring of attitudes quickly left those distinctions behind. Writers such as Donald Campbell argued that values *were* attitudes, so the previous distinctions among beliefs, intentions, values, habits, and preferences broke down, and all of these came to be seen as manifestations of attitudes. During the twenties and thirties, driven in part by the technology of pencil-and-paper attitude tests (Thurstone 1928), empirical results, together with issues concerning what exactly they measured, proliferated. The concept became central to, and for a while virtually the whole of, social psychology. The concept, however, was methodologically puzzling. What were attitudes? Real mental entities? Real because they predicted? In the end, attitudes were conceived of as latent structures with distinct mathematical properties, with which measures of attitudes were understood to be more or less isomorphic, and whose reality was shown indirectly by the predictive relations among the various tests. As mental objects, they were understood as minidispositions, and the theoretical problems they presented lay in understanding their mutual relations at the psychological level. But as McGuire observed in a key review article at the end of the sixties, none of the major approaches to the central problems of the relations between attitudes "seems to have a great deal of empirical validity" (1969, 271).[2]

In recent work, the analytic autonomy of attitudes—the idea that attitudes are mental objects having various properties that can be theorized about—has been undermined by cognitive science, and it has been argued that "attitudes" are better thought of as nodes in connectionist learning networks. What is the methodological significance of such claims? The significance becomes clear when we consider the argument that attitudes are real in the sense that they are mathematically isomorphic with the structure of predictively useful measurements (leaving aside the fact that the predictive utility was "situational" and attitudes never rose to the level of a coherent model of mental life).[3]

2. The nub of the problem was the gap between attitudes and behavior. Later psychologists came to argue that this gap was a result of "situational" conditions for the expression of attitudes in action, and since "situations" typically supplied reasons for not acting on attitudes, or on acting in particular ways, this suggested that reasons played a large role in explaining what people do. This change became explicit in Azjen and Fishbein's "theory of reasoned action." The authors made the point that people often arrived at their attitudes by reasoning, especially by thinking about the consequences of behavior prior to being faced with opportunities to act (1980). They used the language of reasons and intentions, treating them as autonomous from attitudes, and treating attitudes as a codeterminant, with reasons, of intentions. Ironically, this marked a reversion to a model like Thomas's, and implicitly rejected Campbell's reduction of values to attitudes. But from the point of view of the present discussion it represented an attempt to remain with the concepts of ordinary language rather than to replace them.

3. This effort is summarized in Eliot R. Smith's *Handbook of Social Psychology* article (1998, 393–402; cf. also 402–35).

What disappears, once we have evidence about what is inside the black box of cognitive process, is the "realistic" notion of an attitude as an independent entity. The whole machinery for justifying the reality of attitudes, the whole business of validating measurements in order to validate claims about the reality of the things measured, also disappears. Why is it no longer necessary? The situation, to put it simply, is comparable to the situation of the child who has a theory about how clocks work, but no knowledge of the mechanism of a clock. One can imagine constructing robust, predictive, and refined models of the internal works of a clock on the basis of its outputs. But if one is then presented with evidence about the mechanism that established that the clock has moving parts, one of which is a balance wheel, these theories would need to be revised: no amount of predictive power, simplicity, or whatever would make the part irrelevant. The theoretical concepts are putatively real, and their hold on reality depends entirely on their predictive success, but the part is prosaically real. Prosaic reality "wins" in the sense that it has to be taken into account, whereas only the supposed manifestations and indicators of the theoretical concept need to be taken into account. To the extent that we take mechanisms like nodes and links to be prosaically real facts about the brain, they are not merely rival theories, but privileged parts of the topic. The privilege here is not so difficult to explain.

Consider a quite different case, from the history of medicine: the discovery of the cholera flux, the mechanism for the transmission of cholera in water. Before John Snow it was supposed, on the basis of statistical evidence, that cholera was transmitted by air, miasmatically. People who lived at higher elevations, when other differences were controlled by a natural experiment, were much less likely to succumb. When Snow established one different mechanism, namely something that could be isolated in water, the miasmatic theory was not refuted—both could have been true. But the miasmatic model was in big trouble and soon succumbed. Why? It was not easily refutable as a *possible* alternative mechanism, and there were those endless statistics that seemed to support it.

The story is a long one, but the bottom line is this: salvaging the idea of an alternative mechanism of transmission became much tougher as a result of Snow's discovery. It was not simply that the new evidence excluded the mechanism of miasmatic transmission: it did not, directly. But indirectly it eventually did, simply by raising the degree of complexity of the problem that the miasmatic theory had to solve to remain *at all* in the running as an account of the transmission of cholera. And these problems are analogous to the problem of salvaging the traditional concept of attitude.

What sort of new complexity is there? In the first place, one needs to account for the relations between the two types of mechanism. In the case of cholera flux, one of Snow's important results was to show that it was soluble in water but also heavier; therefore it settled. To square this with the miasmatic hypothesis would require increasingly complex and fantastical auxiliary hypotheses—that this heavy stuff nevertheless floated in air; that there were two kinds of cholera material, one heavy and one light; that the one might transform into the other, so that the difference was undetectable at the level of symptoms; and so forth. Not surprisingly, the defenders of the miasmatic model quickly gave up as new evidence made the burden of inventing new auxiliary hypotheses too heavy.

"Attitude" is a theoretical concept. Reasoning about it involves an inference to its existence from the evidence of prediction derived from measures with a given structure. This is a very restricted situation, like the restricted data situation of statistical observation alone that favored the miasmatic hypothesis. When we have something more to define the situation, such as evidence about what is in the black box of mental processes, the situation, and consequently the demands, changes. What was a simple hypothesis now must become a complex hypothesis.

Other social science theoretical concepts, of which practices is an example, are subject to the same discipline. One commentator on *The Social Theory of Practices* ridicules what he wrongly thought to be the claim of the book: that a thinker like Pierre Bourdieu was obliged to produce a "complete psychological theory capable of accounting for the transmission of *habitus*" (Gross 1998, 127). Actually, the claim was rather different: Bourdieu's account ought to be consistent with a conceivable set of mechanisms. The book demonstrates the difficulty of this task: the recognition that at least some significant subset of the cognitive processes that work to produce *habitus* are connectionist poses the same problem for *habitus* as for attitudes. If connectionist learning—with fairly rough, diverse inputs that fail to obliterate difference—is part of the mechanism, and is the only mechanism with a reasonable claim to fit the observed facts that Bourdieu supposes to be the manifestations of practice, the situation changes. Bourdieu can either reconcile this mechanism with his own account, for example by claiming, as with cholera, that these are dual mechanisms, or give up his account. Perhaps it is true that there are multiple mechanisms, for example in relation to language. But for Bourdieu to avail himself of these hypothesized mechanisms he would need to greatly complicate his argument. To do otherwise would be to say, "I don't care how brains work; I am concerned with 'reality' in my own special sense." This is the path of spiritualism.

This dismissal, however, is a bit too simple. There is a legitimate problem here, bearing on an important complex of dualities having to do with mind and body, "spiritual" and physical, and particularly with the status of ordinary-language mental concepts. Philosophers of cognitive science have come to call these concepts "folk psychology." The legitimate issue is this: folk psychology is not merely a "good bad theory," a useful but wrong account of mental life. Ordinary language, of which this is a part, is constitutive of the objects of explanation in social science, and this relationship, as Max Weber famously insisted, continues to define the problems of social science—regardless of how far "science," with its distinctive concepts, advances. The problem holds for the mind/body problem as well: defining the abnormalities to be explained by neurological explanations, for example, requires ordinary-language "reasons" terms (Huff and Turner 1981).

Hence social science concepts have a peculiar status here, one that is worth discussing before taking up the central issue of concepts in the practices family. Social science concepts are dependent, in various ways, on the preconstitution of their objects in ordinary language. Concepts such as attitudes are constructed on the basis of our "lay," or, as ethnomethodologists say, "members" knowledge. In a sense, these concepts can never shed this dependence. However clever your measure of an attitude is, you need to know whether the terms mean what they meant in their original setting when you apply them in a new setting. It is well known that Germans and Americans respond differently to questions about how many friends they have; it is also well known that the terms mean different things to them. If you don't know this, you can't tell whether your predictive results fit with your previous results, whether a statistical difference is meaningful, and what it means. And there are many other aspects of dependence—so many that there has been a strong current in philosophy of social science since Peter Winch, and in sociology since Aaron Cicourel and Harold Garfinkel, of thinking that social science can never really get beyond the investigation of these constitutive concepts.[4]

But concepts like practices and attitudes are *secondary* concepts. They depend on the prior constitution of objects, in ordinary language, but don't do the constituting work on their own. So even if we are stuck with the job of accommodating to folk psychology, or to the mind/body problem in its various forms, we are not stuck with the job of accommodating to concepts like attitudes, practices, culture, society, and so on, except, so to speak, as "folk social theory"—in other words, as part of ordinary language. As theoretical concepts, these terms are perfectly appropriate candidates for the most drastic

---

4. A. R. Louch, for example, argued that the general notions of sociology themselves depended on the logical relations between the ordinary meanings of the terms (Louch 1966). This argument referred to theories that are no longer discussed. But there is a broader point to be made along these lines. It is undeniable that the major concern of social theorists from Althusser to Habermas has been with the changing application of social, political, and economic concepts. Indeed, in a sense, the central problem of social theory has been to argue about the applicability of the standard concepts of liberalism—the individual, freedom, human nature, and so on—typically dividing between those who say that they no longer apply or never applied, and those who agree with this but who argue that liberalism can be understood differently, in better terms, such as the concept of a tradition of civility (discussed in chapter 9).

sort of elimination. To be sure, the line between lay and scientific concepts is hazy. But as "social and behavioral science" concepts they are in play: they need to survive competition with alternative explanations, and are subject to the problem discussed above, of theoretical complication in the face of new evidence about the causal world.

THE CENTRALITY OF PRACTICES

Inevitably the focus of a discussion of this sort will involve the concept of practices, or rather two large families of concepts, one comprising notions such as frames, worldviews, and paradigms, and the other including *habitus*, embodied knowledge, skills, and mores, among other things. The problem of what all these things are is taken up in various ways throughout this volume, so I will not attempt an overview here. But a brief discussion of the problem of practices and its various solutions is necessary to understand the issue as I discussed it in *The Social Theory of Practices*, and as it has evolved since then.

Begin with a box:

SOCIAL

COGNITIVE/SOCIAL

paradigms, *Weltanschauungen*, presuppositions, structures of consciousness or meaning, collective consciousness, systems of collective representations, tacit knowledge, the 'rules' model in conversational analysis, the Searle of *Speech Acts*, etc.

SUBCOGNITIVE/SOCIAL

skills, *habitus*, *mores*, "forms of life" and life-world, etc. conceived as "collective" (perhaps tradition in an Oakeshottian sense, probably in Shils's sense), Kripke's rules, collective intentions

NONSOCIAL

COGNITIVE/NONSOCIAL

artificial intelligence rule and symbolic representational model without sharing of rules

SUBCOGNITIVE/NONSOCIAL

habits, skills, etc. as the "tacit" part of an ensemble in which there are explicit parts (activities, rituals, performances, etc.) to which the individual adjusts.

The social/nonsocial divide refers to what can be thought of as location, whether a practice or worldview is understood to be located in some sort of supraindividual place, such as "the social," or is no more than what exists within individual brains and bodies. A Kuhnian paradigm, presumably, is social and cognitive, because it is "shared" rather than individual, and because it consists of something like beliefs or premises, or frameworks for seeing that are understood more or less on the model of premises. These distinctions are not very precise, it must be said, and in many settings not much hinges on separating, say, skills from beliefs. The families are closely related. But there are characteristically different emphases.

The "cognitive" family employs notions such as rule, premise, structure of consciousness, collective representations, tacit knowledge, and so forth that involve close analogies with what can be directly articulated as rules, propositions, and so forth. What I am calling the subcognitive, or "skills," family emphasizes the nonarticulable, that which may be indicated explicitly, such as the "judicial sense" of a good judge, but cannot usefully be described in terms of rules. One way of drawing this distinction is between propositional and nonpropositional knowledge (cf. D. Smith 1996). The distinction between the two forms of nonsocial cognition will not concern me here, but as I have said, it would be possible to reach much the same results as I reach in this book from a symbolic processing starting point as well.[5]

The most common and familiar usages in both branches of the practice family are social rather than individual. It is essential to the argument of Bourdieu, for example, that individual properties, such as dispositions, are constituted or produced by collective processes. One can quibble endlessly about what all these terms mean, but the basic point is this: practices have both a causal primacy and a kind of autonomy in relation to the individual, what Émile Durkheim called externality. There are, however, those who seem to reject this kind of objectification of collective notions who nevertheless also seek to employ notions like tradition and skill, and who also accord the "tacit" a large and significant role, such as Michael Oakeshott or Michael Polanyi. In these cases there is often a question of how, or whether, they avoid a collectivized or supraindividual concept: in designating something like a tradition as a continuing phenomenon, it might seem, one necessarily makes "it" supraindividual. But it can be argued that what appears to be supraindividual continuity is in fact fully comprehensible and explicable without giving it the kind of autonomous status and causal or constitutive power granted it in the more common usages.

The box indicates a set of possible solutions to a fairly common explanatory problem, but not the whole set. There are some "outside-the-box" solutions, as well as denials of the problem itself. Before turning to these, it will be useful to consider some of the inside-the-box issues that the outside-the box-solutions are attempting to avoid, and to explain, briefly, the argument of *The*

5. One reviewer of *The Social Theory of Practices* took the view that the problem of norm identifying that figured in the book—the fact that people need to have cognitive or subcognitive access to the rules they were supposed to be following—could be resolved by supposing in essence that people were endowed with little search engines (presumably based on symbolic processing or rules) for identifying them. The problem with this solution is that the results would be, from what we know about social life, greatly underdetermined. To put it differently, the search engines for the tacit social rules in situation X would produce lots of matches, and different ones depending on how the search was framed. So the result would be the same.

Social Theory of Practices. The first issue has to do with psychological agency, which is a problem especially for supraindividual accounts. Actions are individual and so are brains, so there must be some individual psychological processes through which the objects—such as practices—operate. This relation may be as simple as the following: language is a real substantive normative structure beyond individuals that individuals internalize or habituate in order to speak, form verbal thoughts, and the like. "Internalization" and "habit" are nevertheless facts about the individual language user in whom something must happen. So the structure is not causally autonomous in its operations, nor does it exist in a different collective dimension, or in an unrelated category of reality, of spirit.

The second issue is the problem of continuity or identity, which is a problem especially for individual accounts. Whatever a tradition is, it cannot exist solely in the individual, because the individual dies. There is no direct continuity from brain to brain or mind to mind—only continuity mediated by speech, objects, and activities. But a tradition seems to be something more than the sum of such parts. Or is it?

The Social Theory of Practices was concerned with the solutions to these theoretical problems inside the box. It argued against the social, or "shared," solutions. To say that people "share" presuppositions or practices means that they have the *same* presuppositions or practices. The usual argument for this is transcendental: people do something, such as communicate; they could not communicate unless they shared the same framework; therefore they share the same framework. This argument, which shows its neo-Kantian origins, mimics a standard strategy used by Polanyi and many others to argue that explicit rules are never sufficient and need to be supplemented by something tacit. But the argument that something extra (and tacit) is needed to explain, for example, communication or scientific discovery, *is not the same* as the argument for a shared framework or for the possession of the same practices. The argument for "sharing" or sameness requires us to believe that there is some mechanism by which the same rules, presuppositions, or practices get into the heads of different people. But if we consider the various possible strategies for solving this problem of transmission, we soon see that it is insurmountable. The claim that the *same* practices, presuppositions, and the like get into the heads of many people requires a means of transmission that is little short of magical.

The details of this argument are too complex to repeat here, but the point may be seen in a simple consideration. Ordinary communication is difficult, even if we use the full range of available explicit language, as anyone who has tried to write an instruction manual knows. One version of the tacit-knowledge hypothesis, which I attack, makes the following astounding assumption: that people can (and routinely do) obtain perfect reproductions of the tacit possessions of others. In other words, people "share" extremely complex common frameworks. Moreover, somehow they acquire these frameworks through means that are radically less error prone than ordinary explicit communication is. Indeed, to really share they must be error free. The means in question must be much more effective than ordinary "training," which is, of course, imperfect. My questions related to these hypothesized means, and I concluded that they were phantasms: that acquiring the tacit possessions that people need is an imperfect, traininglike process that could not guarantee that people would "share" anything tacit, but could only, like training at its most successful, assure that people had certain habituated capacities to perform. Training of this sort only affects external similarities of performance; it tells us nothing about sameness of tacit possessions. Learning "from experience" is likely to produce an even greater diversity than formal training.

The "habituation" alternative to "sharing," once we look carefully, seems to accord better with what we know about the causal processes that actually operate in the world and with the known facts that practice theories purport to explain. This alternative account of what is going on when people learn to communicate, make scientific discoveries, and so forth, is more plausible as an explanation because it does not appeal to any quasi-magical processes of transmission. Individual habituation (with the term being broadly construed to include all acquired learning that is tacit), I argued, does explain the same things, and we can even make some sense of such mysterious things as our common feelings by reference to the role of rituals and performances in inducing habits. This approach inverts the usual explanation of a tradition, for example, not by saying that its rituals are performed because people share a common framework, but by saying instead that rituals are behavioral technologies that produce a certain uniformity of habits—a uniformity, however, that is literally superficial, a matter of external similarity, with internal or personal consequences that vary from individual to individual. For example, prayer has effects on those who pray, but the effects vary from person to person.

My way of thinking about this problem is summed up in the slogan I used at the end of the book, which revised Stanley Cavell's famous saying "We learn language and the world together," by which he meant that the processes of learning the one are inseparable from the processes of learning the other. I said that we should add to this that "[n]ot only do we learn language and the world together, at the same time as we learn them we acquire habits that enable us to be more or less proficient in using both language and the world" (Turner 1994, 121). By this I meant that the processes of learning "objective," explicit, or public things were inseparable from tacit processes of habituation. My point was that the feedback mechanisms of experience that produce habituation are personal, or individual, but at the same time bound up with learning an idiom and experiencing the world.

Something important, however, does get lost in this argument, and lost on purpose. There is no place in this model for a notion of hidden purpose or collective purpose, such as Bourdieu claims to find when he theorizes that the practices of various dominant social groups "accumulate cultural capital." This is not the place to discuss whether this is seriously meant by him as a teleological account in which practices not only serve purposes but are actually manifestations of a kind of intentional behavior or "logic of domination." Suffice it to say that many users of the concept of practices and its variants have such a notion, and this is part of its appeal. There is, however, an objection, nicely formulated by Jon Elster, that I consider fatal to such theories. Elster says, essentially, that to have a notion of purpose, it is a minimal requirement that some sort of feedback mechanism exist by which the activity in question can be modified as a result of changes in circumstances in accordance with the purposes (Elster 1983, 105–7).

Without a feedback mechanism, Elster suggests, there is nothing to the notion of purpose, at least in the sense of a purpose that has effects on, and guides, behavior. If I have a thermostat on my air conditioner, it might be said that the thermostat has the purpose of regulating a temperature and acts to switch the power on and off in accordance with this purpose. But thermostats have feedback mechanisms. They are connected to thermometers. The thermometers feed back to the switching mechanism when the temperature reaches a particular point in a range. Arguably, of course, such mechanisms can be characterized entirely in causal terms. But having a feedback mechanism is, so to speak, an essential condition for asserting that something has an inherent purpose or a purpose of the sort that practices are supposed to have, that is, one that guides what people do. The problem this creates for these practice theories will be discussed shortly.

OUTSIDE-THE-BOX SOLUTIONS

The arguments of *The Social Theory of Practices*, I think, are fatal to the shared, or "social," solutions, or at least to the standard ones. They favor the "individual" solutions. But there are some solutions seemingly "outside the box" that deserve serious consideration as well. One possible outside-the-box approach to these problems is to simply reject the idea that *practice* is a term with any cognitive or psychological implications, and to identify continuities elsewhere. Typically this involves the idea that a practice is an appeal to an ensemble of some kind, involving objects, activities, and so forth. Andrew Pickering has pioneered this approach, and it has some obvious attractions. If a practice is simply an assemblage of objects that people employ, that has no inner directionality, then there is no problem of understanding its inner directionality or psychology. Continuity is simply a matter of the fact that people use or extend the use of the same assemblage of objects, or even vary the assemblage by replacing one object with another without replacing them all.

This argument is discussed in chapter 8, but it should be noted here that despite my critical comments on it, it obviously points to an important feature of the *sociology* of practices, which is that they are often carried on around physical objects whose diffusion requires people to develop skills, habits, and other means to adapt to them. Thus the riding of horses by American Indians was certainly skilled, but perhaps owed little or nothing to European equestrian traditions, theories, and so forth. It was nevertheless a "practice," and whether anything were borrowed along with the horses themselves from these European sources hardly matters much. The horse allowed for a new style of life, new modes of warfare, consumption, and residence: a new culture. So one is tempted to get rid of the "allowed for a new culture" and just say, as Andrew Pickering does, that the machine consisting of the people and the objects— this cyborg—is all there is to the practice. His concern is primarily science, but the point may be generalized to the problem of the way of life of the horse-riding Indians. In its negative form, it is this: nothing in the way of special mental content, collective or individual, is essential to the notion of practice, or for that matter "culture." In its positive form, it is this: practices, cultures, and so on are ensembles, with no essence, whose elements change over time, but that persist or have continuity by virtue of, and only by virtue of, the persistence of the elements themselves.

Pickering's argument points to a key idea about which we agree, but which is emphasized differently in our arguments. Since this idea has something important and problematic in common with a large number of other conceptions, such as the idea that practice can be collapsed into *Dasein*, it is important to make the relationship clear. As I suggest, the difference between Pickering's conception and mine is that for me there are mental elements, including both nontacit things, such as articulated theories and ideas, and tacit things, which I understand as individual habits, that are part of a "practice." The issue, in part, is whether these mental elements should or should not be considered part of the ensemble. The issue can be seen a little more clearly with another outside-the box-solution, with some similarities to Pickering's, of assimilating the notion of practice to the lifeworld, Heidegger's *Dasein* (Cf. Stern 2000).

We can think of ensemble notions of practice, my own version of which I will discuss shortly in somewhat greater detail, as being of two basic types. Since the two types correspond to the individual and social side of the solutions in the boxes, it is not clear that they escape the box after all. The difference is in the type of glue that is thought to bind the ensemble, to make it into an ensemble in the first place. Is there something collectively mental that is a kind of glue that holds the ensemble together? *Dasein* can be thought of either as experience governed by shared mental content, such as shared tacit modes of apprehension of the world, or as a common world that is shared yet is apprehended by each of us in our own way, the product of our distinctive histories and bodies. The motivation for having something "shared" in these arguments is to have something serve as the ensemble's binding agent.

The notion that practice is equivalent to *Dasein* provides a clear illustration of the issue. One way of taking this line of reasoning might be that the ensemble of objects and people, relationships, and so forth that make up *Dasein* or the lifeworld are simply objects, relations, people, and so forth, as seen from the point of view of ordinary lived experience. There is nothing intrinsically "social" or "collective" in this notion of *Dasein*. However, if one wishes to make the further claim that there is some sort of mode of taking or apprehending objects that is common to people within a lifeworld, that is a collective mental notion essentially like that of practice itself, it is open to all of the objections formulated in *The Social Theory of Practices*.

The same problem arises in a more complex form in feminist theory in relation to the concept of a standpoint. Some feminist epistemologists have, or at least have articulated to me, a view of standpoint theory that is, so to speak, purely informational. The epistemic advantages of the oppressed, in their view, arise from the fact that the oppressed have access to information that the oppressor does not have, and this information forms the distinctive standpoint of the members of the category oppressed or particular categories of the oppressed. This can be understood purely individually, in that each individual has access to different information by virtue of different experiences, such as being a maid, or as a result of being identified by others as and treated as members of particular categories. Nothing collective and tacit is needed here. When the people who have these experiences articulate explicit ideas about their experiences and share these explicit thoughts, we are no longer in the tacit part of the ensemble that makes for a practice but in the explicit part; thus it is possible to think of a standpoint as a practice, in the ensemble sense, without a tacit collective mental element.

How does this fit with the usual notion of a standpoint? Dorothy Smith, who uses the notion of experience, explains her position as follows: "The authority of *experience* is foundational to the women's movement (which is not to say that experience is foundational to knowledge) and has been and is at once explosive and fruitful" (1996, 394, emphasis supplied). But experience is not information. "The knowledge people have by virtue of their experience is a knowledge of the local practices of our everyday/everynight worlds. It is for the most part what Michael Polanyi calls 'tacit knowledge'—a knowing that is the very texture of our daily/nightly living in what we know how to do, how to go about things, and what we can get done" (ibid.). So standpoints have a tacit element. But tacit knowledge can be understood as "shared" or "personal" (which is Polanyi's own phrase).

Which does Smith have in mind? It turns out that tacit knowing becomes "a knowledge," which for Smith is a term analogous to "a practice" or "a worldview" when there is an *explicit* element:

> Such tacit knowing, of course, becomes a knowledge only at that point when it is entered into the language game of experience, that is, in the course of telling. For the most part, it remains the secret underpinning of everything we do. We discover it vividly as we learn from small children that they truly do not know the same world that we do or when we travel among a people whose everyday/everynight living is radically different from ours. (D. Smith 1996, 395)

Telling is making something explicit. So this secret underpinning of everything we do becomes a knowledge through a public performance. And this kind of performance is a political method for "the women's movement," which, using "its methodology of working from experience began to unearth the tacit underpinning of gender" (ibid.). So one could think that there is no collective mental content here. There is telling, the explicit, and there are private things that we "know" tacitly and sometimes can and do make into something explicit by "telling." But one might also interpret the element of tacit knowledge in a collective way, so that the element that is added here to make standpoints more than merely the product of information input and individual experience plus explicit discussion—the glue that holds this ensemble together—could be understood as a shared element that shapes experience. But in the course of becoming a "mental" element it is already becoming the subject of individual processing, and this de-collectivizes it.

THE TELOS OF PRACTICE

Other feminist authors, such as Patricia Hill Collins, explicitly emphasize the idea that standpoints are political, and arrive for us through the agency of developing a collective intention to struggle against oppressive practices (Collins 1997). This version of standpoint theory is no different from the classical Destutt de Tracy notion of ideology, namely the idea that one needs to formulate a correct collective system of ideas in order to properly understand reality and act politically, except for one important feature. The important difference is an idea that is common to many of these thinkers, figuring especially in Michel Foucault's version of practice theory. It is that the reality of dominant practices is shown by their actual power over us; this power is revealed, and reveals its properties, when we struggle against it. Practices in this sense are characteristically understood telically or purposively, as oppressive practices, which are "telic" because oppression is an intentional notion. The unbearable heaviness of practice is taken to be evidence for and of both practices and their oppressive characteristics. This is such a powerful political idea that many people have felt that to give up on this notion would be tantamount to accepting oppression.

All telic notions of practice, however, have the troubles that I pointed to earlier, and from the point of view of the argument of *The Social Theory of Practices* it is double trouble. The argument there was directed essentially at the idea that people can in effect download frameworks or practices from some collective server. The assertion was that there is reason to find completely implausible the very idea of a mechanism that downloaded the same mental contents into different minds. This is essentially similar to W. I. Thomas's point about such explicit things as laws and individual attitudes, but applied here to the supposed collective mental content of practice theories and their variants. Telic practice theories need this kind of mechanism, so this is an argument against them.

Telic practice theories, however, require something more: feedback. So there is not only a problem about the mechanism of downloading, but also an additional problem of, we might say, uploading. Information, like temperature information for a thermometer, must somehow be fed into a practice to enable the practice to keep on its oppressive course. This uploading problem is fatal, for parallel reasons. Herbert Spencer was, I think, on the right track when he said that language is the sensorium of society, an idea that John Dewey liked. But the truth in this phrase is that language and the application of terms change as situations change, not in the notion (that Dewey didn't like) of society as an organism with a sensorium. Applying words in new ways is something that individuals do and succeed in making a part of language by having what they say understood by other individuals. Socially telic arguments tend to collapse into one of the two "social" categories in the box, at least if they are sufficiently elaborated to deal with the standard questions of social theory, such as social oppression.

The reason for this is that "oppressive practices" are not the only explanation available in these cases. Consider the simple notion of a "glass ceiling." It may be that it is *as if* there were a glass ceiling. There is plenty of room for "political" condemnation of this on egalitarian grounds. To claim that there is some systematic and oppressive force is different and shifts the locus of condemnation to an anthropomorphized, intentional "it." And this "it" is the subject of, and its claim to reality depends on, an explanatory theory in which "it" works to produce the result. But the theory may be wrong. The "as if" glass ceiling may be the indirect result of many minor causes, all "individual" yet producing the same result. Struggling against "oppressive practices" in this case may simply be struggling against a phantasm. Certainly, collective struggle against a misconceived oppressive cause is not a novelty in history Revolutionary theory recognized this long ago: Georges Sorel cut the link between revolutionary ideology and truth claims with his idea of revolutionary myth, which need not be "true" to be effective. "Struggle" as such, successful or otherwise, validates nothing.

STRAW MEN AND REAL BRAINS

The Social Theory of Practices (especially as I have summarized it here) hinged on an argument about sameness. In a sense this was a very narrow and exotically "philosophical" argument. Worse, it may seem like an argument against a straw man. Who actually claims anything about the sameness of mental contents, aside from Durkheim, Sumner, and various other figures from the distant past? Couldn't it be that sophisticated versions of these theories, such as ethnomethodology, the practice theory of Bourdieu and Anthony Giddens, Foucault, or Sherry Ortner, escape entirely from this problem? Or is it the case that the problem runs through the history of social thought; that it bears on many of the contemporary covert appropriations from this tradition in contemporary philosophy, such as the notion of collective intentionality; and that the "sophisticated" variations on the concept are actually evasions that do not escape the problem, but mostly aggravate it?

Is it reasonable to simply revise our notions of what is "out there" to overcome these objections? A crude version of this revision is to simply declare that practice is temporal or mutable, or has no essence, is neither subjective nor objective, and so on. Every time an objection is made, one can add to the list of declarations to the effect that the new concept does not have the objectionable property. The sociologist Pitirim Sorokin once proposed this as a solution to the problem of social change: just declare change to be "immanent." The problem with these declarations is that they need to be backed up by some sort of real change in the concepts that were claimed to have the defect. And this is not without cost.

If we consider a classic "structuralist" statement about language, we can see how the downloading problem can be solved if we leave out change. Here is Michael Dummett's assertion:

> We communicate our thoughts by means of language because we have an implicit understanding of the . . . principles governing the use of language. . . . In order to analyze thought, therefore, it is necessary to make explicit those principles . . . which we implicitly grasp. (Dummett 1978, 442)

The downloading problem is formulated in the phrase "implicitly grasp." The structure, its rules and so forth, is simply there: individuals accommodate it, learn to cope with it, master or partially master parts of its operations, and so on. It need not be understood as a "shared mental content," at least in the sense that it is shared as a whole, since we might add that not everyone implicitly grasps all the principles. The principles are nevertheless there to be grasped. They are like a constraining object. But explaining change or even the possibility of change becomes a problem with this kind of collective object. By making the object autonomous, separate from the operations of individual users, unaffected by their choices, actions, usages, learnings, trainings, and so on, it becomes separated from the usual causal processes. This was the source of one objection to "structuralism": change became a mystery, as did the source of the structures themselves.

If we solve this problem by making the relevant structures into "practices" and endowing practice with various properties, such as changeability, looseness, telic directionality, temporality (meaning continuity but also continuous change), and so forth, we "solve" the change problem—and perhaps some of the epistemic problems of structuralism, such as the nagging small detail that no one could quite agree on what the structures were. If "practice" is *not* a rigid thing, partly mastered by individuals, and in some sense "out there," what is its relation to individuals? If the relation is that it causes or produces or constitutes individual dispositions, *how* does it do so? Does every change in the big structure appear instantly in each individual? Is the whole evolving, telic, changeable thing present in each individual? If not, what is the relationship with individuals? Are they merely "affected" by practice? If each person's mastery of the collective thing is different because it is partial, and the collective thing is constantly changing, what is the relation between the changes in the individual and the changes in the practices? If mastery by a given individual—an elderly person, for example—reflects a prior state of the structure, then different people will have (partially) mastered different things; and the content of their "mastery" is different not only because each has only partial mastery, but because they have mastered something that is different: the practice at time t rather than time $t + 50$ years, for example.

Neil Gross, in an attempt to respond to *The Social Theory of Practices* in defense of Bourdieu, argues that newer practice theory solves these problems by raising the locus of explanation to a higher level:

> The process of coming to develop practical mastery is, at one level, a matter of emulation. But what is emulated is not the performance of any one individual, or even of any number of individuals. The object of emulation is instead the logic that is common to the field itself. Each field, in other words, has a set of "structuring dispositions" appropriate to it, but no individuals operating on the basis of a particular *habitus* possess the entirety of that set. . . . While agents may act in reference to the total logic of the field in enacting practical mastery, this logic is never directly available to them, at least in its totality, in the actions of any empirical individuals. It could only, therefore, be the logic of the field itself, and not merely the performances of particular individuals, that agents internalize in the process of gaining practical mastery. (Gross 1998, 124)

"Act in reference to" and "internalize" are the downloading terms here. And now it is "the logic of the field" that is downloaded. So this solves the problem of sameness, the problem of reproducing mental contents in each head so they are shared, by putting the active principle, the logic, at a higher supraindividual level, making it, so to say, a cause of causes, a producer of dispositions, something one can act in reference to, internalize, and so forth. "Logics," like other terms in the practice family, are mysterious entities that are supposed to be shared in some fashion by the participants in some collectivity or, if one prefers, field, and which explain the individual manifestations and activities.

Does this work? It makes things much more complicated. We need to add a whole set of causal links, or other links, from this abstract object to the things that actually do the proximate explanatory work, such as helping to explain actions, dispositions, the reasons people have for acting, and so forth. The issue of sameness remains, but now it is the sameness of the alleged common cause or source of such things as dispositions. Dispositions are theoretical objects themselves. So there are two theoretical links between a "logic" and anything actual. We must postulate the existence of a mechanism by which logics create dispositions. But this mechanism has the same problem as other supposed downloading mechanisms from the collective to the individual. So all this maneuvering makes no progress at all in avoiding the argument against the plausibility of these mechanisms. Indeed, it "solves" the problem by making it much worse.

In short, the price for all these evasive maneuvers is staggering theoretical complexity. But of course the problem of complexity is never addressed. It is "solved" by designating these processes as *terra incognita*. But there is no *terra* there at all. There are merely problems artificially generated by the theoretical gimmicks allowing their users to sustain their commitment to supraindividual explainers of this increasingly strange kind. At this point, it must be said, the notion that there is a thing out there being mastered begins to look rather forlorn and unnecessary. What people master depends on what they need to do to get around, to cope, to adjust. Each person winds up with something different out of this process, and gives something different back in the form of feedback to others. There is no need for a complex process of uploading and downloading from a collective object.

THE FUTURE OF SOCIAL THEORY AND ITS PAST

The challenge of cognitive science to social theory is for the most part one sided. Cognitive science and its development is a reality to which social theory needs to adjust. We are in the position that figures like Hobbes were when they saw that the social theory of their time needed to adjust to the mechanization of the world picture. But the challenges are not all directed toward social theory.[6] As I indicate in chapter 3, the casual use of the category of culture by, for example, developmental psychologists and modelers in the simulation/theory theory debate and elsewhere is the source of serious potential problems in their own accounts of their own subjects. In these respects and, I think, many others, social theory is and can be the source of significant puzzles for cognitive science, different in character from the puzzles posed by language and consciousness, which have produced so much effort. To some extent the relation may become more balanced, allowing for revision and extension of the one in light of the problematics revealed by the other. This is something like the relationship that traditional experimental psychology now has with cognitive neuroscience. As Searle's efforts, discussed in chapter 2, show, the relationship with social theory is in its infancy.

But now we can see some of the ways it will grow. One of the most striking features of the rise of the philosophy of cognitive science is that it has led to a reconsideration and revival of problems and positions which, thirty years ago, were thought to be quite dead. Locke, Descartes, and Hume become interesting as theorists of mind whose views pertain directly to the problems of cognitive science with mind and the mental. Social theory has a rich tradition as well, and it would be surprising if there were not many sources within it that could shed light on the theme of this book. The sheer dominance, not to mention the luxuriant variety, of the conception of social life that now appears to us as practice theory has hidden this past. The final chapter, on Edward Shils, tells the story of his encounter with the postwar reconsideration of "tradition" in England, inspired in part by T. S. Eliot, which was shared by Oakeshott, Polanyi, J. P. Mayer, and more peripherally by Isaiah Berlin and Karl Popper. It is a story that illuminates some of the "political" implications of these issues. But it also shows how some of these issues have been hidden within the mainstream of academic social theory, and how they relate to other issues.

Who looks different in the past of social theory? Certainly Max Weber, who Parsons reinterpreted to suit his own views, and who can now be seen as the most prominent figure to reject collective objects in social theory. He constructed a theory of action in which customary usage was sustained not by any external force or tacit idea, but by the fact that it was inconvenient not to follow it, and was made more convenient by habitualization (Turner and Factor 1990). But there are others, such as G. H. Mead and Gabriel Tarde: they appear in chapter 3. Others who more explicitly targeted "the theory of society" might be cited as well. Hobhouse wrote that "essentially the subject matter of

6. I express my admiration if not entirely my solidarity with the pioneering efforts of such ethnomethodologists as Jeff Coulter in their attempts to expose the inadequacies of many of the shortcuts that cognitive science thinkers have taken in the explanation of mind. I think these challenges are important to articulate, and cannot as yet be easily met.

sociology is the interaction of individual minds" (Hobhouse [1924] 1966). The idea was expanded by Charles Ellwood, a student of Dewey's and Mead's, who insisted that "[t]he whole development of human society, so far as it is *human*, has depended on learning processes in individuals, and interlearning processes among individuals" (Ellwood 1938, 560). Ellwood broke with his student, Herbert Blumer, the father of symbolic interactionism, over the relative importance of culture, which Ellwood conceived in terms of these processes of learning.[7]

These thinkers, and others, such as Axel Hägerström (who is discussed in chapter 4 and again in chapter 6), become newly relevant, especially for the alternatives they provide, in his case for the problem of normativity. Approaches that rely heavily on the notion of tacit conventions can profitably be rethought, as "contextualism" of Quentin Skinner and others is in chapter 7 and one kind of "social constructionism" is in chapter 5. Any radical rethinking of the concepts of social theory will, because of the weight and complexity of the tradition, necessarily be a historical rethinking as well. These essays are a beginning.

7. What marred the thought of Hobhouse and Ellwood was that they recognized the depth and significance of cultural difference, yet they fell into a kind of evolutionism that made the adjustment and accommodation that Ellwood called "interlearning" into an ethically informative principle, akin to utilitarianism; this made social change into ethical and cultural improvement. The error is a salutary one, for it is common in discussions of the implications of cognitive science as well: pushing a good idea too far.

one

THROWING OUT THE TACIT RULE BOOK /
Learning and Practices

"Practices" talk, I have argued elsewhere, gets into trouble over the notion of "sharing" (1994). The idea that there are "shared" practices requires some sort of notion of how they come to be shared, and this notion in turn dictates how practices can be conceived. If we decide that these difficulties are insurmountable, I argued, we can dispense with the notion of sharing altogether. Practices without sharing, to use a phrase favored in the nineteenth century, are habits—individual rather than shared. Habits are simply the part of the phenomenon described by the term *practices* that remains when the idea of people possessing the same shared thing is eliminated. *Habits,* however, is a potentially misleading term, especially if *habit* is thought of as a generic alternative explanation rather than simply as the residue of the concept of practices once its objectionable elements have been eliminated. In what follows I will try to avoid this potential misunderstanding by restating my argument against the "social" conception of practices in somewhat different terms, without appealing to *habit* as a concept, and by locating the argument in relation to recent work in cognitive science.

Practices, for the sake of the following, is defined as those nonlinguistic conditions for an activity that are *learned.* By "*a* practice" I will mean an activity that requires its genuine participants to have learned something of this tacit sort in order to perform. What I intend to discuss are some general features of learning that constrain our conception of practices and therefore of a practice which depends on them. Ordinarily, the tacit stuff is not all there is to a practice. Most cases of a practice involve explicit communication or even explicit rules. Rules are not self-applying, so in the case where there are explicit rules, such as the law, the relevant practices are the ones enabling a person to follow the rules—for a lawyer or judge to interpret the law, for example. Sometimes there are no explicit rules, but there is explicit discussion. Painting a house, for example, can be done correctly or incorrectly, and there is a fairly elaborate vocabulary of evaluation and description of mistakes. Some kinds of "knowing how" that might be called "a practice" may have no such elaborate vocabulary of appraisal, and perhaps may have none at all. The practice of flirting, for example, before it was theorized about, presumably lacked such a vocabulary, and small children who flirt presumably have no vocabulary with which to discuss it—but it nevertheless has to be learned. My concern throughout will be with the tacit parts of a practice.

THE LINGUISTIC ANALOGY

Language has always exercised a regulatory role in discussions of practice. Any account of practice that fails to account for language will be defective, because linguistic practices are part and parcel of many other practices and because linguistic practices are in principle not sufficiently different from other practices to regard them as likely to have a radically different character. The usual understanding of what is involved in the case of language is this: we communicate by virtue of sharing in the possession of this highly structured whole, a language, including the nonlinguistic learned conditions for the use of the language, the practices. This notion can be put in a much more cautious way, as for example Davidson does when he speaks of "sharing a language, in whatever sense this is required for communication" (1977, 166). The "required sense" of sharing may be minimal, and may not consist of shared tacit rules. In what follows, I propose to deal with the question of what the "required sense" is, and how it can be squared with a plausible account of learning.

Davidson's remark is fairly conventional stuff in contemporary philosophy, but the argument that informs it is elusive. Is this a kind of unformulated transcendental argument, which amounts to the claim that the "sharing" of "language," in some unspecified sense of these terms, is a condition of the possibility of "communication" in some unspecified sense of this term? Or is it a kind of inference to the best explanation in which there are no real alternatives—an inference, so to speak, to the only explanation (which is perhaps not a bad definition of transcendental argument)? There are good reasons to be suspicious of arguments of this form. Yet this general picture, of some sort of shared (and presumably tacit) stuff at the basis of language, is highly appealing, and so is its extension to practices generally. The claim that there is some class of things that couldn't happen, were it not for the existence of some sort of shared practices, is a commonplace, despite—and perhaps because of—its vagueness.

SYMBOLIC AND CONNECTIONIST MODELS OF HIGHER COGNITIVE PROCESSES

As I have said, the Achilles heel of transcendental arguments is that the unique explanation to which the *explanans* point may not be the only explanation. In this case the argument establishes nothing. There is a close analogue to this kind of argument in cognitive science, and it has recently succumbed, at least in the view of many, to the demonstration that an alternative explanation suffices. The argument is this. People have the capacity to reason mathematically and speak grammatically. We can represent mathematical reasoning and the grammatical structure of a language explicitly, in terms of formal proofs and grammatical rules respectively. The fact that people can do in their head what can be done by formal proofs or in accordance with grammatical rules is a fact of the same kind as communication. It is the sort of fact that seems to require that the people who reason mathematically or speak grammatically possess capacities which pretty closely resemble, and operate like, those of formal proof. In short, people, in thinking mathematically or speaking grammatically, must be employing some sort of mental analogue to the rules of inference and axioms that go into mathematical proofs. The problem for the cognitive theorist is to model these capacities by identifying the tacit rules and axioms that are employed.

In cognitive science, this problem leads to a specific difficulty, the "central paradox of cognition," stated by Smolensky, Legendre, and Miyata as follows:

> Formal theories of logical reasoning, grammar, and other higher mental faculties compel us to think of the *mind* as a machine for rule-based manipulation of structured arrays of *symbols*. What we know of the *brain* compels us to think of human information processing in terms of manipulation of a large set of *numbers*, the activity levels of interconnected neurons. Finally, the richness of human *behavior*, both in everyday environments and in the controlled environments of the psychological laboratory, seems to defy rule-based description, displaying strong sensitivity to subtle statistical factors in experience as well as to structural properties of information. (Smolensky, Legendre, and Miyata 1993, 382)

In this case there is an alternative explanation or approach, namely connectionism.

Connectionism refers to the claim that the appropriate model for the computation occurring in the brain is not, as a once dominant viewpoint had it, the operation of logic machines that process symbols, but rather is the parallel distributed processing that is used on various actual computer applications (such as flight simulators) and requires very substantial computing power. The "symbolic processing" model worked as follows: the mind acquires, either by genetic preprogramming or learning, rules for processing inputs, in a manner familiar from ordinary computing, in which symbols come in well-defined forms and the computer program operates as if computational "rules" are "applied" to them mechanically to produce predictable outputs. Connectionist models work differently. The computer is given a learning algorithm, but no detailed "rules." The computer is then "trained up" by feeding it data and then giving feedback for "correct" answers. This is very much a Humean rather than a Kantian machine. Everything that is inside, except for the most basic capacity for forming "expectations," is a result of inputs, or experience. The inputs are not symbolic, but simply impulses originating from various sensory sources, which are distributed through the brain in pathways made up of "connections" that are formed statistically, by the association of impulses of one kind with impulses of another kind. These are modeled mathematically as "weightings" of the impulses, which travel from "node," or pathway link, to "node" and which modify the link by passing through it, just as a person walking in the forest makes a path, increasing the likelihood of future impulses of a similar kind being distributed in a similar way. The changes in the likelihoods are "learning." These computer methods actually work: this is a model based on actual computer achievements, in which parallel distributed processing systems learn to do such things as detect cancers by being trained entirely empirically with inputs of images and feedback for correct predictions. No theory is needed, and no rules are identified or used in this method. The processes are statistical, and the capacities and outputs of the computer depend on what has been fed to it in the form of data and feedback.

The problem for modelers attempting to deal with human cognition is whether this approach can account for higher mental processes. The general explanatory problem is the question of "how . . . competence that is highly systematic, coherent, compositional, and productive" can be achieved with the specific kinds of "finite and fixed resources" that connectionism employs (Smolensky, Legendre, and Miyata 1993, 383). The highly influential paper by these authors from which these quotations are taken presents some technical results that bear on this problem. Indeed, in the opinion of most cognitive scientists and philosophical observers, these results represent a decisive turning point in the resolution of the issues. Briefly, what Smolensky, Legendre, and Miyata establish is that a connectionist account can be given of certain kinds of grammatical rules previously thought to be impossible to account for without reference to internalized formal rules. Their strategy is to show how "a fully distributed pattern of numerical activities" of a connectionist kind can be "the functional near-equivalent of a symbolic structure" (382). That is, they show how something like "rules" can be the product of "learning" through the simple mechanisms of spreading activation employed by connectionist accounts of the brain. The key idea in their analysis is that there is a kind of purposive process which occurs "when the . . . activation spreading process satisfies certain mathematical properties" (383), a process they call maximizing Harmony. The strategy of the paper is to make rule acquisition, by which they really mean the acquisition of functional equivalents to a rule, into a special case of connectionist learning generally. This raises an obvious possibility: that practices too may be special cases of this kind, or, alternatively, that practices may be better understood not as a special case of the same kind, but in light of the general properties of connectionist learning. In what follows, I will suggest that the latter is the most plausible conclusion.

I take it that there are two main implications of interest to the study of social practices of connectionism generally, one flowing from the other. The first is that because learning starts from a system state in which some learning has already occurred, we would expect that learning is always a product of a transition between a state A and state B such that the transition between another state in another machine and a state B^n which is functionally equivalent to B will be a transition from a different starting point to a different end point. In short, the mechanisms in question, even if they are governed by the same basic simple mechanisms, are individuated by the history of the mechanism. And, in general, the simpler the mechanism and the longer the chains of links between simple mechanisms, the greater the diversity produced by differences in, so to speak, the training history. Like paths from one point in space to another, the connections in a net that produce the "same" competency may be different in structure.

The implication of this that bears on the theory of social practices or the idea of shared practices is that two individuals with an ability to perform the general kind of task may go about it in ways that are quite different on the level of neurocognitive description. Put more simply, if we throw out the idea that there is a rule book that people tacitly master in order to, say, communicate, we also throw out the idea that there is some single thing that people must all have in order to communicate. The approach taken by Smolensky, Legendre, and Miyata modifies this implication, for it suggests that something very much like "the same" rules of grammar may result from the fact that there is, in effect, a common end point to the process of mastering a grammar, namely maximal Harmony. But the approach also raises the question of when and where this notion of functional equivalence is applicable or relevant.

It suggests the following answer to the question: when information is plentiful and structured in such a way that "optimizing Harmony" or some other quasi-purposive system goal can lead to the same rule-like results. The general point supported by connectionism is the idea that the simpler the mechanisms that are the building blocks, the longer or more complex the total structure producing the result will be. Unlike rule books, these various complex individual mental structures are built up over time on the basis of different learning events. Ordinarily, there will be a significant diversifying effect: the individual facts of the history of the acquisition of many cognitive skills will differ in such a way that the results differ. The question is where the result is rule-like and the rule-like structures are shared, and where it is either not rule-like or not shared. I note, incidentally, that Smolensky, Legendre, and Miyata say nothing about the question of whether more than one individually generated reduction of complexity can be functionally equivalent to a grammatical rule. However, there seems to be no reason that more than one result might be optimally Harmonious. Moreover, actual speakers do vary, so there is no reason to think that there is even one set of rule-equivalents that the process of harmonizing would necessarily tend toward in any given language.

We cannot, of course, answer questions about the existence of shared functional rule-equivalents directly. But some light can be shed on them by considering the ways in which "rules" are learned. Consider the child's acquisition of the ability to perform simple arithmetical tasks. What is it to "be able" to add 2 + 2? Is it merely to parrot the correct answer? Presumably not. Indeed, there may be no "criteria" in a Wittgensteinian sense for the possession of this competence. Obviously, a child does not master arithmetic immediately or all at once in the sense that the capacity is turned on like a switch. Other things must be mastered first, such as counting, and these are often things that (it is quite unproblematical to suggest) are mastered in different ways. Some children may count on their fingers. Others may learn through singing the numbers, and others may master a great deal of material by rote without knitting it together, and only later make connections between the numbers of a mathematical kind. In short, students come to the learning of 2 + 2 = 4 from different starting points. They are then put through a series of experiences; naturally, each student's experience is slightly different, as is each classroom's experience.

The differences, however, are not supposed to make a difference in the performance of the capacity. There are right answers, and the point of the various experiences with students having various prior experiences is that the experiences taken together transform the child cognitively in such a way that the child is able to perform the cognitive task correctly. Almost everybody manages to do this. At the period prior to mastery, the cognitive architecture that supports the child's efforts will be, according to the picture I have given here, different. Different children will have different experiences on the way to mastery, and the cognitive architecture will be a product of the path and the experiences along this path that the child takes from its starting point to the goal of mastering the cognitive task. The purposes of children will vary as well. There may be a complex heterogeneity with respect to the goals. Some children may wish to avoid the embarrassment of being brought before the blackboard and humiliated for making mistakes. Other children may have a more positive experience of mastery and pride in achievement. These differences, like differences in the history of learning, do not have any effect on the competence itself.

The question is, why? On the account of mastery that fits best with the tacit rule book model, the reason for this is essentially as follows: mastery is no more and no less than "getting" the basic rules of arithmetic, which are the same for everyone. The student tries this and that, gets corrected, gets told that the answer is correct, and does all of this without understanding. But at some point something clicks, and the student "has" the rule. The history of acquisition is irrelevant because the important moment is the moment of clicking on to the rule, of getting the rule. This model of learning, what I will call the snap-on model, makes the history irrelevant. There is a radical difference of kind between the period before acquiring the rule and the period after, and the learning events of the first period have no effects in the second.

This is obviously an appealing story. It fits well with a certain view of Wittgenstein, and indeed may—though I doubt it—represent the most plausible explication of his notion of rule following. I do not wish to take the issue up here directly, but I will note that in the history of the reception of the *Philosophical Investigations* there was a period in which something like the account I have given here was purveyed by Wittgenstein's students and interpreters.[1] Nevertheless, I think it misleads us about practices generally, misleads us into looking for "criteria" or "agreements" where there is nothing of the sort to be found. The main reason for this is that mastery—however one wishes to think of it—is in most cases *not* the same thing for different people under different circumstances. It is purpose relative, and the purposes of individuals involved in the activity vary. It is also situation or experience relative, in the sense that it depends on the materials to which the rules are applied.

Differences in purpose lead to differences in experience, and this means differences in the information that is fed into the system. Diversity is the normal result, but diversity is nevertheless consistent with a great many kinds of cooperation, and indeed, I think, with communication. In what follows I will consider some examples, and suggest that most of those we call practices are more plausibly thought of as the common activities of people with diverse learnings than as activities made possible by the sharing of the same rule-like

1. "We see that we understand one another, without noticing whether our reactions tally or not. *Because* we agree in our reactions, it is possible for me to tell you something, and it is possible for you to teach me something," as Rhees puts it (1970, 56). This is impeccable Wittgenstein (cf. Ambrose 1979, 89), up to a point—the point at which agreeing in our reactions is made into something like a criteria of the existence of a rule.

structures. Obviously, there is no room here for knockdown arguments. Indeed, the complexity of the processes involved assures, I think, that they will always be opaque to analysis. But something may usefully be suggested about the probable effects of differences in purpose on the cognitive side of practices.

Notice a few unusual features of instruction in arithmetic. Children are tested on their mastery of multiplication tables, and there is clearly a right and a wrong answer to such questions. Children are then disciplined or drilled in these right answers, and indeed in days gone by, the times tables were simply mastered by rote, with no attempt being made at giving the child some sort of conceptual understanding of multiplication. This kind of training is anomalous if we consider the universe of "practices." Whatever this universe might be taken to consist of, presumably it includes such "practices" as the standards of etiquette that Norbert Elias describes; the habits of moderation and compromise that are the means of assuring the fruitfulness of parliamentary discussion that thinkers from John Austin to Michael Polanyi and Michael Oakeshott have supposed to operate at the heart of British parliamentary politics; and perhaps many other things, such as the means by which laboratory scientists identify objects, as well as the examples I have given here of flirting and house painting.

Does the snap-on account of learning fit these cases as well? One difference is this: in these more complex cases, perhaps with the exception of flirting, there is a large spoken or explicit element, a vocabulary of appraisal or even theory about the activity, in addition to its tacit base. In the case of elementary arithmetic there are theories, but they are known to mathematicians alone and are not part of the activities of making change and the like in which elementary arithmetic is used. Another difference with the case of arithmetic is that in these "complex" cases, the means by which information about right and wrong is conveyed is different, and the purposes that the parties to the practice have are diverse and lack a common core, such as making correct change. So it would be a bit surprising if a model in which these differences had no place made much sense of the learning of the practice. If we see the teaching of arithmetic as the employment of various behavioral technologies that are designed to produce absolute consistency of response, it is no surprise that such things as the differences in purpose among learners have no effect on what is learned—that is one of the incidental consequences of a behavioral technology that is designed to eliminate differences. But the behavioral technologies that serve to convey information about right and wrong with respect to these other bodies of practice do not work in this way.

Grammar is learned without behavioral technologies of the same explicit kind. But like arithmetic, the effects of diversity of purposes are overwhelmed, by the quantity of redundant information and, perhaps, by the structure of the information on which learning operates. Flirting, in contrast, is information poor, and the starting points of individuals vary enormously. So it would be odd to find functionally equivalent rules there. Nevertheless, flirting, or at least a personal way of flirting and responding to flirting, is learned, and thus fits the model of a practice with which I began. Similarly for politics. One simply doesn't have the vast amount of experience necessary to overwhelm the diversifying effects of differences in experiences, differences in starting points, and differences in purposes. The explicit rather than the tacit parts of politics, the vocabulary of appraisal, the body of political and historical discussion, and explicitly formulated beliefs of various kinds, do the work of making the practice hang together. A practice such as scientific discovery, built around training that is oriented to enabling a person to participate in discussions involving highly specialized terms and employing common apparatus, may in some respects be more like arithmetic, with its explicit behavioral technology of tests, at least with respect to the mastery of techniques. But scientific discussion itself often skates on the border of mutual intelligibility, and not infrequently goes beyond it. And explicit discussion, not the training base, pulls the practice in new directions and toward new goals and experiences.

PRACTICES IN THE SOCIOLOGICAL SENSE: SOCIAL ORDER

The characteristic way in which sociologists have analyzed social practices in the past has been in terms of patterns which are observed, in which the analyst can say that people behave as if they are following a particular rule, and in which the analyst can point to some sort of sanction or response to violations of the "as if" rule that indicates that some behavior is deviant. Expressing disapproval is a much different means of conveying information than correcting arithmetic tests. Take the practice of dressing for the beach. Beach-dressing practices differ from country to country and place to place. Moreover, they differ fairly systematically. What is appropriate in one place, or for one sort of person, is not appropriate for another. There is no place in which one can look up these "rules." One may be entitled, from this, to conclude that there is among beachgoers in particular places some sort of tacit "code" which forbids certain kinds of attire or defines appropriate attire. But this is a very peculiar sort of conclusion. It seems to be little more than shorthand for saying that if one does various things, some people will express disapproval. One can get quite an elaborate account of the whole business of approval and disapproval, of the distinctions that are implicit in the pattern of disapproval and approval, and so forth.

But it is far less clear that we are all attempting to master the same tacit rule book, or indeed that there is some sort of common thing that is being mastered here. Are we simply trying to dress for the beach in accordance with various purposes, one of which may be—but may not be—to avoid disapproval? Could it be that the apparent structure of the activity is simply the results of different people with different purposes and a variety of attitudes acting and expressing approval and disapproval? The tacit rule book model requires us to think that, as with arithmetic exams, we face social life as an exam which we respond to in terms of approval and disapproval. If we meet with approval, we may take it as a sign that we have not violated the tacit rule book. Disapproval represents failure in mastering the tacit rule book. We learn from the experience what is in the tacit rule book or how to apply the tacit rules. If we retain the image that what we have here is a vast tacit rule book of great complexity, then we can think of individuals as having mastered, though not very satisfactorily, elements of or approximations of this tacit rule book, as having incomplete or unsatisfactory mastery.

But this seems rather strange, for a variety of reasons. Go back to the child's performance of addition in a schoolroom. The child's goal may be for the most part to avoid embarrassment. Getting the right answer is simply a means to this and doubtless other ends. Satisfactory performance from the child's point of view is one that manages to achieve enough of the things the child wants to achieve or to avoid the things the child wants to avoid. Of course, children manage to satisfice in the classroom in lots of ways, such as by becoming the class clown to deflect embarrassment. In short, because goals are heterogeneous, "mastering" is also a heterogeneous notion.

With the usual sorts of things we think of as social practices, such as dressing to go to the beach, our goals are heterogeneous. What counts as satisfactory will be different for different people. And this has implications for the experiences the person has, and consequently the information that person receives as a result of these experiences. The beachgoer who avoids arrest and is satisfied with the knowledge that enables him or her to accomplish this is different from the beachgoer who is satisfied with admiring glances or with being ignored and thus avoiding social disapprobation.

Why should this make any difference to the question of whether there is a tacit rule book of beach attire, or flirting? Arithmetic problems are odd in that optimal mastery is necessary with respect to the large number of usual goals, such as avoiding humiliation, that children bring to the situation of learning elementary arithmetic. Ordinarily, matters are different: different goals dictate different results, because the pursuit of the goals leads to experiences that are different in kind. Sometimes, however, there are intermediate goals that are the same, or demand functionally equivalent conduct or understandings. Language seems to be a case like this. Intelligibility is an intermediate goal that is shared by a large number of people. The mastery of a language is necessary for the achievement of this goal. People have very diverse linguistic experiences, but the quantity of linguistic data with which they operate is so immense that it obliterates many of the differences. In the case of beach attire, matters are quite different. It simply overstates the case to say that people have to internalize a norm of dress in order to participate in the activity. There is no single "norm" corresponding to the various "mastering" strategies that people exhibit while responding to the problem of appropriate beach attire. Not only do people have different explicit ideas about what is appropriate and what is not, they *respond* differently. And their different experiences lead them to have quite different kinds of information on which to operate, information that is different in kind, and not redundant and overwhelming in such a way as to produce the same results. Yet there will be something recognizable to us, as analysts, as a social practice.

If this is a possible explanation, it is a better explanation than the idea of a tacit rule book. The experience of social life—in the absence of a massive amount of information or of highly structured experiences, such as the learning of arithmetic—is simply too diverse, and too thin, for the individual to derive from it anything so determinate as a universal set of rules. Even if there were such rules, and even if individuals optimized in acquiring functional equivalent rule-like responses to the material presented to them, it is reasonable to suppose that the material on which each individual works is too limited—in all but the exceptional cases—for them to acquire the same rule-like response as the next person does.

THE DOMAIN OF PRACTICES

If people are "master" learners who start from different points, acquire what they learn through different sets of experiences, and satisfice according to different goals which may change over time and thus direct the path of experiences and learnings in different ways, it may appear that the real mystery here is how there could be any such things as social practices or "social order" at all unless there is massively redundant information structured to produce functional equivalents of the same rule in all parties to the practice. I think that this is indeed the right question, and the answer to this question needs to be not that there is a tacit rule book and that the problem is to figure out how people acquire it, but rather that the kinds of patterns and regularities we regard as social practices are nothing more than that which people learn, in a rather heterogeneous way, are the best ways or the satisfactory ways to negotiate the paths toward to the fulfillment of whatever purposes they might have. What this suggests is that what sociologists call practices are lessons enabling people to do particular things, such as go to the beach and be comfortable with the responses of other people, or at least get responses from others that they consider satisfying.

This gives us the basis for a crude taxonomy of practices. The learning of some practices is indifferent to the purposes for which they are learned, or, rather, "optimizing Harmony" makes them the same for everyone. For other practices, in contrast, mastery is purpose relative. Neither case, I have suggested here, *requires* the model of a common tacit rule book. It is mistaken in the cases in which mastery is purpose relative because it is simply the imposition of the sociologist—no one learns it, and there is no plausible way for a complex scheme of tacit rules of the hypothesized kind to be learned. It is mistaken in the case in which optimizing Harmony results in the sharing of rules that are functionally the same for everybody because it involves a mistaken inference from the explicit form of an activity to a supposed cognitive basis with a similar form.

the thesis of the Background does not show that theorizing is impossible, on the contrary, the Background itself seems to me an excellent territory for theorizing.
    —John R. Searle, *The Rediscovery of Mind*

"Papa! What's money?"
    The abrupt question had such immediate reference to the subject of Mr. Dombey's thought, that Mr. Dombey was quite disconcerted.
    "What is money, Paul?" he answered. "Money?"
    "Yes," said the child, laying his hands upon the elbows of his little chair, and turning the old face up towards Mr. Dombey's; "what is money?"
    Mr. Dombey was in a difficulty. He would have liked to give him some explanation involving the terms circulating medium, currency, depreciation of currency, paper, bullion, rates of exchange, values of precious metals in the market, and so forth; but looking down at the little chair, and seeing what a long way down it was, he answered: "Gold, and silver, and copper. Guineas, shillings, half-pence. You know what they are?"
    "Oh yes, I know what they are," said Paul. "I don't mean that, Papa. I mean what's money after all?"
    —Charles Dickens, *Dombey and Son* (1855–57)

The Construction of Social Reality purports to answer little Paul satisfactorily for the first time, at least to the extent that his question is meant as a question about the reality of money. John Searle's ostensible subject is the reality of the social institutions, of which money is his paradigm case, that are part of everyday situations, such as the ordering of a beer in a restaurant. He claims that this subject, the ontology of social life, has hitherto been inadequately explored. This will come as a surprise to social theorists, and even to readers of Searle, who will recognize that what he says about the subject now has a great deal to do with what he said about it three decades ago in *Speech Acts* (1969). Searle says little about the tradition of social theory other than to dismiss it for having failed to anticipate his solution to the problem, and for showing what a bad answer would be. He says even less to explain the evolution in his own use of the same basic argument. The book, however, introduces some novel and deeply significant ideas with potentially radical implications both for the whole tradition of social theorizing about these topics and for his own past thinking. Searle, however, is more concerned to contain the implications of the argument for his own past claims than to explore them.

THE PREHISTORY OF THE PROBLEM IN SEARLE'S WRITING

The Concept of the Background

In *Speech Acts*, in a four-page passage, Searle outlines a distinction between brute and institutional facts. Institutional facts, such as "Jones was convicted of larceny," are said to be distinguished from brute facts, like "I weigh 160 pounds," by virtue of the fact that the former depends on institutions, understood as systems of constitutive rules. Searle then holds that "[e]very institution is underlain by a (system of) rule(s) of the form 'X counts as Y in Context C'" (1969, 52). At the time, he was impressed by the fact that "no one . . . would try to offer a description of football in terms of brute facts, and yet curiously enough, people have tried to offer semantic analyses of languages armed with only a conceptual structure of brute facts and ignoring the semantic rules that underlie the brute regularities" (52–53). *Underlie* is a term with spectral reference. As we shall see, Searle later tries to give it body.

At the time, the "brute facts" strategy seemed to him to be easily disposed of: the obvious explanation for the brute regularities is that "the speakers of a language are engaging in a rule governed form of intentional behavior" and the "rules account for the regularities in exactly the same way as the rules of football account for the regularities in a game of football" (1969, 53). One problem with this line of argument is that while there are rules of football, to be found in a rule book, together with a whole apparatus of enforcement and judicial decision making, the constitutive rules underlying many social institutions are partly or entirely tacit. Similarly for the intentionality of the behavior. Football players presumably intend to play football, and in this case the intentions are conscious. But beyond these paradigm cases, matters become more murky. It is less plausible to say that males intend to perpetuate patriarchal domination, and not plausible at all to say it is done, as in the case of choosing to play football, with conscious intent. What seems to have dawned on Searle is that there is a general problem about the status of tacit mental things, a problem that arises in cognitive science, where a renovated "brute regularities" strategy, connectionism, seems to be the winning solution.[1]

Connectionism doesn't challenge the football model of institutional facts directly, but it undermines a traditional, though rarely voiced, answer to the problem of the ontological status of the institutions of a society, which we might call the linguistic model. The model has roots in ideas like Durkheim's notion of the collective *conscience* as the repository of the shared ideas that are the source of the reality of social institutions. Put crudely, the linguistic model holds that the rules of the game are in people's heads, and they share these rules in the same way that they share the rules of grammar. If cognitive science deprives us of the "rules" model of the tacit contents of people's heads for grammar, as it threatens to, it undermines this version of the reality of social institutions, which was plausible only by analogy.

Searle long ago abandoned the rules model of mental contents. As he says, he himself established that "the notion of deep unconscious rule-following is incoherent" (1995, 229 n. 2). He continues the attack in *The Construction of Social Reality*. But he does not give up the football analogy. And here there is a problem. If we give up on the idea that the mind can be characterized all the way down in representational language, what about the representational language of the football analogy, the "rules" picture of institutions? There is a sense in which Searle need not answer this question, for he never embraced the mental aspect of the linguistic model of social institutions in the first place. But the model solves, however badly, a question that an ontologist of social institutions would have to solve about the status of the rules that "underlie" social institutions.

Searle never says that his problem in *The Construction of Social Reality* is to salvage the rules model in the face of these better models of the mental. But this is precisely what his new account would do, if it were successful. It builds a bridge from a model of the mental that is consistent with cognitive science to the old model of social institutions that parallels and replaces the linguistic model. To understand it requires us to retrace the steps of his own attempt to rethink the notion of tacit knowledge in the face of the challenge of cognitive science, and especially connectionism.

In *Intentionality* (1983), Searle began to respond to the problem of the tacit with "the hypothesis of the Background." The Background is a bunch of non-

---

1. For an introduction to the strategy, see Hubert Dreyfus and Stuart Dreyfus, who make the point that connectionism, in contrast with AI approaches, does not "assume that there must be a theory of every domain" (1988, 37), and thus implies that cognitive processes are themselves nonintelligible, a matter of sheer patterns rather than patterns underlain by implicit theories.

representational, preintentional capacities that are required for such things as understanding the simplest sentences (1983, 145–46).

> the sentence "The cat is on the mat" only determines a definite set of truth conditions against a Background of preintentional assumptions that are not part of the literal meaning of the sentence. This is shown by the fact that, if we alter the preintentional Background, the same sentence with the same literal meaning will determine different truth conditions, different conditions of satisfaction, even though there is no change in the literal meaning of the sentence. This has the consequence that the notion of the literal meaning of a sentence is not a context-free notion; it only has application relative to a set of preintentional background assumptions and practices. (145)

The concept of the Background, however, produces some problems. It can't be made up of just more stuff of the same kind as that being explained, such as more sentences made explicit. "If we try to spell out the relevant parts of the background as a set of sentences requiring further semantic contents, that would simply require yet further backgrounds for their comprehension" (148). In short, if the Background is the same sort of thing, such as rules, as the contents, we have an infinite regress, which we know to be impossible, given the actual limitations on human cognitive capacity, which can't contain an infinite set of rules, assumptions, and the like at once. In any case, if ordinary explicit rules are not self-interpreting, how can *tacit* rules be self-interpreting? Apparently they must be, unless we believe that there is a kind of tacit interpretation of the tacit rules that goes on unconsciously (152). This way lies madness, in the form of even more infinite regresses. Yet we have no other way of talking about the Background except representationally or mentally, for example in terms of "assumptions" that take the form of sentences or beliefs. This problem about how to talk about the contents of the Background produces a situation in which we know we are speaking misleadingly about the Background when we speak representationally, and are forced to employ oxymorons, metaphors, and neologisms, such as the term *preintentional* (156–57).

Searle begins to work his way out of the problem of the nonrepresentational true character of the Background by considering skills, such as skiing. Here it becomes clear that the relation between "rules" of the sort that one might find in a ski instruction manual or attribute to the tacit knowledge domain of an individual and the actual performances of individuals cannot plausibly be pictured as either a matter of the individual providing an interpretation of the ski manual or of possessing and applying a large set of tacit rules. A better picture is that the skilled skier has replaced the causal functioning of a representation with something else that is better, for example a body trained to take account of variations in terrain (1983, 150–51).

Skills, like skiing, involve automatic responses. So where does intentionality fit? The usual picture is that "automatic" and "intentional" are opposed pairs. Searle needs to undermine this opposition, which he does by separating the notion of intentionality from consciousness, or at least from complete consciousness. In the case of the skier attempting to win a race, Searle suggests that "on my view, the body takes over and the skier's intentionality is concentrated on winning the race. This is not to deny that there are forms of Intentionality involved in the exercise of skills, nor is it to deny that some of this Intentionality is unconscious" (1983, 151). But it is to deny that all that is intentional is consciously so, and that the automatic character of skilled responses makes them nonintentional.

The positive picture of the mind has the elements of Intentionality and what Searle called the Network and the Background arranged in a certain way:

> we do have Intentional states, some conscious, many unconscious; they form a complex Network. The Network shades off into a Background of capacities (including various skills, abilities, preintentional assumptions and presuppositions, stances, and nonrepresentational attitudes). The Background is not on the periphery of Intentionality but *permeates* the entire network of Intentional states; since without the Background the states could not function, they could not determine conditions of satisfaction. (1983, 151)

Put more simply, intentionality is a larger domain than either the domain of the conscious or the representational. The Background, in other words the elements of the processes of mind that are not representational, or not open to explicit articulation, are necessary for all the mental processes of interest to us—conscious, unconscious, representational, and otherwise.

One effect of this line of reasoning is to separate Intentionality from particular mental contents, such as conscious beliefs. Intentionality reaches back into the preintentional, nonrepresentational Background, as in the case of the skier. When a competitive skier is given instructions, the instructions and the intentions "presuppose a huge underpinning of Background abilities" (1992, 195) that are, so to speak, brought into play by the intentional state. Our intentional states, conscious or unconscious, which form the Network, can be thought of representationally. But the Network "shades off" into the Background, which we can't really think of representationally, at least not without stretching the point. The two aren't really separable, functionally: the things we can think of representationally depend on the continuous operation of the things we can't really think of representationally, such as skills. The effect of this is to undermine the following kind of argument: so and so can't have intended such and such because she didn't possess or think using the relevant representations. The reasoning is this: if the skier didn't think such thoughts as "I will keep balanced by shifting my weight slightly to the right ski when I go over the next mogul," this does not mean that the skills this phrase describes are not really there, or that she didn't shift her weight intentionally.

Collective Intentionality

The possibility of replacing the causal functioning of a representation with something else may seem to be an arcane subject, having little to do with the reality of social institutions. But it takes on a large significance if it is conjoined with another idea. The idea, collective intentionality, plays a large role in *The Construction of Social Reality*, but the case for it is not argued there, but in an earlier paper, "Collective Intentionality and Action." There Searle is more explicit about the problem that underlies *The Construction*, which is put as "what role does the Background play in enabling us to function in social collectives" (1990, 401). Collective intentionality, we will see, provides Searle with the means of reconciling the football model with the hypothesis of the Background. Collective intentionality will eventually be stretched to support the football analogy, and perhaps stretched too far.

The paper begins with some intuitions. One is that "there really is collective intentional behavior as distinct from individual intentional behavior." Searle says that "you can see this by watching a football team execute a pass play or hear it by listening to an orchestra." Another is that there can be no "group mental phenomenon except what is in the brains of the members of the group." Searle thinks the solution to this apparent conflict is likely to be found in some feature of the mental component of collective behavior, namely "in the form of the intentionality" (1990, 402).

Searle argues that we-intentionality is irreducible to I-intentionality, meaning to any set of I-intentions. The argument proceeds as a simple piece of analytic philosophy. There are English language statements of the form "We intend X." Available analyses of such statements into sets of I-intentional statements fail, because they do not succeed in distinguishing cases of cooperation from cases in which people do the things they individually intend, but do so without cooperation. The simple and compelling alternative to these laborious and unsuccessful analyses into sets of I-intentional statements is this: "We simply have to recognize that there are some intentions whose form is: We intend that we perform act A; and such an intention can exist in the mind of each individual agent who is acting as part of the collective" (1990, 407). Statements of this form are primitive.[2] They can't be analyzed into

---

2. The idea that statements of we-intentions are primitive leads to various oddities, such as the result that with collective intentions we may be mistaken about what we are doing—mistaken that anyone else shares the "we-intention." Searle insists that the possibility of such a mistake does not make the intention itself any less a we-intention (1990, 408), but as we shall see, the fact that such a mistake is possible suggests an alternative explanation of we-intentional facts in terms of acceptance.

I-intentional statements. But in accepting them, "we are not required to suppose that there is any element in society other than individuals. . . . It is consistent with the fact that there is no such thing as a group mind or group consciousness" (ibid.).

Our capacity to form we-intentions is ultimately rooted in biology, but the fact that we can form them has some implications for the contents of the Background. In order to form we-intentions, we must at least have "a Background sense of the other as a candidate for co-operative agency; that is it presupposes a sense of others as more than conscious agents, indeed as actual or potential members of a co-operative activity" (1990, 414). These "are not in the normal case beliefs." Searle suggests that this Background sense is fundamental to collective life and even to conversation, so that "certain attempts to understand the character of society must be wrong," such as those which hold that "speech acts in conversation are the 'foundation' of social behavior and hence of society" (415).

The problem of ontology arises in a particular way for collective intentions. He asks, "how could there be any group mental phenomenon except what is in the brains of the members of the group?" (1990, 402), and answers that there can't be. But intentional phenomena are themselves real.

> Intentional phenomena such as rule-following and acting on desires are genuinely causal phenomena; but as intentional phenomena they are essentially related to such normative phenomena as truth and falsity, success and failure, consistency and inconsistency, rationality, illusion, and conditions of satisfaction generally. In short, the actual facts of intentionality contain normative elements, but where functional explanations are concerned, the only *facts* are brute, blind physical facts and the only norms are in us and exist only from our point of view. (1992, 238–39)

Intentional phenomena are real, in the sense of being part of the causal world, and at the same time cross the "normative" barrier. If collective intentional phenomena are in the minds of each individual in the collectivity, they are real too.

With this argument, we have a new, or at least slightly altered, set of tools to deal with the problem of the nature and "reality" of social institutions. We have the concept of the Background, which serves as a substitute for a number of older ideas. When Searle says that the "Background sense" of others as potential cooperators is fundamental to collective life, he is using it as a kind of philosophical anthropology, not dissimilar from Hobbes's use of the notion that people are naturally disposed to keep promises to solve a regress problem in his own contractarian theory of society (the problem that promising is an institution that itself needs to be created and sustained socially). By extending the reach of the notion of intentionality to the Background, in the case of skills, he peels it away from the notion of possession of concepts. This is an important but obscure step. It is a staple of a certain tradition in analytic philosophy that one cannot intend what one cannot conceive, and one cannot conceive what one does not possess the concepts for.

The notion of collective intentionality is a shortcut around many of the problems faced by Hobbes and his successors, who thought that one had somehow to build up social concepts, such as the state, from individual materials, and found this a difficult task. But the explanatory burdens—and the sheer absurdity—of notions of group personality and group minds have often deterred Hobbes's successors from taking this particular shortcut. Searle's change to the notion of intentions lightens this burden, since it does not require a group mind, just an "intention . . . in the mind of each individual agent who is acting as part of the collective" (1990, 407). His use of the Background lightens it even more, since what needs to be in the mind of each individual agent no longer needs to be presently shared concepts but simply shared goals, whose conscious or conceptual content may be as limited as, for example, just wanting to win a football game. The Background may contain a functional substitute for conscious or conceptual content. If one puts Searle's two arguments together, one creates the space for a new set of possible accounts: in which collective intentions can figure without being burdened by, or at least burdened by an overliteral interpretation of, the limitations imposed by the consideration that even a collective intender, a "we," cannot intend results that this "we" does not possess a concept of. The idea that every member of the collectivity must have this intention in their individual mind and brain, something needed to avoid the notion of a group mind, would, taken literally, be at least puzzling: how exactly do people get the same intentions in mind? The legitimacy of the football analogy without the help of something like the linguistic model, an interpretation of the notion of "underlies," is still an unresolved issue. But one can begin to see how Searle might use these arguments to salvage it.

SOCIAL REALITY AS THE PRODUCT OF ENACTMENTS

In *The Construction of Social Reality,* Searle employs exactly the same model of institutional facts that appears in *Speech Acts,* the model I have been calling the football analogy, after Searle's own example (which he continues to employ). Constitutive rules of the form "*X* counts as *Y* in Context *C*" create institutional facts. They have some other properties that are useful, notably the fact that once iterated, they can produce more and more institutional facts. Some of the things that Mr. Dombey thinks of when he thinks of how to explain money are the products of iteration. One can't have such things as junior subordinated debentures, for example, without taking a long series of "counts as" steps away from copper coins. But they too are a form of money. The same ontological results hold in both texts: institutional facts are the product of rules, and are, accordingly, real in a special and secondary way, and thus differ from brute facts. But the Searle of *Construction* adds a great deal to his discussion of the problem, and alters it to deal with the problem created by the fact that these constitutive rules are mostly tacit. This is an important step. In *Speech Acts*, the rules are just there, "underlying" institutional actions. In *Construction*, Searle addresses the problem of where they come from, and what sort of reality they have.

In *Speech Acts*, Searle already claims that human beings have the capacity to create social institutions by making declarations with the particular logical form "*X* counts as *Y* in Context *C*." He now suggests an ontological reading of this formula: that the "counts as" form is one in which a particular person speaking for a "we" in a particular context assigns a particular "function" to a particular physical manifestation. The assignment of a function creates a real institution.

The example Searle returns to throughout the text is money. Money is in some sense "really" money and hence real. It is part of the waiter's ontology. The question Searle wishes to answer is in what sense is it that it is real. The striking thing about money, for Searle, is that on the one hand it is a physical object, and on the other it is money not by virtue of its inherent properties as a physical object but by virtue of a function that we have assigned it. It becomes money only once we assign the function to it. When we cease to assign this function, it ceases to be money. The picture this suggests to him is that the "we assign" part of the process of a physical object becoming an institutional fact is the key to the answer, and our assigning a function is a matter of possessing a collective intention to treat something as something else.

When Searle claims that his account is completely novel, he seems to mean that one of his additions to the notion of enactment makes it novel, namely the notion that the original assignment of function is always assignment of a function to something physical or nonsocial. What he has in mind here is this: things that are real because they are the products of iterated enactmentlike statements, such as junior debentures, have a kind of derivative reality. A junior debenture is a promise about future money under certain circumstances. Creating such a thing requires that there be such a thing as money in the first place, and it assigns a moneylike function to a piece of paper under certain circumstances. But this trick doesn't work for money itself: we must assign the function to a physical object, such as Mr. Dombey's coppers and guineas. I will return to the general ontological implications of this argument—Searle's claim that this reasoning justifies the claim that an objective, publicly accessible, brute reality exists—at the end of this chapter. For the moment, it will be enough to consider the origins problems on their own.

Although Searle does not say so, this theory of institution formation is little more than a generalization of a very old model of legal enactment. Consider the following:

> Be it therefore enacted by the Queen's most Excellent Majesty, by and with the Advice and Consent of the Lords Spiritual and Temporal, and Commons, in this present Parliament assembled, and by the authority of the same, That whensoever the Death of a Person shall be caused by wrongful act, Neglect, or Default . . . the person who would have been liable if Death had not ensued shall be liable to an Action for Damages. (White 1973, 220–21)

This is a real law. It has the following elements: a statement of enactment, that is, a statement that this is an action; a statement of who is enacting and on what authority; and a rule that classifies something in some category which makes it a subject of legal action, or in Searle's terms assigns an agentive function: a function that is not, like the normal function of a screwdriver, part of the thing itself, but is a power granted to it by something we as agents do.

Formulae such as "The king in Parliament is sovereign" or "The pope speaking ex cathedra is infallible on matters of faith and morals" are second-order statements that specify the leader's context and powers and in effect assign functions to the leader's commands. The commands of the king are law when the king speaks "in Parliament," that is, with the consent of Parliament, to which the Victorian formula quoted above refers. The king's sayings to his dogs are not law, nor are just any sayings law. Sayings of a particular kind, namely commands of a general character, spoken in Parliament with the consent of Parliament, are, however, laws. These sayings thus create a new fact, namely a law.

But what does the *form* of enactments tell us? One could argue that form has been the great red herring of the history of legal and political theory, for the simple reason that it has tempted people to look for enactments behind the enactments, and seek authorizing authorities behind the authorities. We may smile at Filmer for thinking that Kingship had to be justified by acts of prior kings, and that when one returned all the way to the beginning one got to God, who had to be the original authorizer of authority and the original authority. We may cringe at Rousseau's substitution of the "general will" for historical authorizers. But these are answers to the question that the iterational character of enactments raises, the question of the original authorization.

Recall that institution-founding rules in *Speech Acts* seem to be tacit rules without a rule giver. Searle replaces this with a form of sentence that says, "We assign function X to object Y," in other words a sentence that refers to actual agents, the "we." He argues that, set in the right context, the formula is a genuine expression of "we-intentionality" or collective intentionality, and that such expressions are the foundation of social institutions such as money. On its own, this argument just pushes the legal formula back to the prelegal stage. And if these formulae are not actually spoken by anyone, are purely fictional, then it may seem that we are no better off than we were when they were disembodied, tacit rules, as they were in *Speech Acts*. But Searle now has some means of dealing with the notion of collective intentionality and tacitness that he did not have in *Speech Acts*. To use these rules, of course, he must establish that there is something to the notion of collective intentionality that does not result in implausibilities about group minds and world spirits.

The way he did this earlier is not entirely adequate to the purposes of this new argument. In the previous article, his way of establishing the notion of collective intentionality was simply to ask whether statements involving we-intentions could be analyzed into statements of individual intention, that is, in terms of individual *expressions* of intention. To say "*I* will treat this as money" does not establish anything as money. Ten people saying it, by the same token, does not make it so either. What is needed, Searle argues, is a we-expression making it so. If such statements are irreducible to individuals' statements, what we have established is the irreducibility of we-intentionality to I-intentionality. The next step is to show that institutional facts *are* the products of we-intentionality.

As any historian of political thought knows, of course, we-intentional statements are themselves the subject of a large theoretical literature concerned with the notion of representation. A we-intentional statement such as the law quoted earlier depends for its acceptance on its according with a doctrine of representation which gives the king, with suitable qualifications, the right to speak for "us." This seems nicely to accord with Searle's analysis, in that the king as sovereign is speaking within a particular context and so on. Where the analysis diverges is in the question of what it is that the king is doing. For Searle the answer presumably is that the king is expressing genuine we-intentions and that what makes those we-intentions effective and makes them into laws our acceptance of them as valid expressions of we-intentions. Thus, laws are not a matter of commands that we obey so much as they resemble statements like "Let's call blue poker chips 'dollars,' alright?" with the response "Alright." Searle even describes the breakdown of law and order in the L.A. riots as an example of the forcelessness of the law if acceptance breaks down. But he also uses this example to make the point that social institutions cannot rest on force, because there simply is not enough force around to compel people to obey the law. Acceptance, then, is necessary most of the time.

Even in this modest example, one can see that there is a certain vagueness about the notion of acceptance. The fact that most people follow the law without coercion tells us what, exactly?

1. That they know the law explicitly, and accept it explicitly?

2. That they accept it in the sense appropriate to Searle's notion of the "network," meaning that if asked, they would say that they knew and accepted the law, even if they ordinarily didn't think explicitly about it?

3. That they behave as though they accepted it, but can't articulate very much about their beliefs if asked, and not nearly enough to account for their actual behavioral conformity with the law?

4. That they do so more or less, at least most of the time, and not precisely as the law exists in the lawyers' sense but close enough not to get into legal trouble and close enough to what other people do to not have too many issues arise during ordinary interaction, and can articulate something about this, but what they can articulate typically doesn't match up very closely, and certainly not exactly, with what other people can articulate?

5. That they have behavioral regularities consistent with the law, but can't articulate a thing about them other than self-observations about their regular conduct?

6. Or any of a dozen other possibilities in between these?

MONEY ON THE BRAIN

Searle's argument establishes one form of we-intentionality, the case of explicit agreement, or a version of (1), which he wishes to extend to the tacit case not by claiming that knowledge of the law is tacit, but that acceptance is, so that being accustomed to the law amounts to accepting a we-intention. The focus of his book is the puzzle of how this works: "How can it be that the rules of the institution play a role in our dealings with the institution, even though we are not following the rules either consciously or unconsciously?" (1995, 137) This formulation points to a problem posed by Searle's own account of collective intentionality, which holds that this intention must "exist in the mind of each individual agent who is acting as part of the collective" (1990, 407): namely the question of *what* exists in the mind of each individual agent. Something must, Searle thinks, but not the rules of the game per se.

The idea that shared beliefs are the basis of whatever is collective (that is, options 1 and 2) is ignored. Searle understands perfectly well that to say that all the people in the collective literally have the same beliefs about money, for example, would be absurd: Mr. Dombey and little Paul, for instance, have quite different beliefs, though they may overlap enough for them to carry on in most situations. So Searle looks elsewhere for a solution to the puzzle of what is collective. He says that his "basic idea" is that "one can develop, one can evolve, a set of abilities that are sensitive to specific structures of intentionality without actually being constituted by that intentionality. One develops skills that are, this means, functionally equivalent to the system of rules, without actually containing any representations or internalizations of those rules" (1995, 142). "Without actually being constituted by that intentionality" means that the core idea of the collective intentionality article, that it has to exist in each individual brain (1990, 407), is being relaxed to allow for the possibility that there is no actual mental analogue to the constitutive X is Y in C rules "in the mind of each individual agent."

Searle argues that this must be the *usual* way in which actual social institutions work. Money is again the example: "We don't stop and think, consciously or unconsciously, 'Ah ha! Money is a case of the imposition of function through collective intentionality according to a rule of the form "X counts as Y in C" and requires collective agreement.' Rather, we develop skills that are responsive to that particular institutional structure" (1995, 143). The virtues of this explanatory strategy are very significant. It frees Searle from the problems of showing that something exists in the minds and brains of all of the members of the relevant collectivities that corresponds to the institutions, the burden that he himself imposed in his earlier discussion of collective intentionality. It fits with a realistic phenomenology of experience with institutions. We become, as he suggests, accustomed or familiar with institutional life, which is a quite different thing from internalizing rules. And, of course, his strategy fits with connectionism.

But how do rules figure in this discussion? Can we say simply that people act as if they are following the rules, but the rules actually have no causal role at all? On this point Searle expresses some unhappiness with the alternatives. He distinguishes "rule-*governed*" behavior—of the sort envisioned in the linguistic model, in which the rules actually play a causal role in determining behavior—from "rule-*described*" behavior, conduct described as if rules were being followed without their having any actual causal force (1995, 139). What we need, he suggests, "is to see that the Background can be causally sensitive to the specific forms of the institutions without actually containing any beliefs or desires or representations of these rules" (141). The way this happens is that the abilities and know-how we get in dealing with institutions such as money and that become "ingrained are in fact a reflection of the sets of constitutive rules whereby we impose functions . . . through collective agreement or acceptance" (142).

Searle sees that this skates very close to behaviorism, the view he stigmatizes in *Speech Acts* for explaining by reference to brute facts. The issue is over the status of "as if" accounts. He invents an interlocutor who points out, "Aren't you really saying this is 'as if' we were following the rules. But then that doesn't really explain anything, since if there is no real intentionality, the 'as if' intentionality doesn't explain anything" (1995, 146). His response is twofold. First, he suggests, we need to add a diachronic or evolutionary element to our account of the causal mechanisms (presumably meaning the real connectionist mental innards of a given individual mind that has adapted to the rules). Second, we still need to appeal to "a socially created normative component," to account for the fact that we "accept that there is something wrong with the person who doesn't recognize any reason to do something after he has made a promise to do it" and similar normative responses. This normative element "is accounted for only by the fact that the institutional structure is a structure of [normative] rules" (147). The *normative element,* then, is accounted for by collective intentionality, or agreement. So what this argument really amounts to is yet another tacit analogue model, in which common intentions are tacit, together with an unstated quasi-transcendental argument to the effect that such a thing as money could not exist unless people did in fact agree—at least in some extended sense, such as by "developing skills that are responsive to that particular institutional structure"—to the constitutive intentional rules that Searle attributes to the institutional structure. Somehow the normative element needs to be inserted into the causal story. In the account Searle gives, it is, so to speak, already there; and when we get accustomed, we get accustomed to it: "where human institutions are concerned, we accept a socially created normative component" (146). The football analogy holds because it *has to* hold if we are to account for normativity.

ACCEPTANCE AND COLLECTIVE INTENTIONALITY

Arguments that such and such is the "only" explanation tempt fate. They are refuted by the production of an alternative explanation. In the case of money, as we shall see, nothing needs to be specially constructed as a counterexample—the *standard* explanation itself, found in a classic text, does not appeal to collective intentionality, and indeed shows why, in the case of money, there would be no point to doing so. Searle's argument fails if this alternative account is true, and continues to fail if it can be extended to other social institutions. But this last qualifier is important. Even if the alternative account of money is true, money may simply have been a poor choice of example. The argument may hold for other institutions. In fact, Searle's argument is simply a case of a more popular and indeed pervasive idea about the nature of normativity, which Searle happens to apply to social institutions. The use of the notion of normativity, the idea that there is such a thing as a "normative element" that plays a genuinely explanatory role, deserves closer scrutiny if only because it appears in Searle in an unusually explicit form.

Searle's attempt to accommodate cognitive science in its connectionist form is independent of claims about normativity, and it constitutes a genuine advance in the discussion. His rearrangement of the problem of the explanation of social institutions does two things. First, it introduces the Background and argues for its pervasiveness. Second, it greatly reduces what is to be explained. The Background does much of the work that formerly was done by ideas about shared tacit presuppositions, internalized rules, and whatnot: what I called the linguistic model. We can now see that this model and its problematic terms are not needed. The mechanism of accustomation and the replacement of conscious rules with the casual structures of the Background that produce skilled performances do much of the work once performed by the "internalization" model. Explicit beliefs, the things Searle puts in the Network, do much of the rest of the work. Indeed, only one small but important thing remains. Thus, one of Searle's real achievements in this text is to radically shrink the thing that remains to be explained, shrink it down to the size of the "normative element."

What exactly is left? Searle wants to insist that the Background cannot perform some explanatory tasks, particularly the task of providing the "normative element" which changes an "X counts as Y in C" sentence from a description of behavior to a genuine rule—in other words, that enables us to distinguish right and wrong uses, counting or not counting, in a sense not reducible to individual opinion. He claims that "we-intentions" that are not reducible to individual opinions create this normative element, and it can be created in no other way.[3]

If this is the nub of the argument, it turns out to be a familiar nub: the problem of the mysterious origin of collective normativity. Invoking "we-intentionality" is not so much a solution to this problem, if it is indeed a problem, as another way of stating the problem, one which by his own admission Searle sees as a dead end, an unanalyzable primitive. And this seems to be where other arguments about intentionality and normativity also end, in embracing a mystery and insisting on its insolubility.

The problem of money is a way into these issues. For Searle, the story is this: there is a collective agreement to count, say, cowrie shells as money, which amounts to saying, "Cowrie shells count as money for transactions between us Weegie Islanders." If someone tries to use a coconut for money, she can be corrected. What *normative* means here is that she is corrected on the basis of a real rule, not just my opinion or your opinion about what counts as money. The collective intention to count cowrie shells as money is the source of the supraindividual normative element that makes the behavioral regularity, the usually predictable bartering conduct of the islanders, into a real rule.

3. One might ask many other questions about this model, such as these: *how* do we-intentions create normativity? How does *intending* to be normative make something actually normative for us? The basic thought behind the model seems to be that in the case of our own intendings there is no place for error: we are right about our intentions because to have an intention includes being right about what it is. So the fact that we can intend something normatively, plus the fact that normativity is just a matter of intention, means that we can't be wrong here, at least about ourselves, though perhaps we can be wrong about the others that make up the "we."

When people individually stop accepting cowrie shells as money, it ceases to be money. The institution vanishes.

The standard story is that there are two phases in the history of money, before and after coinage. After coinage, money is constructed by derivatives of coins, by promises redeemable in coins, and so forth, right on up to junior subordinated debentures. Before coinage, the definition of money is this: "a unit or object conforming to a reasonable degree to some standard of uniformity, which is employed for reckoning or for making a large proportion of the payments customary in the community concerned, and which is accepted in payment largely with the intention of employing it for making payments" (Einzig 1966, 317). Note that intentions figure in this definition, but not collective intentions. Customs also enter the picture, but customs that are, from the point of the individual user of the money, behavioral regularities on which the use of money for the purpose of payment relies. To be sure, someone originally had to have some beliefs that could be made explicit about the things being used as money (or, in Searle's language, contents of the Network), namely beliefs about their future usability in barter.

In this version of the history of money, then, there is a role for accustomation and a role for explicit individual beliefs and intentions, but no role at all for collective intentions, and no role for collective beliefs in Searle's strict sense of being in *all* the individual minds of the collectivity. This definition, and indeed money itself, doesn't even require a collectivity. Community is mentioned in the definition, but only in connection with the loose criteria that the primitive money in question be used for a large proportion of the payments that the individuals in the community make. This is a matter of a behavioral frequency. It is enough that a sufficient number of others will accept the goods in barter. Indeed, one can have the first instance of money, in this model, with only one person intending to use the goods as money.

Coinage works a little differently, but only because it is set in a legal structure and involves authority: you can force people to pay debts in real money, for example. But legal authority involves the same problems over collectivities. One can argue that legal authority requires nothing collective either, but simply that individuals have beliefs of whatever kinds necessary to provide for obedience most of the time. These beliefs may be highly various, as the motives for obedience usually are. The difference between having a state and not having one is not, on this view, a matter of there being anything collective, such as a collective intention, but simply the content of the beliefs that individuals have. If enough of them believe in things that are like the things we recognize as "state" beliefs, such as ideas about sovereignty, and they act more or less in accordance with these beliefs, they have a state. This was Weber's solution to the problem, and it is the main rival to the collective object model.

An alternative to "collective intention plus Background cum beliefs" explanations, then, is Background cum belief explanations. Belief explanations appeal to things that occur in what Searle calls the Network, the realm of articulable beliefs and goals. The case of money turns out to fit this alternative model very nicely. People, like Dombey and his son, believe any number of things about money. Some forms of money are legally significant. There is more to the institutional fact of money than can be accounted for by the articulable beliefs that people have about money. Some of this "more," however, is nonarticulable because, in Searle's terms, it is part of the Background, and is a matter of accustomation. Some is only articulable by legal experts and is not part of the list of ideas about money that ordinary people have.

To recapitulate: what Searle needs to argue is that these explicit beliefs (and individual intentions), together with the habitual ways of acting that are bound up with them and are produced by accustomation, are *not* sufficient to account for the institution of money or some other institution. The usual alternative account relies on a particular kind of belief, namely beliefs that hold something to be true or authoritative. But for the purposes of explaining an institution, such as the state, the alternatives say that an "as if" is sufficient: for example, if enough of the individual subjects to a king believe that the king rules by divine right for the "king" to function as a king, his king-ness is explained. The normative question of whether he actually has divine right is a matter for theology, and thus a mystery *stricto sensu*. Explanation, according to this view, can ignore this mystery. Searle needs to argue that it cannot, that any account of this kind must lack a crucial ingredient, namely the "normative element," that can only be supplied by collective intentionality.

Why does Searle think the alternative account won't work? The reason is to be found in his repeated comment that "[t]he intensionality-with-an-s of the sentence form 'X counts as Y in C' is a clue to the intentionality-with-a-t of the phenomena . . . we have good reasons to suppose that the 'counts as' locution specifies a form of intentionality. The possibilities of creating institutional facts by the use of this formula are limited by the possibilities of imposing new features on entities just by collectively agreeing that they have these features" (1995, 95). Roughly, he thinks that the problem of what needs to be explained is the phenomenon of having something count as something in a particular context can't be solved any other way than by reference to collective intentionality. But is it true that counting something as something, and doing so in terms of correctness, requires something collective? Aren't *beliefs about the correctness* of some pattern of behavior enough, taken together with habitual behavior in applying the beliefs?

The point is an arcane one, but it is central to Wittgenstein and to the interpretation of Wittgenstein on following a rule, a paradigm case of which is counting as something. A Wittgensteinian story that I favor says that following a rule is different from acting habitually, but acting habitually is part of following a rule. The difference is this: following a rule requires training, in which a trainer tells the trainee whether the trainee is right or wrong, the trainee habitualizes her responses, and also is able to habitually distinguish right from wrong. The trainer has to have beliefs, in a minimal sense of the word, that something does or does not count as something else. So, once trained, does the trainee: minimally she needs to be able to respond to the words and thus to distinguish a correct response from an incorrect one. But there is nothing "collective" that happens in this process of training. There are, rather, explicit sayings together with patterns of behavior that are the subject of sayings about whether something does or does not conform to the rule, or "count as." There have to be explicit sayings, because the act of training requires that something is explicitly articulated.

The "normative element" here is the distinction between right and wrong, or the hidden thing that makes this distinction possible. But if the distinction is simply a matter of individual trainers' and trainees' ideas about right and wrong, it is "normative" without being normative in some sort of special sense that requires "collective intentionality" as an explanation. Nothing *is* hidden in the acts of training and being trained: the trainer says "right" or "wrong" and the trainee becomes accustomed; the former is explicit, the latter a personal, Background phenomenon. That some way of acting or "counting as" is "right" is, in any case, a matter of belief separable from the activity of counting. One needs only to be able to count "as if" one were a Weegee Islander to be able to "count as" quite successfully.

In some cases, such as the tacit rules of grammar that Chomskians claim we speak in accordance with, "correctness" is not a matter of explicit rules. But in the case of social institutions, as Searle imagines them, something *does* need to be explicit. In the standard case, "collective intentions" need to be accepted and in some sense agreed upon, at least initially. Only afterwards can there be an intentional structure to which one gets accustomed. The act of acceptance secures the normative element: it is a condition for the intentional structure's being collective and thus for being "normative." But acceptance requires something explicit, like the articulation of a goal or constitutive rule. Telepathic acceptance is not known to cognitive science. And this poses a serious problem for Searle: he cannot separate the normative element that rests on collective intentionality from the necessarily explicit accompaniments of "acceptance."

The point here can be made more simply. Every time we have an institution, we have a bunch of beliefs. Some of these beliefs are "normative." But "normativity," at the level of articulable belief, is something of a mish-mash. There are political beliefs in such things as justice and the divine right of kings, religious and magical beliefs about taboos, beliefs about correct talk and incorrect talk learned from parents, and so on. "Normativity" is inseparable from these beliefs precisely because acceptance is bound up with beliefs.

Searle needs to make social institutions into the sorts of things that depend on something more than belief and accustomation. But he cannot escape belief. And beliefs always threaten to do the explanatory job that he needs a "normative element" to do, and that he must say cannot be done without such a normative element.

This difficulty is shared with a well-developed puzzle in the law. Is there such a thing as "legality," or is legality ultimately no more than legitimacy, what people accept as legal or as part of the legitimate order? Is there legality as such, separable from what people believe? In some sense there is: the legal order that is accepted may dictate, out of considerations of consistency that are themselves accepted parts of the legal order, conclusions about what is legal about which no one previously held explicit beliefs. But this does not establish that there is such a thing as the legal order, or make it "legal." The legality of the law in the sense of the legal order depends on extralegal considerations, such as legitimating beliefs, and the acceptance of the legal order that results from their acceptance. The normativity of the law, in this view, is wholly derivative from beliefs that the law is normative. If they change, for example as a result of revolution or the breakdown of acceptance, the normative character of the law vanishes.

Searle cannot easily show why the same is not true for the normativity of social institutions generally, and this is the curse under which his account operates. Where there is a Searlean "normative element" to be explained "only" by reference to collective intention, there is also and always a normativizing belief. The belief, or rather the diverse bunch of individual ideas on which people acting together typically operate, is an alternative explanation of the institutional facts that we actually observe—in other words, of what people do when they act institutionally. *The alternative explanation, consequently, is always at hand, its presence necessitated by the dependence of collective intentionality on acceptance and acceptance on explicit ideas, ideas that are normativizing, in the way that legitimating beliefs are.* Searle needs to say that these ideas cannot do the work of explaining the normative element of social institutions. If they can, the sole prop on which the argument for collective intentionality rests, the "only," vanishes.

The irony is that Searle's own efforts to rearrange the task of explanation, especially his argument that the Background and accustomation suffice to do most of the explanatory work once an institution has been established, minimize the explanatory job, and thus make it easier for beliefs to perform it. These are very powerful arguments, and radical in their reach. For Searle, there is a moment at which screwdrivers and hammers are created on which people "impose a function by collective intentionality. But subsequent generations are simply brought up in a culture containing screwdrivers and hammers. They never think about the imposition of collective intentionality: they simply take it for granted that these are certain types of useful tools. What was once the explicit imposition of function in a collective intentional act is now assumed as part of the Background" (1995, 126). If we accept this persuasive account of the role of the Background, the burden of explanation for explicit normativizing beliefs is similarly lightened. Like conscious collective intentions, they need play a role only in the initial creation of an institution that may be subsequently experienced solely through accustomation. And these normativizing beliefs are always there to play such a role, since, in reality, and as Searle seems here to acknowledge, acceptance requires that something explicit needs to be said.

Searle's argument for the role of collective intentionality comes down to the quasi-transcendental claim that the normative character of institutions is explicable *only* by reference to collective intentions. The only reason he gives is the "only" reason, in that some features of institutions, their normative character, can *only* be accounted for by reference to collective intentionality. If it is not the only explanation, if it has to compete with alternatives, it is a very dubious one. His vision of an Adamic moment in the history of each social institution in which functions are assigned is utterly implausible (apart from legal contexts in which "assignment of functions" is justified by procedures rather than "collective intention"), precisely because one of the elements of acceptance is persuasion. The alternative explanation, its noncollective *Doppelgänger*, is more plausible on every point. All of the institution–creating persuasion we are familiar with involves normativizing beliefs. The sayings of Jesus become law for his followers because they believe him to be the Son of God. Collective intentionality is either superfluous or the incidental by-product of common belief. If the football analogy hangs on the thread of the actual and necessary operation of collective intentionality in social institutions, it cannot be salvaged.

The concept of collective intentionality is itself highly problematic. Searle places great stock in the argument that intentions and mistakes are conceptually bound up with one another. But the concept of mistake works quite differently in the two types of intention: one ordinarily cannot be mistaken about one's own intentions; one can be mistaken about "collective" intentions for many reasons, including mistakes about the beliefs that others have which give meaning to their intentions. The difference in the two cases parallels the problem of explanation. Wherever there is a mistake about collective intention, there is a mistake about the individual intentions of others.

BRUTE FACTS

Searle adds to his argument a claim about ontology that has attracted considerable attention as an argument against "social constructionism." Searle is happy to concede that we could assign functions to things that are the product of previous assignments of functions. We can, for example, distinguish between junior subordinated debentures and checks only after we have established the notion of money in the first place. But at the beginning of this iterated extension of schemes of assignment of function that is the essence of social institution building, there needs to be some non–"assigned function" fact to which the first function can be assigned. You need paper, gold, or some physical object to which the function of money can be assigned. Searle thinks that if one concedes this argument, one has conceded the existence of distinct worlds of brute fact along with fact by agreement or thing by agreement, thereby creating a hierarchical ontological order, which can then be used to answer the question the book is nominally about, namely where institutional facts fit into the general hierarchy of being. Searle then uses this distinction to attack social constructionist analyses of science, among other things, as well as to attack philosophers who reject realism about the world, such as Rorty. He gives no extended analysis of their arguments and indeed denies that they have any arguments at all.

This is a most peculiar performance. Characteristically, authors such as Rorty have accepted some notion of reality but denied that this notion does very much if anything to enable us to distinguish between, say, true and false scientific theories of the world, or to validate our particular ways of describing the world by saying that our ways as distinct from other people's ways correspond to reality, while theirs do not. Searle's notion of brute facts doesn't seem to do any of this work either, so it is not clear how he thinks his is different from theirs other than by virtue of his sheer insistence on the bruteness of these facts. Searle's claim is that social constructionism is self-refuting because social construction, at least if it means enacting assignments of functions to things, requires things that are nonsocial or brute to which functions can be assigned: "the iterations must bottom out in an X element that is not an institutional construction" (1995, 191).

There is an apparent way out for the constructionist: she can concede the point of circularity and argue that this circularity is nonvicious or at least unavoidable, and that any alternative account is similarly circular. Searle himself argues that in the case of money there is an apparent circularity that takes the following form: part of the definition of the institutional fact of money is that money must be "thought of, or regarded as, or believed to be money" (1995, 52). How can one believe something to be money prior to there being money to believe anything at all about? Searle says that

> the resolution to the paradox is quite simple. The word money marks one node
> in a whole network of practices, the practices of owning, buying, selling, earn-
> ing, paying for services, paying off debts, etc. As long as the object is regarded
> as having that role in the practices, we do not actually need the word money in

the definition of money, so there is no circularity or infinite regress. The word money functions as a placeholder for the linguistic articulation of all these practices. To believe that something is money one does not actually need the word "money." It is sufficient that one believes that the entities in question are media of exchange, repositories of value . . . etc. (ibid.)

Why this argument does not work for the objects of science is not immediately clear. In the case of money "we avoided the vicious circularity only expanding the circle by including other institutional concepts. We are not trying to reduce the concept 'money' to noninstitutional concepts" (1995: 52–53). What Searle seems to be conceding here is that one needs concepts to make concepts. In the case of institutional concepts, one needs institutional concepts—barter and the like—to form the concept of money.

Searle says that this case is obviously completely distinct from knowledge of the scientific world. What is strange about this assertion is that aside from medium-size dry goods, knowledge of the physical world in its most advanced reaches depends just as much as the world of finance on the complex interlocking set of practices. The best evidence we have of the inner workings of the physical world according to advanced theory is precisely squiggles and remnants on detection devices; these are evidence for anything only by virtue of extremely complex linked sets of experimental practices. This makes the idea that there is some radical difference between the objects of institutionalized scientific knowledge and those of institutionalized financial dealings somewhat suspect, and certainly not as obvious as Searle takes it to be.

The difference between Searle and the social constructionists is more subtle. Searle treats ontology as a prior to conceptualization, and runs together the problem of whether the existence of something depends on people believing in its existence with the question of whether anyone has a concept of the thing. Thus he thinks that because the truth of such assertions as "Mount Everest has snow and ice near its summit" does not depend on what people believe about Mount Everest, these facts are unlike institutional facts, which do depend on what people believe and to which constructionism thus correctly applies. Representations have to be representations of something, brute or social, and that means that having a concept of representation implies an ontology. For constructionists, the ontological questions depend on the conceptual ones. If people have a materialist conception of Mount Everest, for them the question of whether Mount Everest has snow and ice near its summit depends on people believing in the existence of Mount Everest would be answered, of course, just as Searle answers it. If they were a tribe of Berkeleyans, they would presumably answer differently. Ontology recapitulates conceptualization, and *concepts* are socially constructed. The difference between institutional concepts and concepts of the brute world, in short, is internal to the conceptualizations that social constructionism explains, and not prior. Searle doesn't deny that it takes concepts to make concepts. For him, the consideration is simply irrelevant. For social constructionism, it is primary, and accounting for concepts of medium-size dry goods and of institutions begins in the same place: what Searle himself calls "a whole network of practices."

IMITATION OR THE INTERNALIZATION OF NORMS /
Is Twentieth-Century Social Theory Based on the Wrong Choice?

The dispute between simulationists and theory theorists follows a basic pattern in philosophical discussions of cognitive science: various theoretical principles pertinent to mind, which commend themselves to us for some reason, conflict and must be reconciled, both with one another and with some partially understood or stable domains of fact (such as the empirical phenomenon of language learning), that are taken to be especially significant or problematic. For the most part this has been psychological and linguistic material. The theory/theory-simulation dispute, as well as that over connectionism and rule/computational models of the mind, has handled conflicts over such "empirical" linguistic and psychological findings in the following way. One side shows that their account is capable of "explaining," or at least of being consistent with or of excluding the opposite of some experimental or linguistically observed finding, and argues that the alternative explanation either cannot account for or is inconsistent with the finding. Sometimes the argument takes the more limited form of showing that a given approach would face particular novel explanatory burdens in attempting to explain something; the response is often to show how these burdens might be lightened.

To be sure, there are findings, such as the psychological experimental findings that make up the core of the discussion, that need to be accommodated by a successful theory. What this means in practice is that the focus of debate is

This chapter was completed while the author was a Fellow at the Swedish Collegium for Advanced Study in the Social Sciences, whose support is gratefully acknowledged.

narrow, and on each side's efforts to explain the same things. This tends to narrow the discussion. This chapter, like some other contributions to the debate, will attempt to broaden the range of relevant phenomenon, and in this way to alter the balance of explanatory burdens. There is nothing sacred about the list of domains taken to be relevant. In this chapter I will extend the discussion to some different incompatibilities among principles and some different domains of "stable, partially understood facts."

My perspective is social theoretical, and my aim shall be to bring some of the topics of social theory into the discussion. Here, as throughout this book, I proceed from a specific thought that not all social theorists share: that certain standard accounts of culture, namely those which treat culture as a shared tacit theory, are problematic pseudo-explanations (Turner 1994). The theory theory has a peculiar relationship to these standard views of culture, which I will explain here. It appears to be compatible, but on examination, and in relation to some more or less stable facts, it turns out that it is not. The incompatibility is so difficult to resolve that it suggests that an alternative approach to mind, such as simulationism or some variant of it, is more plausible, and also that the standard account of culture is not viable. These issues become particularly apparent when we examine a set of stable, partially understood facts about the differences among psychological language in different cultures.

ENCULTURATION

Appeals to the notion of enculturation frequently arise in the theory of mind literature, though they are rarely pursued. One very interesting suggestion, made by Peter K. Smith, indicates the reason these issues might be much more relevant than hitherto imagined. Smith notes that the best evidence for mind-reading by chimpanzees "comes from those exposed to a symbolic language code," and observes that "if the labeling of IVs [i.e., the intervening variables in behavior that correspond to what were traditionally called 'mental states'] is a crucial step, this might suggest that the presence of words (or symbolic codes) for mental states, such as desires and beliefs, in the language of parents and care-givers may be crucial." He goes on to argue that "the availability of such codes is crucial for the developing individual to develop mind-reading abilities. . . . Various aspects of the care-giving environment will facilitate their use." Having a theory of mind, in this view, is dependent on being part of a "theory of mind"–possessing community (P. Smith 1996, 353–54).

This formulation quite directly poses several problems that are common to social theory and the theory theory-simulation debate: What is "enculturation," and what is "culture"? Is a theory of mind a cultural artifact, and is acquiring one thus socialization into a community and its culture? Suppose that it is. Smith himself thinks that "the explicit use of such codes by care-givers is likely to be important." But the specific language of mental states—belief, intention, desire, feeling, and so forth—varies quite extraordinarily among cultural communities. And the language of "facilitate," "crucial steps," and so forth is open to interpretation: Is the culture merely an aid to the more rapid acquisition of a capacity that would eventually be reached independently? Are the various languages for mental states just different expressions of the universal human theory of mind that would be arrived at, or is in some sense already possessed by the normal human? Do different cultures possess different theories of mind, or merely different modes of expression of a common underlying tacit "theory"? Are the variant "codes" constitutive or descriptive, and if descriptive, what are they descriptions of? If they are descriptions, could one culture's theory, or mode of expressing a universal underlying theory, be said to be better than another's? These are not idle questions, for there is a serious problem about the universality of the folk psychology and theory of mind that the theory theory is concerned with: the terms of the folk psychology do not have translational equivalents in all the languages and cultures of the world, an issue whose significance and relevance will become evident in later sections of this chapter.

UNDERSTANDING AND NORMS: THE CONVENTIONAL VIEW

Questions about the nature of understanding are not entirely the product of the debate over theories of mind: social theorists and philosophical writers on interpretation have long written on these topics. The discussion of the problem of understanding in social theory has developed in two traditions: *Verstehen,* or empathy, the German tradition of Dilthey and Weber; and taking the role (or attitude) of the other, originating in the thought of G. H. Mead. Each regards understanding as both an activity of theorists (or historians and other analysts) and of human beings themselves in the course of their dealings with one another. The problem of culture or norms takes two basic forms as well. The dominant one, rooted in Durkheim and Parsons, treats norms, or culture, as a shared body of rule-like cognitive objects that are understood to be tacit.[1]

The connection between the problem of norms and the problem of understanding, though close, is rarely discussed. Stated as a thesis, the conventional view is this: understanding, properly speaking, presupposes the sharing of

1. As we saw in chapter 2, the model figures prominently in the philosophical literature as well; perhaps its simplest statement is to be found in John Searle's *Speech Acts,* in which it is claimed of language that "the speakers of a language are engaging in a rule governed form of intentional behavior" and the "rules account for the regularities in exactly the same way as the rules of football account for the regularities in a game of football" (Searle 1969, 53).

norms. Usually, this is stated even more strongly as the claim that communication (or some other feature of human interaction) would be impossible without the sharing of norms. There is also a close and rarely discussed affinity between the problem of norms and cognitive-science models of mind that treat the mind as a rule-governed machine. To the extent that norms are thought of as akin to linguistic rules, and rule-governed models of mind as the best approach to explaining the way in which individuals are able to master and follow rules of grammar, tacit social norms may be thought of in the same way. The connection is implicit in the commonplace analogy between tacit societal norms and tacit linguistic norms.

Some social theorists have been skeptical of the "culture as rules" model, and a few have provided alternatives to it. Among the skeptics was Durkheim's main French rival, Gabriel Tarde, who proposed a theory of "imitation" to explain most of the same phenomena. The basic idea behind this alternative is present in Nietzsche as well. Children, Nietzsche observed, were natural apes, and primitive human beings were, he argued, the same. A herd instinct rooted in or taking the form of a horror of difference was the psychological basis of morality, whose specific contents were acquired by childish imitation. Tarde's notion of imitation was more complex, and included various kinds of imitation, such as "rational imitation." Weber, who was unenthusiastic about the norms model, accepted "imitation" as a genuine phenomenon and also suggested that morality was buttressed by, if not rooted in, a biological urge to conform—a model that was not so different from Nietzsche's.

These alternative approaches are very interesting in connection with the questions raised above about the nature of a "theory of mind." They deal with the phenomenon of social norms without appealing to any notion of an underlying set of rules or rule-like shared mental contents, such as a shared tacit theory. Imitation is wholly external: one can imitate only what one can see or hear; in other words, the externals of an act, thus the content of imitation, are limited by our ability to identify something to copy. We may imitate unconsciously, but this does not mean that we have special powers of unconscious discernment that allow us to discern anything other than the external aspects of what we imitate.

FUNDAMENTAL PSYCHOLOGICAL MECHANISMS: THE ALTERNATIVE APPROACH

"Imitation" is a basic psychological mechanism, so approaches to culture based on imitation proceed by first taking a backward step to the following question: What are the basic psychological mechanisms for such things as understanding, that is to ask what is the basic mechanism with which children build an understanding of minds, and what internal givens and external data do they build with? Mead gave a distinctive answer to this "basic mechanisms" question that conflicts with the theory theory.[2]

Mead's approach is similar enough to simulation and an older "imitation" theory that Mead began his work by criticizing the idea that the three might be assimilated to one another. I will ignore the differences among the three approaches in what follows (though obviously they were crucial to Mead) and call this family of theories the "emulationist" approach. The common idea of the three theories is that social interaction and "understanding" result from the workings of basic psychological mechanisms which enable an individual to emulate another person in thought—for example, to guess what that person is going to do—and to refine his expectations and responses to others on the basis of the external data given by the responses and conduct of others.

Mead's variant on this basic idea arose out of a critique of the notion of imitation with which he attempted to account for the problems with the notion of imitation and, more interesting for our purposes, to replace it as the fundamental mechanism needed for an explanation of certain key facts about individual social psychological development.[3] The topic of imitation became important in American psychology for reasons quite separate from its role in social theory. James Mark Baldwin wrote an influential work based on observations of his two young daughters (Baldwin [1895] 1968). He observed that young children imitate, something that was not controversial then or now: we may take it as a "stable domain of fact" that young children imitate. We may also stipulate the following: Children role-play, and do so endlessly and without apparent motives. They also do various other things, such as repeat; endlessly ask "why" questions that adults find nonsensical; repeat the answers to them, initially without "understanding" them; apply and alter the answers in new settings; and so forth. Moreover, children vary a great deal in what they do.

The issues between Mead and Baldwin were conceptual, not empirical. Mead argued that one problem with the notion of imitation as a *fundamental* mechanism is that it presupposes what it needed to explain, namely conscious agency, since imitating is already an intentional act. This of course is an arguable point. Psychological research on imitation establishes that unconscious imitation does in fact occur. But the issue points to a more fundamental problem for theories of mind about the causal or genetic *priority* of particular psychological mechanisms or phenomena. If we attribute a given capacity to the mind prior to its development through external inputs and attempt to explain other capacities as derivative (for example, by showing how

2. A. F. Goldman has already noted that Mead is a precursor to simulation in "Empathy, Mind, and Morals" (1995, 196).

3. In what follows, I will rely on two useful guides to these issues: Cook 1993; Kessler 1941. Kessler's dissertation was directed by Mead's student and follower A. E. Murphy.

they are produced by the initial capacity operating on inputs, such as experiences, of various particular kinds), we must be careful not to sneak into our account of the fundamental mechanism features of the phenomena to be explained. In the case of either consciousness or intentionality, the temptation is always present, though usually in a concealed form.

Typically this problem arises through, so to speak, reading motives appropriate to developed minds into undeveloped minds. For Mead, imitation was a paradigm case of this problem. People, like the proverbial monkeys, do "copy" the external behavior of others. But the language of copying and imitating is already intentional. We would not say that the accidental repetition of one action by another person or monkey under similar conditions and in close contact was imitation, but we would want something more, some additional mental element to distinguish the accidental from the genuine case. When we begin to describe this additional element, for example in terms of awareness of what the other is doing, we already have imported a minimal notion of intentionality, namely the capacity of the imitator to recognize something as a doing or an action. If we add to this something like self-awareness of copying we have imported a notion of conscious behavior as well. We no longer have a fundamental mechanism, but a mechanism that presupposes a developed mind.

Simulation, imitation, and taking the attitude of the other are similar in a key respect. They are presented as fundamental mechanisms in that they can explain various mental capacities, but do not presuppose or require a great deal of prior mental equipment. Simulation differs from imitation in the directionality of the relationship. Imitation, as I have noted, operates by an external pattern being reproduced by an individual. In simulation, the individual can think hypothetically or off-line about the individual's own behavior or experiences and project the results of this thinking to, say, the outside world, in the form of expectations about the behavior and responses of others, and get feedback about the success of these projections. To understand the anger of another person, for example, it is not necessary for the individual doing the understanding to have a theory, but only for this individual to be able to place him- or herself imaginatively in the other person's shoes and to monitor his/her own reactions to the imagined situation. The capacity enables learning, in that one can act on one's understanding, "test" it by acting on it, and modify one's simulative capacities accordingly.

In each of these accounts, the fundamental mechanisms, plus learning by experience through the employment of the fundamental mechanisms, do the explanatory work. Baldwin argued that infants were endowed with a capacity and drive to imitate, and that they developed mentally through attempts at imitation. Mead, as I have noted, objected to this on grounds that at the time must have seemed persuasive, namely that imitation presupposed what it aimed to explain, namely capacities for recognizing people and consciously copying.[4] The issue is important for our purposes because what Mead is talking about here is precisely the issue raised by simulation theory: whether interacting with other people requires those who interact to have a so-called theory of mind already or whether one's conceptions of other people and capacities for reasoning about their mental processes derived from some prior act, such as simulating the attitudes of others from which one generates, through a process like hypothesis testing, a set of expectations and capacities that are the functional equivalent of a theory of mind.[5]

EXPLAINING OUR CAPACITY TO UNDERSTAND

One reason the question of what is prior is especially important relates to understanding: if the way in which individuals acquire the capacity for understanding others resembles the acquisition of a theory, such as a theory of mind, and if, in the cultural case, it requires the acquisition of some set of normative rules that are interiorized or internalized, the things acquired are assumed to be essentially the same for everyone, and the condition for interaction and mutual understanding is the fact that each of us shares the same theory. Empathy, understanding within a culture, normative action, and so forth are, on this view, like the situation in which two scientific observers in possession of the same instruments and theory are able to make the same calculations and communicate it to each other precisely because they have the same theory. But this describes the case in which people already possess the same theory. The developmental question is, How do they acquire it (or its functional equivalent)?

One problem with the "shared theory" account, from a developmental point of view, is that individuals' experiences in the course of growing up are extremely diverse. In the case of language, the massive quantity of data overwhelms and obliterates individual differences, at least with respect to such things as basic grammar. But for the sorts of things that people have in mind when they talk about empathy, individual differences are bound to be of greater significance. G. H. Mead's account of development holds that children take the attitude of others, and grants that children imitate. What distinguishes children from one another is *content:* the roles that they take and the

4. The conceptual point is important, but in this case the empirical evidence supports the idea that some capacity for imitation is very basic. As one psychologist puts it, "By the second day of life, babies can reliably recognize their mothers; and also imitate facial gestures such as mouth opening and tongue poking" (Ellis 1998, 23). This is imitation preceding any sort of feedback that would enable the infant to learn how to "copy," and thus before having an "intention to copy." For this reason I would be skeptical about any attempt to salvage a pure form of Mead's account.

5. A simple account of the way such a process would work is available in Elgin 1996, 205–11, esp. 210.

things that they imitate. And here experiences are in some respects common and in other respects very diverse. Little boys in the United States a half century ago took the role of cowboys, and little girls took the role of mommies and role-played with dolls, though obviously not all little girls and little boys did these things, and some did both. But in the course of their development children take quite different roles primarily because they are in different social environments and are compelled through this role-playing to master interaction with people who are themselves taking different kinds of roles. Roles are themselves stereotypical, a point to which I will return shortly.

Role-taking understood as a mode of acquiring competencies (as well as imitation understood in the same way) falls into a category that for convenience I will label *diversifying:* the same mechanisms, applied in the actual situations in which individuals find themselves, lead to diverse capacities of understanding. The differences bear very directly on the problem of intercultural comparison and understanding, and provide a simple explanation of the main problems in this domain. The reason we don't have empathy for, say, historical figures in ancient Rome is that we simply do not understand the roles that they are enacting; we never enacted these roles ourselves. Thus we are inclined to reinterpret empathically the activities of Caesar or Cleopatra in the stereotypic forms of the roles that we have in excess, so that Cleopatra presented on the big screen consists of historical figures behaving in stereotypic ways associated with lovers and statesmen of our own era.

These movies are, so to speak, hypotheses about these historical figures in which we, living in the present, make the historical record conform to expectations about attitudes and the like which we have acquired in the course of our own role-taking and role-playing activities. Not surprisingly, it is usually only possible to make these stories psychologically compelling if we fill in the historical record in a way that better fits our expectations—to make Cleopatra behave in familiar ways, with familiar emotions and attitudes. But in real history and archeology, matters are much more difficult: the conduct of the ancient Romans, especially with respect to sexuality, is a constant challenge to our powers of empathy. It is simply difficult for us to make heads or tails out of their attitudes and motivations because we do not share them; and we do not share them, not because we are some sort of fundamentally different human type, but because they acquired their capacities from a pool of stereotypic courses of action that we no longer possess, and which are essentially irrecoverable for us, because the social world in which they acquired them has disappeared.

The Meadian view of understanding is that understanding another person consists in taking the attitude or the role of the other. Indeed, social interaction and its continued enactment and operation depended very heavily, in the view of Mead's followers, on the fact that people could rely on various stereo-typic expectations. If I go into a doctor's office I know how to behave as a pa-tient and the physician knows how to behave as a doctor. By virtue of these roles we understand one another by imaginatively projecting ourselves into the role of the other. If the doctor asks me a personal question, I respond to it by understanding that it reflects and is meant in terms of the role of the physi-cian and not, say, the role of a new acquaintance or a clerk.

In what I have said here I have vacillated between the "stereotypic" aspects of this process and its "diversifying" ones. The literature itself tends to vacil-late in this way, and in one sense the notion of role is extremely congenial to the notion of a culture as a set of normatively defined roles; it is in this form that it entered the thought of Parsons. Roles are simply understandable as en-actments of normative expectations, and norms can be understood as a notion correlative to roles. If you are sick, for example, you must conform to the sick role in order to be "understood." Parsons, indeed, studied precisely these ex-pectations. But everything depends on how one thinks of the stereotypes. One might think of them as common possessions, as a kind of theory that each member of a group acquires. Or, one might think of them as internal mental devices, as a *private* shorthand (consisting, perhaps, of expectations) that is partly structured by public codes, that is, by language, or what Mead called significant symbols. Weber seems to have thought of what he called ideal-types in this way as well: as a private set of simplifying cognitive devices, whose employment, consciously or unconsciously, is demanded by the econ-omy of thought in the face of the infinity of perceptual material. But he also recognized that one could be trained, as a lawyer is trained, in the use of con-ventional ideal-types, such as those of legal categorization, and that one com-municates scholarly findings by constructing such types for others.[6]

This "private shorthand" model preserves the personal or diversifying character of stereotypes. We may each use the same terms in describing a "sick" person, the practical necessities of communication provide feedback, and a kind of public disciplining of our usage occurs through the various en-counters in which we use the term. But the mental content of the term for us is our own, the product of our experiences, and it could hardly be otherwise, since language learning is done through experience and feedback like any other learning.

Two points should be made here to forestall any misunderstanding and to

6. Weber is quite clear that these concepts cannot represent the shared theory of people: the "ideas which govern the behavior of a population of a certain epoch . . . empirically . . . exists in the minds of an indefinite and constantly changing mass of individuals and assumes in their minds the most multifarious nuances of form and content, clarity and meaning." If, for example, the "Christianity" of the individuals of the Middle Ages "could be completely portrayed," he adds, it would be a "chaos of infinitely differentiated and highly contradictory complexes of ideas and feelings" (Weber 1949, 95–96).

prepare the ground for the final discussion. Nothing in what has been said here to characterize the "emulationist" approach conflicts with the thought that, among the basic psychological possessions or starting points of individuals—along with a basic mechanism such as simulation or imitation—are some basic emotions, perhaps associated with basic facial expressions. Indeed, it helps this approach if the basic material with which "understanding" develops includes some common starting points, so that children do not have to learn what pain is and what expresses it, but can instead use this capacity in interpreting others. Common starting points are sometimes called basic emotions, and there is important evidence that there are some universal feelings with universally correlated facial expressions (Ekman 1993, 384–92).[7]

If there are some such common (and noncultural or universal) starting points, it makes it possible for us to create a bridge into another language or into the emotional experiences of others by linking our "hypotheses" about the feelings of others with a set of facts, namely the facts conveyed by facial expressions. There might also be "nonbasic" emotions that are not indicated by facial expressions. These might well arise through various transformations and training out of (or building on) basic emotions. Patriotic feeling, for example, is perhaps rooted in fellow feeling and pride, but is the product of training or the experience of participating in specific rituals, and is nonuniversal and nonbasic. There is no guarantee that such emotions will be accessible to those who have not shared the experiences, or analogous ones. Feelings of sexual attraction, though certainly rooted in something "basic," may also develop in very different and mutually incomprehensible ways, depending on the experiences of the individual.

With these various distinctions in mind, we can consider the question of what it is that people "acquire" through feedback from their experiences with others. One answer would be what might be called the "culturalist" one—that people acquire a culture, in a specific sense of this term. Clifford Geertz, himself a student of Parsons's, famously defined culture as "an historically transmitted pattern of meanings embodied in symbols, a system of inherited conceptions expressed in symbolic forms by means of which men communicate, perpetuate, and develop their knowledge about and attitudes toward life" (Geertz 1973, 89).

We will shortly reconsider this definition with respect to the notion of "inheritance." The feature that is crucial here is the notion of "system of . . . conceptions," which is to say a theorylike intellectual object. In an earlier part of this discussion I asked whether the theory of mind was such a system of inherited conceptions, but delayed answering it.

7. The idea is also found in Darwin, who attributes them to animals (cf. 1988), and has a close affinity to Wittgenstein, who says "the common behavior of mankind is the system of reference by means of which we interpret an unknown language" (1958, §206).

Another answer to the question, What do people acquire? would be this: all that understanding another person means is to be able to interact, and this means to play the relevant roles, to take the attitude of the other in the relevant stereotyped ways, and to employ the significant symbols in this activity of attitude taking. What we "acquire" is no more than the results of our own attempts to interact on the basis of our hypotheses about the attitudes of others, and the feedback that enables us to improve our attempts to take the attitudes of others is the success and failure of our interactions. There is no more than this to understanding, and specifically nothing in the way of "a system of conceptions" that must be "inherited" in order for us to understand.

This "emulationist" account of mutuality is also an account of culture, or rather an alternative approach to the phenomena that are usually explained as "cultural." Acquiring a culture, in this approach, is nothing more than acquiring the ability to take the attitude of others with respect to stereotyped roles and significant symbols. Culture is thus not a system that needs to be "inherited," but a set of learned capacities organized around objects, such as symbols, ritualized actions, and so forth. The capacities are individualized in the sense that personal history of learning is not irrelevant, but disciplining, mutual interaction, and experiences around particular symbols may tend to make people respond in ways that are outwardly uniform.

CULTURE VERSUS PSYCHOLOGICAL UNIVERSALS

The linguistic psychologist Anna Wierzbicka, who works on the problem of the language of emotions, imagines the following dialog between psychologists and linguists:

P: Fear and anger are universal human emotions.
L: Fear and anger are English words, which don't have equivalents in all other languages. Why should these English words, rather than some words from language X, for which English has no equivalents—capture correctly some emotional universals?
P: It doesn't matter whether other languages have words for fear and anger or not. Let's not deify words.
L: Yes, but in talking about these emotions you are using culture-specific English words, and thus you are introducing an Anglo perspective on emotions into your discussion.
P: I don't think so. I am sure that people in these other cultures also experience fear and anger, even if they don't have words for them.
L: Maybe they do experience fear and anger, but their categorization of emotions is different from that reflected in a standard English lexicon.
P: Let's not exaggerate the importance of language. (Wierzbicka 1998, 161–62)

This conflict is important for the theory theory, but for a reason that is difficult to explain. The conflict between the linguist and the psychologist is closely analogous to a conflict between a "culturalist" interpretation of the "theory" involved in the kind of reasoning about the minds of others that is learned by children, and a "psychological" one.

How does one explain the diversity of emotion terms in different languages? Wierzbika considers angst, an emotion that has no proper English equivalents. The problem with angst is this. It is widely reported as an emotion among Germans, but not reported widely in other cultures, and indeed is not part of the language at all in most other cultures. This emotion, then, is "cultural." The psychological theory is that there are certain common basic emotions that all people have. Angst is therefore not "basic." So there is no direct conflict here. But there is a conflict nevertheless, and it is a profound one.

Both theories attempt to explain the same kinds of facts, emotions. The linguistic or culturalist explanation suggests that emotions are in some sense cultural, dependent on the things that language is dependent on. The psychological explanation holds that at least some emotions, and perhaps all real emotions, are universal, and explicable by features of human psychology, biology, and development that are themselves universal. Neither can be completely right. Either the "culturalist" explanation is specious for some emotions, such as anger, or the psychological account is false, a mistaken attempt to turn a cultural fact into a universal feature of psychology. There is a burden on the psychological account to explain such emotions as angst, that apparently are not universal. And there is a burden on the culturalist account to explain why some emotions appear to be cultural and others appear to be universal or noncultural, even though there is no apparent reason that the same cultural explanations that are invoked for angst could not also be invoked for anger.

Of course, there are a variety of possible solutions here. But the important point about these "solutions" is this: they impose additional burdens on the explanation, burdens that are not apparent from the initial explanation. The same point holds in the case of the theory theory, in its relationship to culturalist explanations of "folk psychology," where there is a similar problem about language, a problem that is in some respects more serious. Folk psychological language is theoretical, and for this reason even more varied than emotion language. Four examples can be given. The term *believe*, in which the "false belief" problem is itself defined, lacks good equivalents in some languages—a problem discovered at a practical level, as Rodney Needham has observed, by Bible translators (Needham 1972). In many languages, it is impossible to describe sensations: the locutions for description are literally translated in forms like "Object X stands in relation Y with me." In classical Chinese, it is impossible to formulate statements taking a form analogous to "X believes P," where

P is a proposition. To translate "*X* believes the moon is red," one might say, "*X* uses the moon and deems it red."⁸ In short, many of the elements of folk psychology that make up the false belief problem and the conventional theory of mind are *not* linguistically or culturally universal.

This kind of variation poses a problem for enterprises like the theory theory that can be understood by analogy with the difficulties that arise with emotions. They come down to this. The theory theory is an account of developed intentional thinking, complete with an ability to solve the false belief problem. Its answer is that people, all people (with the exception of those who have genuine psychological abnormalities, such as autism), somehow acquire this theory. The theory, incidentally, is false in that it is a part of "folk psychology" and cannot be developed into a scientific theory of mind. If normal people do not acquire the theory, the theory theory is itself false. If they appear to acquire different theories of mind, as the surface differences in language suggest that they do, then these differences need to be shown to be irrelevant to the validity of the theory theory as an explanation.

It would be convenient for the theory theory if the language of folk psychology were the same or more or less completely and easily intertranslatable the world over.⁹ If so, it could be said that children are aided to acquire this theory (which it is agreed they do not have from birth, since there is a stage in which they cannot solve the false belief problem) by maxims, codes, and the like—the stuff of culture. If all cultures were uniform with respect to these maxims and codes, it would be possible to list them among the universals of culture, and perhaps even to theorize that the reason they are found in the same form in all cultures is that they reflect a universally acquired psychological "theory" which is in some sense not linguistic but is prior to language or in the language of the mind itself. In this case the surface differences of language could be dismissed, in the manner of *P* above.

The fact that the diversity of mental language is apparently greater than this is inconvenient, since it imposes additional explanatory burdens. It could mean that people in different cultures have different mental terms and thus

8. As Chad Hansen explains, "The core Chinese concept is *xin* (the heart-mind). As the translation suggests, Chinese folk psychology lacked a contrast between cognitive and affective states ([representative ideas, cognition, reason, beliefs] versus [desires, motives, emotions, feelings]). The *xin* guides action, but not via beliefs and desires" (Hansen 1998, <www.hku.hk/philodept/ch/>). At least one philosopher, Herbert Fingarette (1972, 37–56), has suggested that classical Chinese has no psychological theory. This would be a quite literal example of a non–"theory of mind" community.

9. It seems that intentional language *is* more or less translatable, but that "belief" language is not. As Needham says, "Belief makes an extreme contrast. It is not a necessary concept, and it is not a distinct capacity of inner state; other languages make no recognition of a mode of consciousness of the kind, and other people order their lives without reference to any such capacity" (1972, 146). "Belief," however, is a key concept in the "folk psychology" that the theory theory purports to explain.

genuinely different theories, each of which happens to enable them to solve the false belief problem, but differently, which is to say that the theories are cultural artifacts. This would mean that the theory theory is gratuitous for its main purpose, explaining "folk psychology," because the specific folk psychologies of particular groups are already explained as distinct cultural facts, as something acquired with and as a part of a culture. But this leaves the explanation entirely at the level of culture and cultural adaptation, and treats acquisition as a matter of acquiring culture, which of course does not occur in one developmental step.

Thus, a new explanatory burden is created by the "cultural" explanation, namely, a problem of explaining the apparent universality of the solution of the false belief problem. Perhaps it is not such a difficult one. It does seem odd that all cultures should develop a false theory, and more or less the same false theory, and that this is the adaptive theory. But perhaps this is merely odd. One can deny that the commonalities amount to much more than the result: the common ability to solve the inferential problems called in English the false belief problem. If the whole business of mental language and "theory" is cultural and culturally relative, it is perhaps surprising that all cultures have the equipment to solve the false belief problem in the form that it can arise in that culture. But perhaps it is not. Perhaps it is simply analogous to the fact that all cultures can in some sense think "causally" without all having precisely verbally equivalent concepts of causation. Both ways of thinking are profoundly adaptive (as a culture of autism would not be), so there simply is no extant culture that lacks them.

There are alternatives that can save the theory theory from reduction to culture, but these create some even more peculiar explanatory burdens.[10] If the universal features of the developmental process explain acquisition of the theory theory, and the theory is false, then one must explain the cultural and linguistic diversity of folk psychological idioms. But how does one explain cultural differences if the mechanisms of acquisition of the theory are themselves general and psychological? The problem is analogous to the problem of emotion terms, but not precisely analogous, since the terms in question are not primary descriptions, but theoretical terms about nonobservable facts. Why would people hold the same "theory" tacitly and nonlinguistically, but articulate it in different ways? One could say "error" and see the folk theory of different cultures as bad theory, like bad science or ethnoscience. But this is overly complicated. It is more plausible in this case, in contrast with the emo-

10. The culturalist account is not free of profound explanatory burdens either. For example, even a culturalist account is forced to posit some universal cognitive machinery. Recall the metaphors of "inheritance" that recur in Geertz's definition of "culture." What is the cognitive mechanism by which "systems of concepts" are passed from one person to another intact, in other words, as a "system"? This question is the theme of Turner 1994 *(The Social Theory of Practices)*.

tions case, to drop the hypothesis of a universally shared tacit folk psychology entirely. Yet dropping that hypothesis leaves the process by which children develop these cognitive capacities, the empirical findings that have motivated much of the discussion, unexplained, and apparently inexplicable.

What this suggests is that both the culturalist and the psychological universalist approach to theories of mind bring in their train serious explanatory burdens. A combined approach would have its own burdens. Chomsky's linguistics is often the model that thinkers in cognitive science have in mind when they consider the nature of the mechanisms they study. But Chomsky's approach carefully avoids this problem, by modeling the relation of the universal claims it makes to the actual diversity of languages on the relation between language and dialects: all human languages, it is claimed, are dialects of the universal language. This is not an option open to theory theorists. Theories are the same only if the terms of the theory are the same, and the problem here is that the terms of folk psychology are not the same, and some of them do not even appear in other languages.

CONGENIALITY AND EXPLANATORY BURDENS

What sort of argument is this? What we have arrived at is a very crude result. The alternatives of the theory theory and simulation have been extended to deal with some more or less stable facts that are usually of concern to social theory. Various lines of development of the basic idea of the theory theory turn out to run into peculiar explanatory burdens, such as explaining the actual cultural diversity of terms for beliefs, intentions, and so forth. When we arrive at these issues, the difficulties mount up. The contrast between "cultural" concepts and a "universal but tacit" folk psychology turns out to produce particularly serious problems, problems of compatibility between explanations. Put simply, the problem is that two "theory theories," a universalistic psychological one and a relativistic culturalist one, attempt to explain the same thing, and thus conflict. Neither can be reduced to or made easily compatible with the other. Neither is implausible.

Simulation and related fundamental mechanisms, however, appear to avoid these problems. They don't rely on "possession of a theory" as an explanation, and consequently there is no conflict between two theories, of different kinds, each of which explains some of the same things. The problem is to see if the basic mechanisms, together with some plausible starting points, such as emotions and recognition of emotions expressed on faces, can account for the things one wishes to account for. And in this case it is plausible, at least for a large range of things. Actual experience, notably the empirical experiences gained in role-playing, imitation, and simulation tested by experience, provides a great deal of the kind of psychological content that is needed to have the capacity to interact socially.[11] And the capacities thus understood are congenial with an alternative account both of understanding and of culture itself—though not necessarily an account in which a culture is a kind of a theory and in which understanding is by virtue of sharing this theory.

I use the term *congenial* for a reason. Though the relationships here are relationships of a particularly loose kind, they are nevertheless meaningful. The relations between the "stable domain of fact" I have appealed to and the very abstract models at stake in the discussion are not so well defined as to make the facts into very persuasive tests of the models. More important, the models can be developed in various ways, on the basis of the internal resources of the models, to account for the findings or facts that are claimed to be problematic for them. But difficulties do arise, and the conflict between the culturalist notion of the "theory" that explains intentional language and the psychological notion of the "theory" that underlies the inferences needed to solve the "false belief" problem is a significant one. The less burdened path in the face of this conflict is to avoid the notion of "theory" in either the cultural or the psychological context, and this is congenial with the path I have labeled the "emulationist" model, which avoids appealing to shared tacit theory, psychological or cultural. It is the path that twentieth-century social theory for the most part did not take. Perhaps the balance of explanatory burdens has now changed, and it is the path that should be taken.

11. And, incidentally, to think intentionally about others, which as we have seen Needham suggests is universal, in contrast to other elements of "folk psychology."

FOUR

RELATIVISM AS EXPLANATION /

One difficulty with even beginning to talk about relativism as a kind of intellectual object is that it is unclear what kind of intellectual object it is. Is it a theory, a metatheory, reflexive paradox, a form of skepticism that insists that any claim (or any first premise) is as good as any other, a methodological principle, a type of inconsistency, a cultural or world-historical condition, a vegetarian expression of nihilism, another word for tolerance as it applies to questions of basic ideologies, a form of the idea of the suspension of judgment, merely another word for the basic principles of tolerance and the acceptance of the possibility of our own fallibility, or an implication that arises from some other philosophical commitment, such as antirealism, existentialism, the fact-value distinction, or any of dozens more ideas?

Settling the question of which it "really is" seems pointless, at least if the point is to vindicate or refute relativism, because whatever disputes arise over relativism are likely to again arise in the course of placing it into one or another of these categories, or in deciding what it means to be in the category. The disagreements that arise about relativism will typically still be there once one puts it into a category. If relativism is just intellectual tolerance, for example, what does this mean when we come to the question of tolerating intellectual absolutism? Is there a relevant difference between, say, the absolutisms of Steven Weinberg (1996) and of the Jehovah's Witnesses? If there is, what is its basis? Suppose we say that Weinberg possesses "minimum rationality" and the Witnesses do not. Why is the criterion of minimum rationality itself anything other than another form of absolutism? Why is religion less "tolerable" than science?

Stalemates of this kind are characteristic of disputes about relativism, and result from the binary structure of the problem: the ability of the relativist to relativize the premises of the absolutist, and the ability of the absolutist to show that the relativist must relativize her own premises as well. Relativistic stalemate in its various forms will not be my concern here, other than to show that it may be avoided. What I will suggest is that by going around to the un-guarded back door of these various versions of relativism, to what I will call the explanatory side of relativism, something new might result.

Although relativism is closely connected to explanation, the explanatory structure of relativism is rarely discussed. This contrasts with the case of philo-sophical skepticism, where the contexts and conditions for the skeptic's claims have come to be seen as critical to the problem itself; and it is generally under-stood that there is something fishy about the extensions of particular skeptical claims, such as the reasonable skepticism about flying saucers or out-of-body experiences, where we have some checks to distinguish real from fake physical experiences or evidences of the presence of physical objects—to the kinds of skepticism associated with Descartes or Hume, which challenge experience in a totalizing way. The difference is perhaps not surprising, for two reasons. The first is that the relativist operates with real differences, not wild hypotheses, and seems to have evidence on her side. The second is that the explanatory claims, though crucial, are rather dowdy and uninteresting. The implications of rela-tivism for "truth" and other such questions, such as the possibility of estab-lishing the ethical superiority of one culture over another, are flashy and dra-matic, and unlike skepticism seem to justify practical conclusions.

Nevertheless, these dowdy little explanations, which frequently are no more than very thin sketches of explanations (typically even less—no more than allusions to categories of explanatory ideas, such as vague appeals to "culture" or "history"), deserve our attention. They deserve a separate in-quiry precisely because they are independent of the conclusions about truth, superiority, and so forth that they are usually taken to ground. As a matter of logic, this means that they may be a weak link in these arguments. This may not seem to be a very likely possibility. But if there *is* an error in one of the rarely discussed steps beyond the facts that relativism rests on, mundane facts about differences, then the conclusions about truth, superiority, and so forth that are supposed to follow might not follow. If the error is a systematic one, one that occurs across the whole range of classes of specific explanations that justify relativism, it may be that relativism is not entitled to its strongest card: the relativistic significance of factual differences in culture, perspectives, frameworks, worldviews, and the like.

THE JESUITICAL CONCLUSION

The case I make here will be in support of what I will call, for reasons that will become clear shortly, the Jesuitical Conclusion. An outline of the argument is this: claims that the validity of particular beliefs is "relative" are, or depend on, explanations, explanations of the fact that people disagree. But people disagree all the time for reasons that do not suggest that validity is "relative." For example, people may disagree about the truth of some proposition that is underdetermined by the data, such as a proposition about which horse will win the next race or what scientific theory about some topic is true. This disagreement may be quite rational in the sense that each of the conflicting claims is consistent with the available data, and no issues about validity arise. So relativistic conclusions are not the only possible implications of the fact of disagreement. This brings to mind a possibility raised by the Jesuit who explained that he was theologically obliged to believe in Hell, but not to believe that anyone was in it. It could it be that relativistic explanations are never needed. If so, there is no "problem" of relativism, other than as a hypothetical possibility. All the actual differences that have been taken to be cases of relativism are something nonrelativistic. This is what I will call the Jesuitical Conclusion.

At first, this may seem like a strange approach to the issue, for difference and disagreement of the most fundamental kind are to be found everywhere: between cultures, genders, scientists and nonscientists, different scientific paradigms, different traditions, different religions, and so on. Difference is the most salient fact of the age, together with the recognition that our beliefs are only one cognitively unprivileged historical possibility out of many. One might suppose that anyone coming to the Jesuitical Conclusion would have to ignore all this, and subscribe to a reduction of otherness to error and inferiority, issuing from a numbing ethnocentrism, unwarranted philosophical self-satisfaction, or discredited anthropological theories of the psychic unity of mankind.

This is very far from my opinion about the reality and significance of differences in belief and usage, so perhaps I should make this clear at the outset. If anything, discussions of relativism in the philosophical (and especially in the ethics) literature seem to be unable to grasp the depth of the issues—to see, for example, that the very language of ethical theory itself, of norms, obligations, commitments, and so on, is culturally and linguistically specific to a Western Christian tradition, and very imperfectly translatable to other traditions, a point I will illustrate below with respect to relativism itself. Even cognitive terminology, such as the term *belief,* varies enormously, as Rodney Needham stressed a generation ago, and perhaps even the possibility of characterizing others as possessors of beliefs is not universal. "Relativism" in some sense seems to be a fair characterization of this situation, and the burden of explanation seems to me to fall on those who pretend that "our" way of talking about these things is right and everyone else's is wrong, or is just a concealed way of talking as we do.

Yet it simply does not follow from examples of differences, however startling, that the differences must be understood "relativistically." The problem is with the "must." The unasked question is this: can one explain the actual differences in satisfactory ways so that no cases actually remain to be accounted for relativistically? If one cannot, is this for reasons of principle, or is it a matter of the inadequacy of our data? If this question is answered in a way that is consistent with the standard attacks on relativism in the philosophical literature, the answer would be that there is truth and error, and anything not true is to be accounted for by an "error theory" which is itself true.

No one, so far as I know, has bothered to try to vindicate this line of argument by examining the empirical cases. It rests on a different argument, which is not about explanation but about the self-referential problems of relativism as it bears on truth. Any other answer, according to these standard arguments, would be self-undermining, because if one asked whether the other answer were true, one would get only the answer that it was true relative to its paradigm, tradition, or whatnot, which is a confession that it is not really true, or not really any better than the alternatives, and therefore falsely presents itself as a generally valid claim. As one can see, this leads directly to an impasse. The relativist can say "So what?" and observe that everyone is in the same situation, dependent on a tradition, whether they acknowledge it honestly or not. And quibbling about whether the situation is itself genuinely a cause of relativistic incompatibility is beside the point. In this respect the person arguing for the fact of genuine incompatibility is like the person arguing for the possibility of the existence of God. If it is true that God exists, it doesn't matter whether it is paradoxical or that there are no good arguments for it. Our arguments and ideas of paradox will simply need to adjust to the reality. Similarly for relativism: if there are fundamentally divergent frames and "rationalities," and our frame or our ideas about rationality cannot be made to accommodate this, the facts win, and it is our frame that collapses into paradox and confusion.

If we go back to the problem of explanation, and wait to leap into the issue of the self-referential paradoxes of relativism until we are forced to by a true explanation with relativistic implications, it is clear that the Jesuitical Conclusion is an open possibility. The question "Are there differences that *can only* be understood relativistically?" is a live question that can be answered only by considering real explanations or types of explanations, and concluding from these considerations that there are such differences. I will suggest that there is no need for the kinds of relativistic explanations that "undermine rationality," that these forms of explanation do not exhaust the universe of possible forms of explanation for the differences, that there are plenty of genuine problems of explanation that these explanations attempt to address, and that both of the sides that lead to the impasse depend on bad forms of explanation.

This is a circuitous approach, with its own problems, but it is nevertheless one that moves beyond the sterilities of much discussion of relativism. The key to the sterilities is this: the very structure of the "problem of relativism" *as a problem of truth* is binary, so that the denial of relativism seems to require the acceptance of absolutism, and the denial of absolutism is the same as relativism. But as a problem of explanation, rather than as a problem of ultimate truth, there are other possibilities. If these other explanations suffice, there is nothing specific—for example, in the way of a fact of irreconcilable difference—to motivate relativism, and thus nothing to motivate its absolutistic denial. The difficulty in establishing this arises from that fact that every disagreement can be turned into a case which appears to be "relativistic," the product of different fundamental premises. Showing that this appearance is misleading needs to be done—if not on a case by case basis, then on the basis of showing that some class of arguments can be better understood differently. And in what follows a large number of potential relativizations will be considered, in each case to make a similar point: that there is no need to accept the relativistic characteristic.

WHAT DOES RELATIVISM DO FOR US?

Classifying relativisms is an instructive first step toward understanding relativism as a problem of explanation. There are two basic forms of classification found in book indexes: in terms of topic, such as moral relativism and cognitive relativism, or by the objects in which the relativism is thought to subsist, that is, the thing that a belief is "relative to," which also usually means "explained by." There is, for example, racial relativism and cultural relativism, and many variants of these relativisms. Historical relativism, for example, seems to depend on the notion that there are different epochs with different views on the world.[1] Historical relativism is both topical—it is about objects that vary in history—and a kind of explanation, in which the fact of living in an epoch is an essential part of an explanation of one's views and opinions.

The Jesuitical Conclusion is a denial that there are disagreements which

---

1. Imagined by Wilhelm Dilthey as a prison:

There are always walls enclosing us; we are always attempting tumultuously to free ourselves from them . . . [yet we must realize] the impossibility of such an attempt, for here, as everywhere, one encounters the fundamental characteristic of all human consciousness: its historicity. (Dilthey 1960, 38) force us into relativism. In terms of explanation, the problem is this: are we forced to appeal to odd objects, such as cultures, paradigms, and epochs, which can only be construed relativistically? Can the actual disagreements be accounted for differently, and better, without resorting to objects such as cultures or paradigms? Or can the objects that the explanations appeal to be better construed in ways that do not lead to relativistic conclusions? One can, of course, envision other possible questions as well, each of which might fit with the Jesuitical Conclusion. And in each case we are forced to ask the same kind of question: whether the new possible answers can avoid relativistic stalemate.

Obviously, "accounting for disagreement" is a problematic notion, but this much can be taken as unproblematic. We have many differences in belief that are accounted for very prosaically, in such terms as the fact of having had one experience rather than another, or having different information. We have a series of categories, such as acts of faith and taste, which we use to classify disagreements, some of which place them apart from reasons and justifications. These are explanatory categories, though there often isn't much to the explanation. We don't know why little Tommy likes oatmeal for breakfast and his brother Billy does not, or why Tommy likes it one day and not the next. *De gustibus non es disputandum* is, so to speak, a maxim of rationality which says that things falling into this category, taste, are not matters for which argument or reasons are relevant. In the case of data or information, the point is different. If we explain different beliefs by analogy to formal logical arguments—and it ought to remain for the moment an open question whether this is a good approach—different information or data provide different premises, and the difference explains the difference in the conclusion.

I need hardly add that there are many other ways in which we use notions like "different experiences" to account for differences in belief. These explanations shade off into others that do not immediately suggest relativism, but might be taken to lead to it. Notions of training, skills, and the like are somewhere between "experiences," data, and information, on the one side, and tacit knowledge, frames, perspectives, traditions, fundamental premises, paradigms, *Weltanschauungen,* and cultures on the other side, which can be, and typically are, given a relativistic interpretation, and have an explanatory role that more or less directly leads to relativistic conclusions. The reason for this can be seen readily in the case of fundamental premises. The data or information provides, in the language of older logic, minor premises, while the major premises are the frames, cultures, worldviews, and the like. The major premises necessarily go beyond and cannot be based on the data, but are needed in order for us to do any reasoning with the data. But this is a purely analogical usage, and the idea that experience produces only data and that the premises come from some other source is a prejudice rooted in the analogy.

Although I will not pursue the vast Kantian muddle that arises from this analogy here, it must be pointed out that acculturation, training, and so forth consist in experiences—systematized and constructed sets of experiences, with feedback, intended to produce some sort of specific capacity in the trainee, and similarly in the acculturee. The "techniques of the body" made famous by Marcel Mauss are the best example of this: performing certain "normal" bodily feats, like sitting on chairs, is learned, and part of the effort of raising children is getting them to learn to do them; a process that begins, with many techniques of the body, in infancy itself. The inputs in both cases can consist in nothing other than experiences, and even if cognitive science were to discover that we come to possess something like premises or frames by biological inheritance rather than learning, this does not account for any of the facts that relativism is based on, unless the differences that are crucial to relativism are explained by reference to biological difference, as with racial relativism.

Consider the possible cognitive science explanations of cultural difference. If the differences are simply a matter of experiences that are so persistently, massively, and systematically different that those who are subject to the different experience regimes come to think differently, it is not clear that this explanation has relativistic implications. Indeed, this is an extended form of the "different data" explanation. And if we consider that other cognitive differences, such as different memories, might also influence perspectives, one is inclined to put all of this on the data side of the line, and not count any of it as relevant to relativism or as having relativistic explanations—that we believe differently because we have had massively different experiences seems unproblematic, but irrelevant to relativism, since in the future we could come to have the same experiences and thus agree, just as if we saw the same data we might agree. The problem arises from the analogy itself.

There is a possible alternative cognitive science model of learning here, one in which trainees or acculturees construct internal rules for themselves out of the experiential material, including feedback, that is given them, which are like premises or, better yet, rules of inference in logic. This model is most plausible in relation to grammar. But in the case of grammar and of many other "rules," people articulate the rules or rules of an articulated kind (don't say "ain't") together with habits that aren't articulated, leading to patterns of behavior that resemble rule-following, and that can be captured by cultural anthropologists and ethnomethodologists. A famous example in ethnomethodology refers to a person who says, in an ordinary setting, "I have got all my usual clothes on today." The idea is that this produces confusion and astonishment because it violates a "rule," and the reaction indicates the existence of hidden rules.

This is simply a bad inference. Children are *told* to wear clothes, to wear their usual clothes, and so forth, often and explicitly. There is no mystery here—acculturation is feedback from experience together with explicit statements of many kinds relating to clothes and when they should be worn, and habituated responses to clothes talk of various kinds. Do these things amount to "rules" that are cognitive science facts in the minds of people? No, or at least it is a bad inference to make. The uttering of the problem phrase is a problem for the hearers. But it is not so much a problem because there is a "rule" in the heads of people in the setting that says something about the inappropriateness of the utterance (and it is difficult to imagine what such a rule could be), but because there is nothing that the utterance does. It does nothing precisely because it is *not* linked to habitual patterns of response or explicit expectations in the minds of the hearers, and does nothing in a setting where people expect utterances to do something.

So there is no necessary direct relation between the "rules" accessible to cultural anthropology and ethnomethodology, which are "as if" rules, that is, descriptions of what some activity would be like if it were governed by rules, and the contents of people's heads, even if these happen also to be rule-like, since the "as if" patterns can be produced by a fantastically wide variety of combinations of things, and a fantastic variety of rule-like things in people's individual heads. This bears on the premises model, in this sense: even if the cognitive contents of a mind are in part rule-like, or can be conveniently represented as rules, there is no reason to think that each of us doesn't have different rules, produced by our different experiences, to produce our overt patterned conduct or our joint, collective conduct—or that we produce these without rules at all.

THE PREMISES MODEL

Perhaps the simplest way to understand the premises model is through a joke. The Georgian wit Sydney Smith was walking through Edinburgh with a friend when they came upon two women on opposite balconies arguing with each other. The friend observed that it was no wonder they were disagreeing, for they were "arguing from different premises" (Epstein 1999, 18). The pun, to be tedious about it, rests on the ambiguity of "premises," an ambiguity between premises in the sense of arguments and premises in the sense of property, but also, and more subtly, on the idea that a difference in premises in the property sense is an explanation of the difference in premises in the argument sense.

Call the explanatory form in which disagreements are explained by citing the fact that people are arguing from different premises "the premises model." The model, along with its usage, is so ubiquitous that we don't notice it. It has a nonanalogical use, namely in the case of two or more explicit arguments from premises to conclusions where there are conflicting conclusions and each conclusion in conflict is the logical consequence of some different set of premises. But in Sydney Smith's case the usage is analogical: we infer that the two women possess beliefs which they are reasoning from that differ.

The premises model leads to relativism if we add the following: the people who are disagreeing are arguing from different premises that can be secured only by reference to other "different premises," which are "fundamental" in the sense that they cannot be secured at all, but represent acts of commitment or other nonrational causes. If the causes are racial, for example, we have racial relativism. The term *premises*, in Smith's pun, is a term that implies fundamentality and the equality of fundamental premises: the reason they will "never agree" is that the premises are unrevisable because they are fundamental, in that they depend on no prior premises, and are equal for the same reason. This is a different kind of equality from the equality of underdetermined hypotheses that are open to determination by new data, or new considerations, for no amount of new data bears on genuinely fundamental premises, and new considerations can only arise from different premises.

What is striking is the problem of how one gets to the point of invoking this kind of explanation. The analogical moment, the point at which the analogy ceases to have the appearance of an analogy and takes on the appearance of a description, is usually invisible. Smith, for example, does not justify it. We are made aware of it because he employs *premises* to make a pun, a pun that plays on the ambiguity between two explanations. But on occasion it is underlined for us. Margaret Mead, in *Coming of Age in Samoa*, uses a variant form of the premises model: "Each primitive people has selected one set of human gifts, one set of human values, and fashioned for themselves an art, a social organization, a religion, which is their unique contribution to the human spirit" (1928, 13). Here the imagery differs from the premises model, but the structure of the reasoning is the same. Human "values" are "selections." But the act of selection is wholly analogical, as is the term *value*. The implications are the same as in the premises model: values, because they are selected, are not given, and are equal with respect to not being given.

Why does this matter? What is wrong with a bit of metaphor here? These explanations imply relativism when the metareasons—such as culture—are themselves held to be equal, or equally contingent. And here is where the metaphor is a trap. Mead also says that each primitive people "fashioned for themselves" an art, a religion, and so forth. Fashion, choice, commitment, faith, value, decision, preference, selection, and so on are terms that are bound up with this whole body of characterizations. But they are all analogical, and the analogies have similar problems. If we think of the Hobbesian story about the origin of sovereign power through a social contract made in the state of nature, we can see some reasons for a problem. One is that the notion of choice is itself an unhistorical imposition. Did any "primitive peoples," as she says, select their values, in some sort of collective act of will? Of course not, in a literal sense. Did they "select" or choose at all? Were they conscious of choice, and what sort of choice was it—rational, or in some sense prerational or nonrational? When they "fashioned" their art, religion, and so forth, did they think they were doing so? Or did they think they were warranted, justified, correct, or doing what was necessary? Perhaps this would not matter if the language of choice and commitment were the unequivocally correct description of the reality of their situation. But if we are trying to assess the language of description itself, specifically to assess the claim that there is no alternative to this language, hence no alternative to the relativistic implications of this language as used in explanation, we cannot prejudge the issue.

We thus arrive here at a new form of the impasse, issuing from the ubiquitous language of choice and commitment, which fits with the premises model so neatly. Why does it seem natural for us to use this language in order to understand cultural difference? One possible answer is this: the reason it seems so natural for us is that it is an extended application of a body of concepts that we use in our own historical tradition to characterize religious differences. The idea that one must believe in order to understand dates to the Christianity of the Roman era. The Reformation, which sought to go back to the early church, revived this way of talking, in connection with such doctrines as justification by faith alone.

The use of the term *faith* to describe a religion followed naturally from this. And the existence of different faiths, equally rational because they were each rooted in different acts of faith, was the hard-won intellectual outcome of the wars of religion. It soon became rooted in political doctrines of toleration. Nothing could be more familiar to us than this tradition and complex of ideas. But it is an act of ethnocentrism to suppose that it is the terminology that uniquely reveals the truth about the matter. That, one would rather say, is a matter of what terminology makes for the best explanation. To be sure, the question of what makes for the best explanation might be supposed to always collapse into relativistic stalemates over the concept of explanation, over the cognitive value that is pointed to by the phrase "the best," and so on. But then again it may not be the case that this is a matter in which there are genuine "relativistic" alternatives either. The premises model would lead one to think that there must be such alternatives, or that the problem is always interpretable solely in terms of the conflict of premises. But this assumes the explanatory adequacy or superiority of the premises model itself. And this is the issue here. But before we can consider whether there are better alternatives we must consider whether there are alternatives at all.

IS THERE AN ALTERNATIVE TO THE PREMISES MODEL?

In this section I will consider some ideas of Axel Hägerström, the Swedish philosopher of law, who supplies two important elements of the argument: first, a model form of a critique of the premises model, and second, an alter-

native form of explanation of differences. The explanatory accounts he gives
are not dependent on the premises model: they are reminiscent of Comte's
Three Stages, or an earlier Enlightenment model of intellectual change found
in Turgot. Those he criticizes are versions of the premises model applied to
law. The criticisms involve the fictitious and analogical character of the explanations of the key notions of normative legality, issues that bedevil the philosophy of law still. In the law this takes the form of the problem of the basis of
the premises of the law, what Hans Kelsen called the *Grundnorm*. The basis of
the law cannot be in the law itself—if there is a primal enactment that creates
the law, for example, it cannot itself be in accordance with the law, for there is,
by definition of *primal*, no law until the primal enactment.

Legal positivism had various ways of dealing with the problem of grounding this object and explaining what it was that made it "the law." The standard
answer prior to positivism was the "will" theory—that the law was the law because the sovereign, or the "people," or some such entity willed it to be the law.
Hägerström's attack on this model parallels my comments on Mead: he took
these assertions quite literally, and showed that they lead to absurdity.[2] He
demonstrated that the law is the law even if the sovereign doesn't like the law,
that the "people" don't need to will the law, either collectively or individually,
that supraindividual "willing" is just another joke, and so on.

The arguments need not be repeated here; they worked by taking the standard explanations of the lawness of the law seriously as explanations and showing that they promptly fell apart, just as Mead's "selection" fairy tale does.
Hägerström then turned to Kelsen's *Grundnorm* and did the same thing with
it. The results are as embarrassing for legal positivism today as when they were
written. It doesn't help to say, with H. L. A. Hart, that "recognition" rather
than will is the basis of law, because recognition just gets us in the same explanatory circularities that will did. If the basis of the law is the recognition of
the sovereign, who recognizes the sovereign as the recognizer of the law? If it
is the individual, obviously people don't actually perform some sort of act of
recognition, and if they ceased to recognize it, individually, the law would still

2. A fair sample of Hägerström's strategy of translating literally to produce absurdities, of
which many can be found, is this comment of the idea that law can be the expression of the general will.

(I)It is not at all certain that the individual would demand that all others should in all respects
observe the rules of law. Do criminals as a rule feel such a burning desire that the judges shall
apply the criminal law to them? (ii) The individual has no adequate knowledge of the rules
of law which hold in his society, and therefore cannot demand that they shall be observed. It
might no doubt be alleged that the general will does not demand in detail the observance of
rules of law, and therefore that it does not need to have knowledge of them, but that it merely
demands observance in the abstract of rules which have a certain formal character. Suppose,
for the sake of argument, that we ignore the element of pure fiction in this whole supposition. Still, no particular rule of law can be a demand of the general will, on this view, since
its special content is not demanded by that will but is a matter of indifference to it. (1953, 21)

be the law for that individual. Supraindividual "recognizers" don't help much either, since they seem to have no reality beyond the job of recognizing and thus validating the law, which then goes on in a mundane way as a closed system (cf. Hägerström 1953, 11–12).

Objects like cultures, paradigms, and worldviews of course have an uncanny resemblance to the closed, gapless, axiomaticlike object of "the law." The reason is simple: both are applications of the premises model. If one buys into these notions, one has the same structural problem. The grounding has to go on outside the system, and it seems it has to be done by providing some sort of single super-reason that serves as the "basis" for the whole thing. But it can't be a reason, at least in the sense of the reasons that are valid within the system, for that would be circular. So it is usually an act—an act of faith, commitment, et cetera. The language is just an echo of the will theory, as it should be. The will theory had already recognized that the only "reason" one would give in these cases was a nonreason, a cause or an action, which explains why one accepts one thing rather than another as a reason.

Hägerström gave a naturalistic account of this process. He took over the utilitarian's notions of association as the basis of sentiments about duty, but in the face of the problem of the diversity of morals and law, argued that the relevant associations are with local and particular legal ideas, and explained notions of duty through their association with these ideas. The utilitarians tended to run the problem of explaining morals and the acquisition of moral sentiments together, especially by arguments like the following: one learned from experience that stealing is bad, that is, one acquires associations between stealing and bad experiences, and at the community level people come to learn that stealing has bad effects and thus come to regard it as bad.

Hägerström's originality comes from his refusal to accept these arguments. He forthrightly treated the law as essentially magical, and the ideas of duty and obligation to which we become attached as essentially magical as well. And this yields something quite different from the premises model, something, I will argue, that is an explanatory alternative, and one that can be generalized outside the law. Suitably understood and supplemented, it sustains the Jesuitical Conclusion, for these kinds of explanation do the explanatory work that the premises model purports to do, and better.

In a major work on Roman law, Hägerström analyzed the notion of legal obligation in terms of these magical contents. To give some flavor of the reasoning, consider the following. If I say, "You are now man and wife" or "I promise that I will pay you one hundred dollars next Monday," I am doing something with legal effect, if the conditions are right—if I and my auditors are in the right state or are privileged to say such things, for example. We would now call these statements performative utterances. As Hägerström saw, that is not quite to the point, especially if one considers the history of legal promising and marriage ceremonial. In fact these are, in their earliest known forms, magical acts, and this is especially obvious in the case of the actual Roman procedures for taking legal action, where, for example, to sell land one had to bring a bit of soil from the land to the transaction. So saying "I promise" or "You are now man and wife" is for Hägerström really more like casting a spell than describing, commanding, and so on.

What intrigued Hägerström is that our present notions of these things, though differently theorized, are the lineal descendants of the Roman magical notions. Like Vilfredo Pareto, he saw that the theories about the rituals changed while the rituals went on largely unchanged.[3] So the appropriate explanation of the form of our present notions of obligation is to trace the changes in the notions. This leads us in a quite different direction. Rather than starting with some sort of generic notion of rationality, within which we operate like rational choice actors to come up with a set of institutions that serve our interests, the starting point is the genuinely magical past, which we have altered or disenchanted in various ways. Diversity may be accounted for within this style of explanation by either the fact of different starting points or different historical paths of alteration.

Hägerström was not especially concerned with diversity, but he had the machinery to deal with it. At the level of explicit legal theory, there were various ways in which the formulae of the past would be modified, improved, and the like, and Continental legal history is the history of these changes and the different legal systems this history produced. But all this history may proceed on the level of explicit theory and justification—there are no moments of "recognition," no places in which the "will" expresses itself de novo, and so forth. Hägerström thought that the law was *still* magical, and that the revisions did not and cannot erase this essentially magical character. It is a bit like this: the lawyer is like the sorcerer searching for the right formula for the results that he wants; one can get better in concocting formulae, and get better results, and have a better theory of the construction of formulae. We are never without law, and at best we have fancier and better theorized spells to cast.

A skeletal form of Hägerström's reasoning is as follows:

1. The ideas through which we conceive the world have a history, with various contingencies.

2. These contingencies include the starting point of the ideas, which are typically magical or superstitious, though only seem so in retrospect.

3. The development of ideas reflects choices about what makes sense that reflect other contingencies. In the case of the Roman law, for example, the way

3. It is perhaps worth recalling that Peter Winch used an argument of Pareto's about Roman lustral rites and the ritual of baptism as an example of the failure to understand the significance of concepts.

in which the notion of the responsibilities of persons for their agents has changed over time has reflected the legal issues that have been presented by particular kinds of events such as the promises made by employees, which have no determinate solution in Roman law itself because the issue does not arise in the same way in past circumstances. Not surprisingly, enactment and theory develop in different ways under different circumstances, and may well lead to conflicts between different legal systems deriving from the Roman law.

4. Neither the legal theorists nor the enactors of the law need be "irrational" in any special sense to come to the different conclusions they come to, though irrationality, interest, and a great many other things may in fact account for the way in which ideas develop differently in different places.

5. In the case of the law, there is a strong magical element at the beginning. This does not "vanish" completely, and indeed many of the notions that become part of the law in the course of change, such as "rights" in the modern sense, derive from other parts of the law and, so to speak, carry a burden of magic—such as the "natural-law" elements in them. The complete disappearance of magic or natural-law elements would be the end of the law.

Why is this significantly different from Mead's picture? One difference is this: nothing Hägerström said depended on the notion of a hidden set of premises behind the premises, a collective selection of values to make a culture, or anything of the kind. The law, for him, was not a system that is "willed" or "recognized" in some sort of mysterious (and fictional) collective act, but rather a body of beliefs, many of which have magical elements and expectations, all of which surround, and are the conditions of, enactment properly so-called. There is no *Grundnorm*, no act of founding, for Hägerström, because he didn't need this fiction. The mystery element of the law that these fictions are designed to explain is already there in the starting point of his account, namely in the magical character of legal rites.

The magic, or more accurately the belief in the magic, explains why people act as they do—in accordance with the law. Nothing additional, no implicit contracts, tacit consent, and the like, is needed. And we can see from his analysis why these accounts are useless as accounts of origins anyway: to make a contract is already to participate in an essentially magical rite. The contract theory was based on historical reality: the medieval practice of creating cities by confraternities based on oaths. This was then projected back to the beginning of legal authority as such. But taking oaths is already a magical ritual.

So there is a second significance of Hägerström's strategy. Not only did he avoid "systems" and the origins problems the notion of system produces, he also avoided the need for historical fictions. His own reconstructions of the development of Roman legal practice exemplify an actual historical procedure. If we generalize it to other cases we are necessarily forming an historical hypothesis. Such a hypothesis is not a fiction. Even Mead and Hobbes could not seriously have believed that people gathered under a casuarina or chestnut tree, as the case may be, and selected values or created a sovereign. But we can seriously believe that primitive people lived in a world of ill-understood forces about which they theorized in terms of magical powers, occult forces, and gods, and that their rituals operated in terms of these forces. We can also seriously believe that our own rituals, such as oath taking, signing a check, marrying, and the rest of legal ritual, are the successors of ancient rituals, and that there was no moment at which there was a break, no moment without any of these rituals, after which someone needed to invent them as a system and enact them through collective action. Not only can we seriously believe all of this, we cannot easily disbelieve it.

For these legal changes, then, we have the following: an account that at no point challenges the rationality of anyone (indeed, even the primitive peoples with their magical theories may be taken to be coping rationally with real data and real uncertainties); an account that does not employ the notion of system in its hidden or tacit sense; and the sense of the premises model (the law itself may be a logical system, with a premiselike structure, but these are explicit premises, not hidden or tacit ones) that does not depend on historical fictions. For the last reason alone, it is a better explanation than its fiction-dependent rivals (I will return to the question of whether "better" is illegitimately used here; for the moment it will suffice to say that *fictional* here means "historically untrue," and no known account of explanation prefers the untrue *simpliciter*).

The rivals depend on a version of the premises model. The familiar reasoning is this: the explicit law, the book of enactments, is of course not "the law," not least because it cannot include its own grounding or conditions for being the law. This is where the whole business of recognition and implicit contracts comes in, since these are the (implicit!) premises or conditions under which the law can be said to be the law as distinct from a bunch of printed words having no legal force. There is more to be said about how this kind of explanation works, and how it accounts for diversity as well as change. But the point of talking about this will be clear once the question of the relation between these explanations and the general problem of explaining difference is itself made clear.

EXPLANATIONS OF CHANGE AND EXPLANATIONS OF DIFFERENCE

Why is this relevant? The category "explanations of change" is a subset of the category "explanations of difference," so the two are obviously closely connected. And it is significant that there is at least a subset of the category "explanations of change" that appears to avoid the usual relativistic stalemate.

The difference between the earlier lawyers and the later ones is a matter of the rituals they employ and the extent to which they take the associated superstitions seriously. This is a difference, so to speak, within a tradition, in which there is continuity and in which some things, indeed a great many things, remain more or less the same—contracts are still contracts, persons are still persons, and so forth, even though the concepts of person and contract evolve and change. But what is the relation between change explanations of this special type and difference explanations generally?

Consider the following answer to this question: the kind of explanation Hägerström gave for law is not merely a subset of change explanations, but a type of explanation that, suitably extended, can deal with all the actual explanatory problems of difference that the premises model and its variants attempt to solve. If we established this claim, we would establish the Jesuitical Conclusion: there would be no cases in which it was necessary to appeal to the premises model or its variants.

This is the case I would like to make—that there is nothing magic, so to speak, about Hägerström's explanations, that they are unproblematic and uncontroversial, and do not depend on any special theory. Our problem here is a metaphilosophical or methodological one. We need to understand these explanations and see why they have the power they have. Once we have done this, we will see that it is the premises model, not Hägerström's, that is strange and unnecessary, and that the problem of relativism that is compelled by the premises model is thus based on a misunderstanding. To make this case, it will be necessary to go back through a series of issues, and see why, under the pervasive influence of the premises model, they have been misconstrued—to abnormalize the premises model and normalize Hägerström's.

This radical strategy is open to a major objection. The kind of evolution and change described by Hägerström is irrelevant to the Jesuitical Conclusion, precisely because it is "within a tradition" in which some concepts remain more or less the same. The problem, however, is to explain differences *between* traditions. But there is a problem with saying this. If we assume that "within a tradition" means "sharing premises," then the objection merely presupposes the premises model, whose explanatory value we are examining. But there is a second sense of "within a tradition" that is purely historical, namely that the things passed on in the tradition have been passed on in a direct lineal sequence, which is a historical matter. It is the significance of this feature—the factual matter of tradition, so to speak—that needs some scrutiny.

The key to the success of Hägerström's arguments is that he could assume a mechanism by which legal concepts change. The problem with this mechanism, for my argument, but not Hägerström's, is that this mechanism only works where there is in fact a historical lineal descent of a concept. The mechanism is simple. A legal concept develops—in other words, is applied to new and slightly different cases in ways that permit its extension to still other cases—to the point that two subjects of legal action that formerly appeared to be the same now appear to be distinct; or, conversely, two that formally appeared to be distinct now appear to be equivalent. In either case, the law develops by equating one thing to another. What appears to be "equal" or distinct is not a matter that can be settled by appeal to the pure concepts of the law, but falls rather into the category of *applicatio*, the application of general concepts. Consequently, a relationship such as the use of the state horse on the family errands of the state official that once appeared to be a right of office subsequently appears to be an act of theft.

One can see legal categories evolving in this way all the time; for example, when someone attempts to deal with the question of whether one's e-mail is private by such expedients as determining what computer it was written or received on. This business of finding legal equivalence and determining what is reasonable is clearly contextual in the sense that the kinds of considerations that go into it are basically casuistic, and the cases that are used to construct casuistic arguments differ in different contexts, leading to different results. One can scarcely imagine how an ancient Roman jurist would have decided this question of the ownership of e-mails received at work, but one can be sure that the relevance to similarities would be conditioned by the kinds of examples that the Roman jurist would have at his command and the properties that could be appropriated and extended as "relevant" from these examples.

These conceptual equivalencies develop differently in different circumstances, since different cases present different things that need to be equated or distinguished. Taking the step of treating two kinds of cases as "the same" and entrenching this equivalence in practice leads to the possibilities of new and different future responses to new cases in which it is necessary to make distinctions or settle questions about future equivalencies. The sequence of solutions to problems of equating and distinguishing constitutes a kind of path. We have no difficulty in saying both that the outcome of legal development is path dependent, and that the legal concepts enforced in any given legal systems are the result of this path, which in common law jurisdictions can be traced through precedent-setting judicial decisions and in Continental jurisdictions through the writings of professors of law.

There are, of course, other ways in which concepts change, and the whole distinction among concepts changing, data producing changes in expectations that change the concepts in other respects, and other modes of change is problematic in various ways.[4] What I have given here is a simplification, but in a do-

---

4. I will give a very simple example here. The inferences we make with "concepts" depend on what sorts of expectations we have; and the "same" concept, "death," for example, can change its role in the inferences we draw if the circumstances and expectations change. It is evident, for example, that the frequency of direct experience with death, of family members, people in the street, and so forth, is much reduced as the result of the demographic transition. What death

main in which simplification is inescapable. The issue is whether the simplification offered by the premises model is inescapable—and the existence of an alternative simplification with a superior explanation answers this question in the negative. If the answer can be extended to the whole domain covered by the premises model, the Jesuitical Conclusion follows. The obstacle, however, is deep differences, notably those that go beyond single traditions.

EXPLAINING DEEP DIFFERENCES

Divergences among paths explain differences, so these are explanations of conceptual difference as well as change. But they are explanations that work only when there is a lineal connection between paths, where a concept can be traced back to a prior node where the concepts were the same—a common ancestor. One might identify this common origin with the idea of the shared tradition. In any case, the issue of different traditions does pose a problem for any generalization of Hägerström's model to the point where it is grounds for the Jesuitical Conclusion. The point may be put simply: suppose that Chinese thought, the thought of the Andaman Islanders, and the thought of the !Kung, as well as the thought of the Indo-Europeans, all have different origins, and employ different concepts. Nothing about the divergences of paths could explain these differences, because the paths, by hypothesis, would have always been different and never shared concepts.

This seems like an insurmountable objection, though once upon a time it would not have seemed so. One might, after all, claim that the origin of human concepts is in one set of concepts and one setting, and that every subsequent concept is a revision of these basic concepts. This is essentially what William Whewell said about the concepts of science—that one needs concepts to make new concepts, but there have always been concepts to revise, right back to the beginning of thought about the physical world. Of course, there is nothing one can really say, empirically, for or against this hypothesis, other than to speculate about the relation between concept possession and archeological evidence, genetic evidence about human origins, linguistic evidence, and so forth. Anthropologists in the nineteenth century were comfortable with these speculations, but in the twentieth century, especially under the influence of Franz Boas, they became unfashionable and regarded as unscientific.

---

means in a culture changes along with this. The Renaissance Florentines' constant contact with death, and the whole structure of religion and religious devotion, reflected this. The images of heaven and hell in the Duomo mean something different in a world in which death was a part of daily experience. Death is not at all part of our daily experience. The change is massive, and probably the consequences—for the role of religion, the functionaries of mortuary practice and belief, and so forth—are massive as well. Did a concept change? Or the data? I don't think this is a very good distinction. We are inclined to say the concept changed when there is some distinct difference in usage in relation to other concepts, but in a sense by then the concept in terms of the expectations attached to its use had already changed.

But there is a connection to the problem of relativism here that makes this change in fashion less than innocent: Boas, Mead's teacher, was an eager promoter of cultural relativism, that is, the application of the premises model to culture. He would have said, as Mead did in the material quoted earlier, that the cultures listed above had different cultural premises, that these premises were equally as valid as our own, and so on. He would not have regarded this as a historical hypothesis, but as a statement about the character of culture. Nevertheless, as we have seen with Mead, this is disingenuous, not to say dishonest. There is a real question, though probably not an answerable one, about the origins of cultures. The "multiple origins" answer has no historical evidence behind it that establishes its superiority to the "single origins" answer. It seems plausible to use only as a result of the plausibility of the premises model itself as applied to current cultures. But this is what is in dispute.

We can better define the dispute in this way. A picture of the problem of cultural change that everyone would accept at least as plausible might be this: there are today multiple traditions, in the sense of complex bodies of inferences that connect to one another. These traditions develop internally, at least in part, by an analog of the process by which legal concepts develop, in that in new contexts, with new objects of comparison, things come to be regarded as the same or different, and their usages become entrenched and form the basis for future changes of usage when new objects of comparison arise in new contexts; these form paths, and the resulting divergences are explicable by reference to the history of the conceptual changes on the path. This, in short, is Hägerström's picture. The premises model does not deny any element of this picture, but adds something to it: that the traditions are based on fundamental premises that are not groundable but are simply chosen and are therefore equal to other such choices, and that there are conceptual revolutions in which new premises are established.

What is in dispute is what to do about different traditions, and whether premises do any explanatory work that a less problematic explanation cannot do. The case of conceptual revolutions is crucial, because this is a case in which it is claimed both that there is an explanatory necessity that only the premises model can supply, and that there is a type of change that Hägerström's model cannot account for. These two disputes can be handled separately. One involves a singular deep difference, between traditions, and the other, a deep difference between two sides of a conceptual revolution. The problem with Hägerström's model as an approach to deep differences between traditions is that different traditions perhaps lack a common ancestry.

TRADITIONS: DIFFERENT ALL THE WAY DOWN?

The idea that different traditions represent radically different conceptual starting points, without common ancestry, appears to be the pons asinorum over which this line of reasoning cannot possibly advance. If there were historically, genuinely different starting points, and if all path development, or at least all that can be explained by means of the nonpremises model, is internal to a tradition, the premises model is necessitated by the problem of giving sense to the notion of different starting points. But this problem is still infected with the premises model, for it is not clear that the only sense that can be given to different starting points is the sense given by the premises model. Indeed, we can just as well invoke error theory at this point, and argue that the original starting points were compounds of what each tradition later regarded as superstition, error, confusion, and bad theory together with bad theology. To say this sort of thing internally, within a tradition, does not require any sort of special "perspective" other than the perspective for which Hägerström's model allows, the perspective of the later results of the tradition.

The problem may be understood as follows: our default attitude to "our own" tradition is that it is the product of conceptual changes (and other changes—in belief, expectations, tools, and so forth) since the beginning of human tradition. The premises model in its various forms, as well as historicism, to be considered in the next section, takes a different view: that each era, or each culture, has premises (value choices, and so forth) distinctive to it. These premises, rather than starting points at the beginning of human culture, are what we ought to compare. So we are to compare our premises with, say, those of the Andaman Islanders, or the ancient Romans. But there is something deeply fishy about this when it is applied to the lineal sources of our own concepts, to "our" tradition. In the case of our own tradition, we have no trouble in saying that it was full of superstitions from which we have emancipated ourselves, false theologies we reject, and so forth. We do not take the idea of the divinity of the emperors of Rome seriously. It is only under the influence of a theory, namely the premises model, that we would say that this is a piece of political theory that is "equal" to our own political ideas.

When we turn to the hypothetical but nevertheless genuinely historical problem of the starting points of "our tradition," however, matters are somewhat different. Our attitude toward our neolithic or preneolithic ancestors is that they were wrong about almost everything "theoretical" and right about a lot of practical things—otherwise they would not have been able to survive and pass anything along. We don't feel any angst about saying that the emperors of Rome were not divinities, for example. And we think essentially the same thing about the lineal ancestors of other present-day traditions. We don't think that the emperors of China or Japan were divine, either. We also see these beliefs as more or less equivalently false. But are we entitled to do so? The premises model says that we are not—that the choices underlying these beliefs are just a selection from the available stock. So why do we feel entitled to reject the divinity of emperors?

Begin with the fact that the apparent inequalities between us and the Andaman Islanders which cultural relativism—using the premises model—denies, do not reach back to "starting points." We would not have expected that the people whose concepts were the source of our concepts were any different from those who were the sources of other traditions' concepts with respect to anything cognitive, the correctness of their concepts, or any other matter. With regard to starting points, we are egalitarian—we think that they are equally erroneous. Are we entitled to think this? If we are entitled to do so with respect to the starting points or distant past of our own tradition, and the alternative starting points are (as indeed they are) more or less similar in the kind of beliefs their distinctive concepts support, is this not all we really need in order to be entitled to make these claims with respect to them as well? Isn't the functional similarity of starting points in the distant past enough to treat them as equally wrong? Isn't this similarity as good, for our explanatory purposes, as common ancestry?

Perhaps the best way to think of this question is to imagine a few scenarios under which similarity—the possibility of translating into more or less similar claims in our own language—did not hold. If we found that the claims did not translate similarly, we would be faced with a difference in traditions greater than exists today, perhaps with a situation in which Western ancestral beliefs, or the ancestral beliefs of what were to become world civilizations, were strikingly different and better than the ancestral beliefs of the Andaman Islanders. In such a case we would be faced with a problem of inequality that went all the way back to starting points. But as far as we know, there are no such differences. Nothing that is distinctive about the West, for example, seems to have arisen in other than intelligible steps.

Max Weber, who is the thinker for whom the problem of Western distinctiveness was central, argued essentially this point in his *Ancient Judaism*. The contribution of ancient Judaism to "Western rationality," he claimed, was its hostility to superstition. But this hostility arose not through any special virtue of the starting point of the ancient Jews, but from an accidental feature of their own ritual practice, which made it necessary for them to develop the practice of oracles differently from their Near Eastern contemporaries. Where other methods of divination allowed for priestly expertise in interpretation—entrails, the movements of birds, and so forth—the ancient Jews cast lots. So the focus of divination shifted:

> the question had to be correctly put in order that the facts and God's substantive will be determined simply by lot. . . . [T]hus the Levite had to acquire a rational method to express problems to be placed before God in a form permitting answers of "yea" and "nay." More and more questions had to arise which could not be directly settled by lot or by "yea" and "nay." Complicated preliminary questions had to be settled before they could be placed before God and, in many

instances, this arrangement hardly left anything to be determined by the oracle. . . . [T]he oracle inevitably became less and less important as against the rational case study of sins. (Weber 1952, 179)

This is a kind of reasoning that is quite congenial to Hägerström's model. It uses the accidents of conceptual evolution, beginning here with the accident of the reliance on casting lots, to account for subsequent conceptual diversity, in this case in the development of Western rationalism itself. But it does not rely at all on notions of premise change to do so.

We do not need to accept this or that particular bit of historical analysis of this sort to deal with the Jesuitical Conclusion. But these arguments still depend on branching from the same source. And this seems to be a fatal limitation. But older writers on cultural evolution were not impressed by this problem, and perhaps they were right not to be. Consider the following question: how much "common ancestry" is needed to make arguments of this sort account for all the differences that need to be accounted for? Is similarity enough? All we need, to establish the plausibility of the Jesuitical Conclusion, is for similarities to be enough to show or suppose that the differences that exist today, however deep, are the result of accidents of this kind, rather than "different premises." If we shift the burden of proof to the premises model, and ask whether it adds anything to a path model that is capable at least in principle of accounting for all the observable differences, however "deep," as the result of accidents of this kind, the issue changes. The implausibilities of the premises model catch up to it, and there is little that it adds.

The model of collective choice of premises is so weird historically that it is not really a competitor with respect to ordinary conceptual change. So the issue with the Jesuitical Conclusion comes down to this: is this addition, the premises model, necessary for some other, extraordinary kind of conceptual change? If the best answer is that it is not, the Jesuitical Conclusion holds. But if actual historical explanations of change—and not just the differences of the kind that the historically weird model of collective choice of premises or values was supposed to explain—prove to require the premises model, the Jesuitical Conclusion does not hold. And this, the issue of extraordinary conceptual change, has been a stronger ground for relativism, in recent years, than the doctrine of cultural relativism.

HISTORY, KUHN, AND PARADIGM SHIFTS

The "accidents" discussed by Weber do not threaten "rationality" itself with relativization, because his account of these kinds of historical changes does not depend on the notion that rationality depends on a selection of premises. That is apparent in his example, because the same considerations and type of explanation would apply equally to the Chinese examples of magical thinking that he believed to have hobbled Chinese development. But later writers, notably Thomas Kuhn and Michel Foucault, and many other heirs of neo-Kantianism, have argued that explaining historical changes requires a model that does depend on the premises model or one of its variants. The notion of paradigm shifts is, of course, the paradigm of these models of change. And the whole point of the model of change is to account for changes that cannot be accounted for in other ways.

Is it true that we are forced into this kind of explanation? It is doubtful that, as a matter of history, there were any "revolutions" of this sort. Despite the radical character of the changes of the scientific revolution, it fits the model of paradigm change very poorly itself. The main feature of the revolution was the removal of teleology from the physical world. But the completion of this process took generations. Kuhn's teacher and mentor, James B. Conant, from whom Kuhn took his interest in revolutionary moments of conceptual change, disliked the notion of paradigms and insisted that a great deal, particularly instrumentation and the understanding of the instrumentation, stayed the same throughout a revolutionary period.

Richard Rorty summarized the appeal of Kuhn by commenting that the exciting achievement of Kuhn was to show that scientific change could occur like the change of political orders. Here one sees, *in nuce*, the central ambiguity of the historical argument: revolution is an analogical notion, as are the other notions that played such a central role in *The Structure of Scientific Revolutions* (1962), such as the idea of Gestalt switches. The problem with these analogies, however, is that they are not only piled on so indiscriminately that in the end it is deeply unclear what Kuhn meant by his famous term *paradigm*, but that each of the analogies is either ambiguous or inapt. Coming to understand a novel scientific theory is simply not the same as seeing the duck after seeing the rabbit in the famous duck-rabbit picture, even though in the course of understanding a radically new theory one might need to make a number of analogous shifts in one's "seeing."

Revolutions in politics, similarly, are not the totalizing events in which everything changes at a stroke: Antonio Gramsci's notion that the new culture had already to be there, available to the revolution, is cruelly mocked by the fact that so little of the political culture changed at all in the great proletarian revolution of the twentieth century. In the French Revolution, the "revolutionary" forms of debate derived, as François Furet showed, from a long tradition of Masonic debate. The totalizing notion of revolution that one associates with Georges Sorel and the revolutionary mythos of the General Strike is correctly called a myth. But it is this fantasy notion of revolution that is the argument for the historiographic necessity of the premises model.

There is, however, a peculiar problem here. The Kuhnian model sought to surpass the ways of explaining conceptual change that figure in textbooks of scientific method, and within the paradigms that are supplanted. Similarly for Foucault: the point is that epistemes or discourses are constitutive of the subject matter and thus cannot be used to account for changes that occur in what is constituted. Their arguments are not against alternatives like Hägerström's, but against the explanations that can be given internally on the premises of the paradigms they are explaining. The problem is that these explanations presuppose the premises model in characterizing the situation that supposedly necessitates the acceptance of the premises model.

The key to Kuhn's argument is that the data of the old paradigm never are enough to explain the transformation to the new, even in cases where the data are anomalous. By *data,* we mean that which is accredited and interpreted as real data by the methods and theories of the old paradigm. Something new is needed, something that accredits the data or interprets this anomalous data and makes it relevant. The problem with this line of reasoning is that it is assumed that the something must be "new" premises. But are actual conceptual changes in science like this—indeed, are any changes in concepts like this? As with the original problem of assessing the question of whether there are disagreements that require, for their explanation, appeals to objects like cultures and other variants of the premises model, we are stuck with disagreements or differences that are already predescribed in terms of the model.

There is, however, a good general reason for doubting the model: it would be difficult to imagine what a genuine conceptual novelty of the required sort would be like, as distinct from the extended application of previously understood concepts. Saul Bellow invents such novel moral concepts in *Henderson the Rain King* (1959), in which Henderson comes to admire the moral leaders of a particular society known as the Women of Bittahness. Bittahness is never explained in our terms, and presumably could not be: it is not intelligible to us. Kuhn seems to be insisting that the same kind of leap beyond intelligibility is required in episodes of scientific change. But despite Kuhn's apparent conviction that scientific revolutions involve shifts into conceptual worlds that are alien to our own, the changes typically are much less mystifying. While they do indeed involve novel theories, with concepts alien to the domain of the existing "paradigm," and new interpretations of data and the meaning of data or even what counts as data, these are not novelties plucked out of the air, but typically are extended applications of concepts that are already intelligible.

SLOW CONCEPTUAL CHANGE AND PATHS

Hägerström's model can be understood easily in application to the glacial changes in such legal notions as the personality, a notion that has shrunk throughout legal history, from including one's slaves—and, for the patriarch, the members of his family—as a part of one's person to including little more than the body of one's person. The conceptual differences may be seen in such domains as what counts as the "self" for purposes of "self-defense." One might reconstruct this process nonteleologically by noting what it was in each case that led the judges or law professors who deliberated the problem to narrow the application of the concept by concluding that a new case either was or was not, for legal purposes, a case of self-defense. At each step, the judges or professors were rational in making these decisions.

The cases involve essentially the same elements. Something comes to be seen as the same or different that formerly did not. The reasons for this change in perception often have to do with background beliefs, or practical implications of a category, that change in ways that affect the judgment of sameness: for example, when an act becomes rash or dangerous, and therefore not merely self-defense, as occurs when the weapons employed in self-defense become more deadly; or when the belief in the purse snatcher's right to a day in court becomes more weighty, perhaps because of a justified sense of the greater danger of crimes involving the use of weapons or of the improbability that the purse snatcher will be seriously punished.

This may seem to be a very limited model. But the limits are not the limits of the model, but a feature of law—the desire for justice and legal certainty requires us to apply the law equally to equal cases. In other contexts, we have different motives for changing or extending concepts, and different results. Paul Churchland (2000) gives a simple example of this, taken from Paul Feyerabend. The Brownian Motion is a phenomenon that seems senseless and "anomalous" from the point of view of classical thermodynamics, and the ceaselessness of the motion conflicts with the Second Law of Thermodynamics. Both Feyerabend and Churchland employ the language of frameworks that I am rejecting, a point to which I will return, specifically in connection with Churchland's comments on the cognitive-science implications of this example. Their point in this case is that a thinker who was a genuine captive of the framework of classical thermodynamics would be stymied. But science nevertheless was not stymied. As Feyerabend points out, from another route, namely "the quite different assumptions of the kinetic/corpuscular theory of heat, its behavioral profile suddenly teems with potential significance. The permanence of the puzzling motion is only the first of many giveaways" (Churchland 2000, 150). The puzzling data can be reinterpreted in terms of the idea that heat is only molecular motion, predictions can be made that cohere with other theories, and so forth.

The moral to this story, for Feyerabend (as Churchland puts it), is "the virtue of the proliferation of candidate theories in any domain" (2000, 151). Churchland has argued that this point can be thought of neurocomputationally in connectionist terms as an illustration of the point that the amount of learning that takes place is *path-sensitive:* from some regions in synaptic weight space, the network is doomed to slide into a merely local minimum from which no series of training examples will ever dislodge it. "That is to say, a network can quite properly learn its way into a cognitive configuration that yields nontrivial performance, but then be utterly unable to profit further from continued exposure to the data. The network gets 'stuck' in a merely local error minimum. It gets captured, as it were, by a false paradigm" (ibid.). The solution to this, however, is to have other paths available, such as the path represented by the kinetic/corpuscular theory.

The point in relation to Kuhn should be clear: the new theory, in this case, is an extension of previously understood concepts on a new path, one that extends and applies different concepts. This is Hägerström's model, too. The puzzling phenomena of the Brownian Motion are "the same," in arguably relevant ways, to the motions of heated gases, and conceived of as the same, allow us to produce theory that coheres with other theories, predictions, and so forth, thus validating the extension of the concepts. The effect of this explanation is to make it into one that is like the slow conceptual change explanations of Hägerström's model. It is faster, because scientists' purposes are different from those of lawyers.

The cognitive-science implications of Churchland's remarks are important for our purposes as well. Churchland is giving a connectionist analogy to the phenomenon Kuhn characterizes in terms of a "paradigm." But he goes on to argue that scientists have, and agrees with Feyerabend that they should have, access to a variety of alternative ways of thinking that allow them not be "stuck" in this way, and provides a cognitive-science model of the kind of thinking in which there can be "on a very short time scale, quite different responses to one and the same sensory input" because there are multiple sources of preexisting biasing connections that we may think of as multiple paths. His examples have to do with recognizing pictures, which we may be unable to do until we are given information that activates the inputs from a preexisting path—for example, a picture that we can make out if we are told it is "a portly floor cleaner with a bucket, seen from behind," which the mind completes by filling in missing information from sources it had not previously accessed (2000, 155).

Why is this relevant? Because it suggests that what Sydney Smith's housewives were doing when they were arguing was not a matter, at the neuronal level, of "different premises," but of different weighted patterns of synaptic connections produced by different inputs and feedback; and that "premises" talk is merely analogical (the stuff it is analogical to is not some sort of distinctive mental content, some sort of premise-stuff). The whole point of the premises model is that the premises are premises, that is, different in kind from mere inputs. It has always been a mystery as to how such premises are acquired. But the whole line of argument in its many variants depends on the idea that they differ. Connectionism, too, depends on starting points, but these are acquisition algorithms rather than premises, and are very far indeed from paradigms, cultures, and worldviews. To be sure, what is learned from new experiences depends on what is already there, namely the embodied history of the training given by experience, in the connectionist model. So this history, not some distinctive mental possession called premises, culture, or paradigms, is what is causally relevant to how each housewife reasons that leads her to reject the reasoning of the other. "Premises" are rough analogies at best, and deeply wrong and misleading analogies when applied to the causal processes of cognition.

DOING WITHOUT PREMISES

For various purposes it may be quite harmless to use these analogies to characterize the tacit basis of argument. To say that people have premises or make assumptions—and mean by this not the assumptions and premises they employ explicitly but assumptions and premises that they employ tacitly—is a device for making sense of what people say. But sometimes the analogy is harmful. The argument of this chapter has been that the problem of relativism comes from taking the premises model literally, and then posing questions about the tacit premises to which it refers as though they were not problematic analogical uses but akin to explicit premises. I have argued both that the premises model is a bad explanation and an unnecessary one, and this requires some amplification.

Begin with the following counterargument: this argument fails because you are not entitled to use phrases like "good explanation" in the first place—such phrases are relative to standpoints, traditions, class interests, gender, historical epochs, disciplines, moral commitments, your relationship to God, and so forth; and your use of this phrase and your acceptance of the validity of this concept of good explanation is just a product of your position. My response to this is simply that this counterargument fails, because it is circular: it invokes an explanatory theory, the premises model, that is a bad explanation and an unnecessary explanation, unnecessary in the sense that we are not forced to accept it because there is no alternative, and it is a condition for the possibility of something for which we need to account.

To make the issues here as clear as possible, they can be put in terms, not of preferences between alternatives, of good versus bad explanations, but of minimal grounds for acceptance. For simplicity, consider only "premises model" explanations and their variants and what I am calling here path explanations. By this term I mean to include not only the explanations exemplified by Hägerström's discussion of Roman legal ritual, but also Weber's discussions of the contingencies in the development of "Western rationalism," plus other nonproblematic explanations, such as changes in expectations resulting from different inputs. The difference between the premises model and the other model is this: the premises model is a fairy tale, useful for enabling understanding, but false. Its falsity becomes clear as soon as one considers the literal meaning of terms such as *selection* of values by a culture. In contrast, the path explanations are historical hypotheses, which are not verifiable in practice, but which can be improved and argued about because they are stated as factual. Moreover, they have factual implications that can be used to support or undermine them in comparison with other hypotheses.

The issue between the two is not so much a matter of preference, of better and worse explanations, as a matter of what counts as an explanation. A preference for a real explanation, one that refers to facts, is not a preference at all—so it is not "relativizable" in the same way as, say, a preference for predictive power over theoretical simplicity.[5] Premises-model explanations don't count at all; they are not in the realm of fact, period. The appeal of the premises model depends on the sleight of hand that occurs when the historical realities (however inaccessible) are ignored—a sleight of hand practiced, not coincidentally, by Boas himself, who promoted cultural relativism at the same time that he attacked his nineteenth century anthropological predecessors for historical speculation. They, however, had real, if perhaps not soluble, problems, which Mead's variant of the premises model "solved" in a bogus way by appealing to a historical unreality, an act of collective selection of "values."

So the premises model is simply a sham form of explanation. It cannot be the ground for a usage that attributes the possession of actual tacit premises to anyone, because there are no such things. This is a crucial point. The only ground for thinking there are such things is explanatory convenience. But something that is not an explanation is not a candidate for the status "convenient explanation." The supposition of the existence of tacit premises cannot be justified on the grounds of inference to the best explanation, because it is not an explanation at all. The usual quasi-transcendental argument to the effect that there must be tacit "premises" for something, such as communication, to happen also fails—to be a candidate solution to a transcendental argument problem, to be a candidate for a condition for the possibility of something, it must be real.

Disqualifying the model as a form of explanation, however, does not put an end to the apparently meaningful objections. I will not try to catalog all of

5. Laudan shows very nicely, in his *Science and Values* (1984), how these "preferences" could be argued about explicitly and revised on the basis of the experiences of scientists in fashioning theories designed to live up to particular cognitive values. His point is that there are rational grounds for revising cognitive values, including arguments resting on "ought implies can" which justified dispensing with a given desiderata when there were good scientific grounds for thinking it unachievable in some domain. The argument depends on the existence of situations in the history of science in which there are moments of factual underdetermination, during which issues about cognitive values become salient and revision can be done—but it is done explicitly, through methodological argument, rather than through Kuhnian collective leaps of faith.

these here, but I will deal with a sample, to show why they are not meaningful after all. One is that excluding nonfactual explanation is a preference that is itself ungroundable. One could imagine a culture, or a coven of postmodernist Wiccans, that prefers fairy tales to factual explanations. To them one could give no compelling reason for the preference for factual explanations, since the group preference is fundamental and ungroundable.

To this, let me first observe that the argument depends on the notion of tacit group premises, here in the form of groups having "preferences." It is thus a circular argument, but one that we can keep from ever getting started. It depends on the contested premise, namely that there are such things as tacit group preferences. Thus, it appears that the relativization here ultimately occurs between two standpoints, one of which prefers the factual, the other having other preferences. But the notion of standpoints is just another group notion. And if it is conceived as an actual thing, which along with (tacitly premised) preferences is taken to explain something, we are back on the grounds not of fairy tales but of fact.

However one argues these points, the same difficulty arises: they cannot be formulated without the premises model. Standpoints, worldviews, and so forth have to be strong objects for the argument to work. Without them, the apparently meaningful objections can't be formulated. Without them, the points cannot be protected from arguments that reject them using arguments of the form "the alternative is good, valid, superior, meaningful, and so on only relative to a certain standpoint," because this argument also needs the notion of standpoint—a strong object.

BEYOND THE PREMISES MODEL: CONTINGENCY AND RATIONALITY

The premises model, by which I mean the use of the model of explicit deductive reasoning to account for reasoning based on inexplicit or tacit premises, is so deeply ingrained that it is difficult to imagine life without it. But there is one benefit, or potentially beneficial consequence, of giving it up. Relativism doesn't arise, and cannot be formulated, if we forgo this talk, because at least in its familiar forms it depends on these concepts—and depends on them being more than bad analogies. To relativize something requires something to which it can be relativized. The problem with getting rid of such an ingrained usage—though I suspect it is less ingrained than one might at first think—is that the issues it was formerly used to deal with are still there. There are still intractable disagreements, but if we now say that these disagreements cannot be the result of tacit premises, because there are no such things, what sense can we make of them?

There is a sense in which this line of argument actually leads to a form of relativism that has many of the same consequences as the argument based on the premises model. Both involve contingencies—one the contingent fact of possessing one set of group premises rather than another; the other the contingencies of historical change, in which paths diverge because at some context in the history of a concept it came to be intelligibly applied in a manner different from what it had been on a different path of historical development. Hägerström, from this point of view, is a relativist, and a real relativist. He is not a premise relativist, so to speak, but a path relativist: the paths of successive revisions of concepts that make legal systems different are such that a revision on path X may not be transferred to path Y. And this means that Hägerström cannot judge the rationality of claims in X on the basis of claims in Y.

Is this "real relativism"? I think that this is a terminological quibble, based on a nostalgia for the stalemate between relativism and absolutism. But it is an interesting quibble for another reason, for it points to a distinction between two ways of thinking about rationality. In the seventies, Robert Nozick argued against John Rawls that the issue of justice could not simply be a matter of end states, but had to be understood in terms of how the end states arose. If they arose through just acts, they were just. This, I think, is the way to think of Hägerström's relativism. He constructed an account in which there are no moments of irrationality, no leaps between worldviews, no acts of commitment, and so on—or at least none are demanded by the model itself. This is not to say that irrationality is not there. It is the ever-present legacy of the dim past and the origins of legal thought in magic. But the legal ideas we arrive at arise through rational revisions. Banal considerations of intelligibly revising the law under changed circumstances leave Hägerström with enough contingency to defeat absolutism without defeating rationality—at least in the sense of the individual rationality of the people doing the revising—along with it.

What is objectionable about this "relativism"? Even if one believes that fundamental categories or criteria of rationality come from God or nature, one is hard put to deny that the discovery of the categories or the establishment of their validity was a process in history, governed by various contingencies. After all, at any given moment the state of our beliefs could have been different. It could have been that Watson and Crick gave up on DNA, and that others also decided their efforts were better spent elsewhere. It could have been that Warren Wilson had never made the investment in molecularizing biology that created the resource base which favored Watson and Crick's efforts. People throughout history had to make the discoveries and do the validating, and they might not have done so. Similarly, someone in the future may overturn previously established truths or categories. We would then recognize, retrospectively, that our past beliefs resulted from contingencies we had not been aware of at the time. We do not know whether our beliefs were formed under the most favorable auspices. The activity of discovering and validating truths and categories, in short, is no more free of contingency, no less path dependent, than other activities. We can leap from one set of beliefs to another as we can leap from one rock in a stream to another rock in a stream, but we have to stand on one rock at a time. We can judge other rocks only from the vantage point of the particular rock on which we are standing—in light of the beliefs we have. Sometimes these beliefs give us reasons for thinking that the beliefs of people who have also acquired them through a series of rational steps are wrong. Sometimes the same will be believed of us.

The law provides many cases of this sort. We have no difficulty in saying both that the outcome of legal development is path dependent and that the legal concepts enforced in any given legal systems are the result of this path, a path that in common law jurisdictions can be traced through precedent-setting judicial decisions and in Continental jurisdictions through the writings of professors of law. There is no "error theory" that makes any sense here except one that would work within a legal tradition in which one can say that a particular judicial decision or a particular scholarly argument which was accepted for a time was in fact wrong and needed correction. This is not to say that one cannot make judgments about legal systems, admire the virtues of other legal systems, or even attempt to import the features or the legal forms and distinctions of one legal system into another. Legal systems are not hermetically sealed off from one another. They often must take cognizance of other legal systems and acknowledge their validity under various circumstances, and in any case are open to the recognition of legal arguments imported from another legal system.

There seems to be, in short, no obstacle in principle to the making of judgments and decisions that reflect opinions about the virtues of various legal usages. Of course, a decision about whether, say, a condominium contract is valid within a particular legal system is an internal decision within a legal system. But here we are on the level of explicit judgments. This limitation does not exclude questions of legal policy that might take the form "Should condominium law be recognized within the legal system?" And one can imagine very long-running disputes over the relative merits of one legal system over another in which neither system proves superior. Once we have disposed of the premises model, however, we are free to treat these as ordinary subjects of discussion and evaluation, over which we can have ordinary disagreements, reflecting our different beliefs and our different evaluations as individuals, and in which new information and experience can change our beliefs and thus our evaluations.

These legal examples show that the genealogical conception of rationality allows for the making of at least some kinds of judgments of systems. But these judgments are never free from the accidents of their own history. We don't have standards of legality as such. We have instead some general ideas about what the law is and does that allow us to recognize forms of action that are not "legal" in the internal sense of our own standards of law in this generic context. Yet our idea of what is legal is in the end part of the history of legal concepts and, like legal concepts, may be challenged by the occurrence of new cases to which our current ideas about legality are difficult to extend, to encompass in a determinate way. If computers featuring a program owned as a matter of copyright law by a particular creator themselves advance to the point of formulating their own group ordinances, complete with sanctions, are these ordinances "laws"? Does the owner of the program own these laws? Are the computers like employees, or like slaves? Can laws be property, or must they precede the concept of property? Questions of this sort, when they arise, lead to changes in our notion of legality of the kind discussed above in connection with Hägerström, and our answers—our conception of legality—have no freedom from the process of historical change he describes, with all its potential for contingency. Similarly for rationality: the genealogical conception of rationality is itself rational genealogically, as a product of a path dealing with particular questions thrown up in large part by accident and in an accidental sequence.

The claims for the second conception of rationality, which asks in a "Rawlsian" way whether we can have "standards of rationality" free from history and genealogy, cannot be dealt with here. But I will give the short response to the usual problem this raises; namely, is the genealogy notion just another standpoint, and if not, isn't it true (rational, superior, and so forth) absolutely? The answer is this: no such notion of rationality is required by Hägerströmian explanations, and there is no reflexive problem for a Hägerströmian in claiming that the genealogical conception of rationality is sufficient to account for the kinds of disagreements that motivate relativism. To be sure, the basic device that the genealogical conception employs to account for difference, the extension of concepts in the face of underdetermination, is "universal." But its universality is innocuous, precisely because it is not cultural, and thus not *culturally* universal. It is not a standard of judgment belonging to a culture, and it is not an empirical thesis to the effect that all "cultures" possess some shared premise like "extend concepts to similar objects" (and it is not because it does not involve cultures or the shared premises model at all). It does not rest on a theory of the psychic unity of humanity in the sense that it supposes that there is some standard set of categories, standard reasons, or any standard cognitive content. It is as basic as connectionist learning about sameness and difference itself.

DISAGREEMENTS: INDIVIDUAL OR COLLECTIVE

Getting rid of the premises model means getting rid of collective tacit, premiselike explanations for disagreement. Can this model of ordinary disagreement account for the kinds of disagreements that led to the premises model itself? Aren't these, properly, Rawlsian disagreements in the first place? Knowing the history of a disagreement and understanding how it arose doesn't enable one to settle such disagreements. But aren't we sometimes forced to settle such disagreements, or to take sides? Isn't agnosticism just a pose like relativism, in the face of Hägerström-explained, Rawls-unanswered cases?

The story repeated by Clifford Geertz (1986) as "The Case of the Drunken Indian and the Kidney Machine" raises precisely this kind of question. The story is of a Native American on dialysis, a scarce medical resource, who refuses to stop drinking, taking the position, as Geertz paraphrases it: "I am indeed a drunken Indian, I have been one for quite some time, and I intend to go on being one for as long as you can keep me alive by hooking me up to this damn machine of yours" (116). The issue that concerns Geertz about this case derives from a theory, the theory he takes to be implicit in the Indian's self-description, and which he shares (though with some reservations), namely that there is a Native American culture within which this is a normatively valid choice, while in the "white" medical culture that is paying the bills it is not only an invalid choice but an act of deep cruelty, since it diminishes the chance to live of others who need this resource, and might kill other potential patients. Geertz is conveniently explicit about this, distinguishing, in good premise-model fashion, between "the doctors' values (that is, approximately, ours) [and] the Indian's (that is, approximately, not-ours)" as though values were choices, or disposable possessions (117).[6]

Is this really a case of disagreement? The alcoholic Indian was certainly just as aware of risks and consequences of alcohol abuse as the ordinary person and, perhaps as a result of being around other victims, even more aware. Yet he is also, in a sense, a victim of whatever experiences and social circumstances lead him and other Indians to abuse alcohol, and because these are not merely personal afflictions but commonplace aspects of Native American life, we are inclined to question the morality of reducing this case to an ordinary case of individual responsibility, however unclear we might be on the causal processes. And, because in some sense the alcoholism of Indians is part of their historical victimization, it seems outrageous to ignore this in the case of a living, breathing, suffering human being. Geertz correctly acknowledges all this, ad-

6. Rorty, in a reply to Geertz (1991), says, "So what?" The institutions worked as they should have, namely by protecting his rights. The fact that the institutions that protected the Indian were part of what "we western liberals" take to be the right thing shouldn't bother us as it does Geertz. He recommends that "we western liberals" forget the idea that "you are being irrational, and probably viciously ethnocentric, whenever you cannot appeal to neutral criteria" (208), and forget the idea of distinguishing "between rational judgement and cultural bias" from which he believes this idea to follow. Appealing to neutral criteria, however, is precisely what the procedures of liberal institutions are supposed to do: without neutrality, there is no liberalism.

mitting to "a more than sentimental sympathy with that refractory American Indian," based on "our knowledge of the degree to which he has earned his views" (1986, 123). And if he left it at this, we would be able to treat this case as just one of those hard cases in which different moral considerations (perhaps weighted differently by different people, perhaps not) pull in different directions. In short, it would be an ordinary moral disagreement, with no easy answers.

Geertz, however, is trapped by the idea, as he puts it, of "one's imprisonment in one's own cultural tradition" (1986, 108) or a culture. And what is added by invoking the existence of a theoretical object, the idea of a culture as a framework? It could be that the doctors, or the "whites," failed to take all this into account. But adding the notion of culture-as-framework, or "our values" to this situation adds nothing substantive. Of course, there is a worry that we might give the name *ethnocentrism,* a worry that we are wrongly judging people whom we don't really understand well enough to judge, or we do in fact understand but with whom we disagree and believe to be wrong. But (as Geertz acknowledges) we have these problems with our neighbors, with the Jehovah's Witnesses who come to our door, and with irritating newspaper columnists. "Wogs begin long before Calais," as he puts it (112). This is the beginning of wisdom. What keeps him from following it up is the ensuing bit of conventional wisdom:

> The perception that meaning, in the form of interpretable signs—sounds, images, feelings, artefacts, gestures—comes to exist only within language games, communities of discourse, intersubjective systems of reference, ways of worldmaking; that it arises within the frame of concrete social interaction in which something is a something for a you and a me, and not in some secret grotto in the head; and that it is through and through historical, hammered out in the flow of events, is read to imply (as, in my opinion, neither Malinowski nor Wittgenstein—nor for that matter Kuhn or Foucault meant it to imply)—that human communities are, or should be semantic monads, nearly windowless. (112–13)

Geertz sees that this is a bad picture, once it is spelled out. He sees that the idea of choosing and commitment—the language he himself uses (112), and uses lavishly—is, if taken literally, vaguely absurd (111). But he shrinks from the implications of this literal absurdity. Hägerström was a connoisseur of such absurdities, for he knew that they were a sign of deeply defective theories.

FIVE /
THE LIMITS OF SOCIAL CONSTRUCTIONISM /

What is social constructionism? Is it a form of relativism that is essentially similar to cultural relativism and historical relativism? Is it a thesis about the contingency of knowledge? What is the point of saying constructionism is "social"? Partly because the term *social construction* originated in sociology, in Berger and Luckmann's influential book *The Social Construction of Reality* (1967), these simple "philosophical" questions have not been systematically addressed. In this chapter I will give a kind of genealogy of relativism in terms of which these questions may be posed. I will distinguish two historically important forms of relativism by labeling them *cold* and *hot*. Cold relativisms are those that appeal to notions like "culture" and "epoch." Cultures and epochs are totalizing notions. But precisely because they are totalizing notions, change is difficult to account for. Hot relativisms are those, like Thomas Kuhn's model of scientific revolutions (1962), in which change plays a more central and dramatic role. But change is a puzzle for Kuhn as well. Does it really always involve a moment of irrationality and the psychology of the mob?

Constructionism solves the problem of explaining changes between divergent "frameworks." The narratives detailing the "social construction" of a fact are accounts of change of the sort missing in both hot and cold relativisms. But the accounts work by appealing, often covertly, to a particular model of social life. Thus, constructionism depends on a distinctive social theory. On the surface, constructionist change narratives appear to be radically different from familiar change narratives appealing to such notions as rational superiority. The "relativistic" character of constructionist accounts, it seems, arises entirely from the importation into these accounts of notions that derive from either cold or hot relativism. Whether these imported notions add anything to a detailed account of the construction of a fact or concept is an open question. In the end, it seems, there are few differences between an account of conceptual change (in terms of reasons that makes some innocuous concessions to the notion of the historical contingency of knowledge) and a "social constructionist" account.

COLD RELATIVISM

Claude Lévi-Strauss made a famous distinction between hot cultures, by which he meant cultures in a constant state of change, those of modern societies, and cold cultures, those of the static world of the "primitive." The latter, he presumed, were structured by fundamental principles of mental ordering that modern thought has transcended. The distinction between our thought and that of cold cultures is dubious. Indeed, Jacques Derrida turned the tables on Lévi-Strauss by suggesting that his whole project was itself an exercise in mythic thinking (1972, 258). But the distinction is useful as a way of categorizing modes of thought about culture and about the objects in terms of which we account for the facts of culture.

The relativism of Diderot in his "Supplement to Bougainville's Voyage" ([1762] 1964) and the relativism of Jacob Burckhardt in his reconstruction of the mind of Renaissance Italy (1975) are relativisms of cultures and epochs respectively. For Diderot's audience, the perspective on sexuality of his (ethnographically quite mythical) Tahitians was exotic, but it was nevertheless open to recapture in the language of eighteenth-century European civilization. Indeed, Diderot valorized it as sensible and humane. Burckhardt's task was defined by the fact that in the nineteenth century an aesthetic sensibility so different from that of the Renaissance had taken hold that the reasons for particular works of art and architecture in the past having been regarded as great had to be reconstructed or supplied by the historian of culture.

Burckhardt was happy enough talking of "the Italian mind" (1975, 279). From Burckhardt's time forward, however, a different locution has become entrenched. The term of choice is *presuppositions*. The neo-Kantians were the first to use *presuppositions* as a term to describe the contents of the mentality of an epoch or *Fach* (speciality, field, or discipline). The idea of presupposition, used in this way, is based on a complex analogy. The model is the missing premise in a formal logical argument. What the neo-Kantian analyst does for a specialized discipline, for example, is to supply the missing premises that would make the discipline's arguments valid; these are its "presuppositions." It was understood that the presuppositions were ordinarily tacit. But it was also understood that the things taken for granted were shared among members of a discipline, such as the law, and that these common things could be identified and recovered.

Presuppositions are cold things. To think that they are shared is to think that something unchanging is shared. Consequently, this model of the cognitive character of culture lent itself to a particular range of cases, such as epochs or disciplines in which there is presumably little change and much commonality. Epochs, however, end, whereas disciplines undergo radical changes. The historiographic convention of constructing periodizations fits nicely with a certain view of these changes, namely that there must be a breakdown of order—a rupture between epochs or a moment of revolution in which the presuppositions of the next epoch are formed.

The model of rupture and revolution fits best with external explanations of change. Presuppositions could be identified with historical classes, and their rise and fall could be accounted for externally by the political or economic fact of the rise and fall of classes. This was the basis of Karl Marx's theory of the *Überbau* (superstructure). The same strategy, of identifying systems of thought with their class-bearers, and accounting for the historical fate of ideas in terms of the historical fate of their bearers, is equally central to Weber. For Émile Durkheim, moral facts (which he conceived of as collectively charged presuppositions) were established in cruciblelike moments of flux and collective "fusion" that marked the transition between epochs.

In these models, change is exceptional—a hot moment between periods of presuppositional glaciation. Ruptures and revolutions are exceptional moments, such as the birth of a new class, a period of moral collapse and ferment, or the emergence of a charismatic leader exhorting a moral or religious ideology. These moments are themselves mysterious, so change itself remains a mystery. What is the source of the bourgeois ideology for Marx? What determines the new moral facts for Durkheim? What is the cause of the charismatic leaders' message for Max Weber? In the case of Marx, there is no answer, other than the general teleological claim that the bourgeois ideology serves to justify bourgeois claims to power and legitimize its scheme of domination. In Weber and Durkheim, the claim is that in general nothing constrains the messages of the charismatic leader or the results of a period of collective fusion.

There has been a good deal of discernible change in Western society that cannot be traced to the rise and fall of class positions, to periods of moral flux, to moments of collective fusion, or to charismatic moral ideologists. Indeed, the dominant "liberal" narrative and explanation of moral development in Europe at the time that these three thinkers wrote was the story of the extirpation of superstition, the slow triumph of rationality, and the advance of secularism. Weber himself was a proponent of this model. For him, the process of rationalization was more or less normal. The explanations of non-Western cultures that he advanced were essentially accounts of the impediments to this process.

HOT RELATIVISM

The inner sanctum of the narrative of secularization, and indeed the putative motor of rationalization, was science itself. Yet the history of science by the midtwentieth century was itself subjected to an analysis of a cold relativist kind, particularly by historians of science influenced by neo-Kantianism. The most important of these was James Bryant Conant (1951), who stressed the idea that the science of a particular period served as a kind of reception device that received and accepted only those ideas for which it was ready, so that a scientific idea born out of its time would need to wait until the discipline had changed enough for new ideas to be received. Conant's teaching assistant, Thomas Kuhn, was to restate these ideas in a way that undermined the rationality and rationalization narratives decisively.

By marrying the notion of periods of flux to the notion that the presuppositions of science change, Kuhn produced the idea of periods of scientific revolution in which the first principles of science themselves were replaced. This was hot relativism, a relativism that recognized not just the alien character of the presuppositions of the dead and distant but the alienness of the presuppositions of the last generation of scientists. Change in fundamental premises was still an exceptional event—"normal" science was the norm. But revolutions were now seen as, if not normal, historically ubiquitous, necessary, and central to intellectual life.

The problem of the mechanism of change, which could be safely neglected by writers like Burckhardt or Diderot, or treated in terms of corruption by outside influences, now became more problematic. There were no "outside influences" on physics, no classes that declined or rose, no *Bau* (or underlying "structure") that changed, no charismatic prophets. What was needed to explain change in presuppositions was some sort of internal mechanism. Kuhn's own attempts to provide such a mechanism, famous though they became in the 1960s, were poor answers. The difficulty Kuhn faced was this: On the one hand, he argued that the world of the scientist was constituted by the presuppositions of a given discipline and period. On the other, he needed reasons that these fundamental presuppositions should be abandoned. But if the reasons were constituted in terms of the presuppositions, they could not be reasons for abandoning the presuppositions. So something had to give.

CONSTRUCTIONISM

Hot relativism was not a machine that could go of itself. It was, rather, a dramatic description of the phenomenon of change in search of a mechanism of change. Social constructionism supplied an internal mechanism of change of precisely the kind that hot relativism required. Constructionism enabled one to explain how facts could be constructed as "anomalies" that gave grounds for abandoning fundamental presuppositions, and thus enabled one to explain how fundamental presuppositions came to be established, how novelties came to be created, and how presuppositions came to be replaced. The secret of constructionism—and the source of its power—is that it provides an account of the creation of conceptual practices.

A characteristic constructivist argument goes something like this. Something is constructed as a fact through means that are available to the constructor. The "means" are such things as practices of representation that are shared between the constructor and the audience of the constructor. By applying these practices or by construing the world or representing it in accordance with these practices, one establishes something as a fact. "Facts," of course, are not the only things that can be constructed. What holds for "facts" can also be understood to hold for moral arguments or claims, practical facts, inventions, "isms" such as racism and sexism, and a whole variety of other things.

A (constructed) fact is also an object of conduct—something to use in relation to others. By treating a novel "fact" as a fact, one allows for the accretion around it of standard actions and forms of reasoning. Facts acted upon as facts become practices—shared between those who act upon them in a similar way and thus open to use among those who share in the actions and forms of reasoning, The step in the reproductive cycle of constructions in which practices result from treating things as facts may be called "embedding": facts become embedded as practices through shared action, successful imitation of the usages of others, and so forth. The power of facts to produce practices through their use by a given group of persons—the ability of facts to become tacitized or embedded as practices—creates audiences having shared practices. The possession of shared practices in turn enables audiences to be persuaded, joint conduct of various kinds to be undertaken, and so forth. Shared practices also makes it possible to establish new facts—in just the way that the original practices were used to establish the fact with which we began.

Fact-making and representation is not the whole of a body of practices, typically, but only a part of the joint uses of the practices. So the bed of practices within which facts are established has a kind of stability that stems from the role of practices in joint actions, and at the same time ensures that practices are community relative, meaning that a given body of practices attains this stability (or facts become practices through their appropriation in action) only within "local" settings.

The relativism of constructivism derives from the local character of practices. Only those who share in the activities, such as the laboratory activities within which facts are created and used, are in possession of the practices in terms of which facts are made. It takes another step, what Bruno Latour calls translation, to turn facts that are the products of joint action within a community into products of joint action in other communities; and typically the actions that come to surround a fact will differ and produce different practices in different communities.

AN EXAMPLE: IAN HACKING ON "CHILD ABUSE"

This structure may not be obvious in all constructionist texts, and indeed may seem like a very inaccurate description of the main work of constructionism, for example in the sociology of scientific knowledge. Especially where these narratives have become routinized, they have become partial, so the larger story in terms of which they have a point is suppressed or ignored. However, if we take a standard case of a constructivist narrative, Hacking's "The Making and Molding of Child Abuse" (1991), we can identify most of these main narrative elements quite readily. Hacking's account, like those of the sociology of scientific knowledge, begins with a showing of the point before the newly constructed idea is established as a fact. In the case of child abuse, Hacking stresses "the malleability of the idea" and the fact that it did not exist in its present, though widely agreed-upon, form even a few years ago (259). The story he tells is one about how, through the use of some very specific techniques of medical representation that were widely accepted in the medical community, a new syndrome of "child abuse" was first established. He then explains how it was, to use Latourian language, translated into the public domain, notably through the efforts of journalists, academics, politicians, and pressure groups; how the definitions were gradually extended; and how various numbers games came to be played with the new "fact" of the prevalence of child abuse. X-ray evidence was only the first in a long series of constructions of child abuse, as Hacking shows. Each step in the extension or reconstruction of the concept of child abuse depended on the establishment of a previous construction. These reconstructions are mostly, in Hacking's account, successful attempts to define things that had not previously been labeled in this way, such as incest, as "child abuse" (276). The creation of a new object of joint action, as I call it, is the point of the constructionist narrative. It is Hacking's point as well. He tells us that his concern is not simply with "the construction of the idea of child abuse" but rather with how "we uncritically and spontaneously 'make up people'" (254). People, he says,

> are affected by what we call them and, more importantly, by the available classifications within which they can describe their own actions and make their own constrained choices. People act and decide under descriptions, and as new possibilities for description emerge, so do new kinds of action. (254–55)

This is a description of the way in which a fact becomes a practice. In this case it is a practice of classification that has a power of constraint. Only some version of the social theory of practices I have sketched above can account for the phenomenon of collective constraint to which Hacking's discussion refers.

CONSTRUCTION AND CONTINGENCY

This dependence on the notion of practices comes in many forms. In some constructivist arguments, the term *practices* is used; in others it is not. The range of concepts that can be used to refer to collectively shared tacit presuppositions, methods of classification, and so forth are quite large, as I have suggested in the history given above. But the appearance of these concepts in constructionist arguments raises basic questions. To what extent do constructionist narratives depend on the notion of practices for their relativistic conclusions? Is the skepticism that constructivist accounts generate a product of convincing narrative, or is it simply a by-product of the role of a relativistic object in the accounts? Does constructionism assume relativism, or are relativistic conclusions the outcome of constructionist analyses? Hacking's explicit aim is to induce a certain kind of skepticism about the constructed fact of child abuse—not to deny that it exists, but to make it more difficult for us to take the concept for granted. If we are, so to speak, constrained by our practices or socially contingent presuppositions to take this notion of child abuse seriously, Hacking offers, if not freedom from constraint, a loosening of the fetters. This is a familiar enough aim—it was Diderot's as well. In each case we show that the usage that we took for granted is historically contingent, in the specific sense of being relative to a specific historical community, and not given by God or nature. One might think that constructionism is an extension of this insight. But there are two quite distinct claims mixed up in this formulation, and only one of them supports any sort of radical skepticism or relativism.

Consider three claims. The first is this: all knowledge is historically contingent, and what we believe to be true about the world is conditioned by circumstances, some of which are beyond our control. The second is that "the world" (and therefore what can be true for us about the world) is constituted for us by culture, language, scientific paradigms, and so forth, and these rise and fall for contingent reasons that cannot be reduced to a uniquely valid story of "rational advance," in part because all stories of rational advance are internal to cultures, paradigms, and the like, and their validity is relative to a particular culture or paradigm. The third claim is this: particular constitutive conceptual frameworks or bodies of practice have a genealogy that involves motives which in some way compromise the practitioners' claim within this framework to truth. One might claim, for example, that the modern idea that numbers are especially objective is a framework that arises and serves the interest of patriarchy.

Contingency alone perhaps justifies a certain form of skepticism, but a somewhat innocuous one. If one is not committed to the notion of ultimate truths or categories, one is free from the worry that present concepts, produced under present circumstances, do not correspond to those "ultimates." One can simply concede that our ideas are what they are partly as a result of contingencies (whose effects are usually unknown to us), and ask instead whether they are the best ideas available, and whether they can be improved.

If "frameworks" or "practices" are what is held to be the products of contingencies, however, it seems that this last activity is itself rendered problematic. Standards of goodness of theories are relative to frameworks; judgments of factuality and validity are internal to bodies of practice. The thought that our evaluations are themselves the product of historical contingencies, however, is only unsettling if we think that standards of evaluation ought to be different from facts, not subject to revision as our beliefs about the world are. If we believe that our cognitive standards are given by God or nature, we are in the same difficulty as those who believe that their categories come from God or nature. The contingencies that, we now think, shaped past evaluations are not different in kind from those that operate today and might in unknown ways shape present evaluations.

Kuhnianism was indeed an unpleasant revelation for those philosophers who thought that standards of theory-choice could be spared historicity. But acknowledging that standards are just as contingent as discoveries is only a problem for philosophers who hold that standards are and always have been not only fixed and universal but universally known. If constructionism is only a club to beat this largely lifeless corpse, it adds nothing to hot relativism. But there is more to it than this. Contingency at the level of basic frameworks seems to imply something more than contingency of factual belief. It seems to bear on the possibility of improving basic frameworks. Hot relativism says that basic frameworks are "basic." We can leap from one to another as we can leap from one rock in a stream to another rock in a stream, but we have to stand on one rock at a time. We can judge other rocks only from the vantage point of the particular rock on which we are standing. Hot relativism thus rules out the possibility that one can improve one's basic framework and be on the same evaluative footing as someone who has not yet improved it. Improvement is a leap; recognizing improvement only comes with the same leap.

The existence of such things as "paradigms," self-grounding cognitive objects shared by some group and conceived as stable, is the source of the difficulty. By definition, such objects are not revisable. Change only comes in the form of leaps, or, as Kuhn called them, revolutions; and piecemeal changes "within" the paradigm do not challenge its self-grounding bases. The problem of explaining change and the problem of "improvement" arise from the same source: the leaps can neither be explained nor justified in a way that is permitted by the theory of paradigms.

"PRACTICES" FOR "PARADIGMS"

The zone in which constructionism's claim to account for change operates is more or less the zone in which rationalizing narratives, progress and improvement narratives, and "bowing to necessity" narratives have operated in the past. In the case of cold relativistic objects, such as the Italian mind, and hot relativistic objects, such as paradigms, there was no such competition. The objects themselves were novel. Because they were such novel objects, there were no existing answers to questions like "How do they progress?" Existing notions of progress and change did not apply to these objects, but rather to such things as errors and superstitions. Constructionism, however, faces a more crowded field. The changes explained by social constructionists are usually already explained, if not precisely in the same terms, by the people who argued for the changes and by historians of science and ideas.

The smaller the object, the more extensive its applications and the more direct the competition. "Italian minds" and paradigms are relatively rare objects; practices are ubiquitous and plentiful. So to turn to the concept of practices to solve the explanatory problems of hot relativism is to invite new problems. We can ask how constructionist narratives differ from ordinary historical narratives and the narratives of participants, and how they lead to apparently different conclusions.

Hacking's account of the making and molding of the concept of child abuse provides a clear illustration of the kind of competition that occurs in this zone. He identifies a series of successful attempts by individuals to define or redefine different phenomena as instances of child abuse. The initial act is the definition of a particular identifiable pattern of bone injuries as a "syndrome" (1991, 267–68), later relabeled "battered-child syndrome." This basic concept is then remade and molded by various people to suit various purposes. Hacking's main effort is spent on the general question of the "contingency" of the concept of child abuse that has ultimately emerged from the battered-child syndrome, but two specific kinds of contingency concern him most. At each step along the path between the X-ray observations and the present concept, Hacking identifies individuals who promoted the expansion of the concept to cover more ills, and stresses the contingent character of the circumstances under which this expansion occurred—that is, under which these individuals "constructed" the concept and under which it was received and accepted by various audiences. One set of contingencies of expansion and acceptance involves power. Indeed, at one point Hacking summarizes his general argument by saying that "in the power struggle over who owns child abuse the doctors triumphed" (287), by which he means that the definition of child abuse promoted by physicians, which employed a medical model and implied that the appropriate expert authorities in this domain were physicians, became the dominant or most widely accepted definition. He goes on to suggest that "this was a foregone conclusion because child abuse is seen in a framework of normalcy and pathology" (ibid.). "Normal," he argues, is a notion that in the nineteenth century replaced "human nature." In another work, *The Taming of Chance* (1990), Hacking gave a constructionist account of the rise to dominance of this concept. So the origin of the concept of child abuse and its triumph depended on the previous establishment of the rhetorical rails on which the argument expanding the notion of child abuse traveled. These rails were simply a set of preexisting practices that had arisen through construction and a subsequent forgetting of their origins, in the same manner as the concept of child abuse itself did.

Despite calling the triumph of the physicians a foregone conclusion, Hacking makes a great deal of the ways in which the details of the molding of the concept of child abuse reflected the existence of particular institutions with particular power interests. He notes, for example, that "the name 'social work' was unknown before 1900" and goes on to say that when social work was established, "a new kind of expert had emerged and insofar as anyone was to be responsible for cruelty to children it was . . . to be the social worker" (1991, 266). This was an anterior condition for one step in the molding of the category of child abuse. It gave rise to a group of people with professional interests. The immediate occasion for one organized effort to promote the notion of child abuse was the organizational need of the Children's Bureau of Health Education and Welfare for something to do: it was "a bureaucracy in search of a job" (267). This bureaucracy, presumably motivated by the need to survive, found the "job" of dealing with child abuse (ibid.).

Hacking also tells the story of the effort to interest the mass media in the new framework of child abuse and its successful promotion as the object of public policy and public concern. The effort, Hacking stresses, also rode along preestablished rhetorical tracks. The terminology of abuse itself was morally loaded and connected to notions of pollution and purification, established elements of the practice of moral representation in American society. Hacking suggests that the connection between the notion of self-abuse and the notion of pollution provided the terminology with a specific moral charge (1991, 279).

These are representative steps in Hacking's argument. The possession of a practice is a contingency. The physicians "won" because they could appeal to the preexisting practice of their audience of thinking in terms of normality. If there were no such practice, there could have been no such successful appeal. There is no reason to think of the audience as duped. In and of itself, this contingency is like contingencies of discovery in science in which one fact or method needs to be discovered or established before another can be. But Hacking wishes to say something more than this. Using terms like *own* and *power struggle* to characterize the wide acceptance of a particular notion of child abuse and appending such institutional facts as the creation of a profession of social work suggest that these other contingencies are neither neutral nor innocuous, and that their role in the history of the concept of child abuse taints it. It is here that Hacking's account collides with its competitors.

At one point Hacking gives an example of what he regards as a particularly risible extension of the notion of child abuse by a physician. The example is a discussion presented in a medical textbook on child abuse written by a pediatrics professor and physician. The author points to the problem of abuse by siblings. From Hacking's point of view, this is another instance of the tendency of physicians and other professionals to assert authority over domains previously left to the family. As it happens, I spoke to the author when he was writing the book, and I can supply some of the context for the point he makes. He is a clinician whose patients are children at a large clinic serving the urban poor of Baltimore. He frequently testifies in court on child abuse cases, and typically is requested to judge whether a particular injury could have been produced by accident, such as falling down stairs. Medical diagnoses do not ordinarily take the form required by the courts: "very unlikely" is not a good enough answer. The problem of identifying physical bases for distinguishing child abuse in a legally adjudicable sense from all the other kinds of injuries to which children are prone is a problem produced by the courts and their procedures. But dealing with child abuse, protecting the child, requires something more of the physician than guarded answers. The physician as caregiver has responsibilities that the cautious researcher does not, so the physician's concern with "nonmedical" aspects of child abuse is imposed by circumstance. Sibling abuse, in which the same injuries are produced by siblings rather than parents or caregivers, is medically indistinguishable from child abuse, and it presents the physician as caregiver with the same problem. What is medical prudence here? Send the child back to be injured again? Report the case as abuse (as is typically required by law)?

Hacking's presentation, of course, ignores this specific context, in effect exoticizing the notion of sibling abuse, lumping it together with a long series of similarly exoticized, out-of-context extensions of the concept of child abuse. These extensions are made to seem like a series of accidents that can be fitted into a pattern of professional power seeking. It is at this point that the accounts collide. The collision, however, is quite unequal. The constructionist account has no attraction once one knows the things Hacking leaves out.

Hacking's larger story, of course, leaves many things out as well. Moreover, it can be told in a less sensitive way. Some physicians identified a series of Roentgenological artifacts, constructed an explanation of them, and thus created a medical notion of child abuse. Other professions with a responsibility for children accepted and then revised this notion, and publicized the idea. Ultimately, the revisions of the idea came into conflict with commonly held ideas about child rearing and parental authority. Such conflicts are not surprising. People under different circumstances will revise concepts in different directions. When, for whatever reason, they come into conflict, the conflicts may need to be resolved by new revisions of our ideas, by institutional changes, and so forth. Child abuse is a typical case of this. Practical considerations— even professional interests—may bear on the process and motivate revisions. One would be surprised if they did not.

Sorting out these conflicts is a genuine problem. Reconstructing the paths by which a widely accepted classification emerged, with attention to the special circumstances under which they developed, may serve a constructive purpose. But at some point the machinery of constructionism ceases to contribute much to this task. We can tell these stories without exoticizing, without reference to "practices" and "interests." When we tell them better in a more prosaic way, by filling in facts and context, we have reached the limits of constructivism.

SIX

MAKING NORMATIVE SOUP OUT OF
NONNORMATIVE BONES /

Robert Brandom's *Making It Explicit* (1994) has revived a problem that has a
long and fascinating history both in social theory and in the history of philosophy, especially the philosophy of law. Brandom's discussion of the problem in
chapter 1 of his book derives from more recent philosophical literature motivated largely by a problem in the interpretation of Ludwig Wittgenstein (1958,
186–201). The problem, put simply, is this: what is the ultimate basis of normative assertion? Brandom replies that explicit normative assertion must be
based on implicit norms, hence implicit norms exist. In this chapter I will treat
his argument from his first chapters as a problem within social theory, specifically within the familiar realm of problems of explanatory structure and
form in social theory. What I will try to show is that Brandom's thesis is in part
a thesis about how norms must be *explained,* and that he needs a plausible solution to the problem of the origins of normativity. In the course of the discussion I will show that his solution to this problem is less plausible than com-
peting accounts. The problem is not merely an issue with Brandom, for his
argument is closely related to similar claims in the history of social theory—
notably Talcott Parsons's in *The Structure of Social Action* (1937, 74–82) that
the "normative" is an ineliminable dimension of all action explanations—and
to the claims of ethnomethodology. The reason for these similarities is quite
simple. Both Brandom and Parsons borrow a notion of the normative from
Kant, and both are faced with the consequences of the Kantian distinction between fact and value. Ethnomethodology shares the idea of the normative as
well, and adds to it (as Brandom does) the claim that there are implicit norms,

which are taken by ethnomethodology to be "resources" for "members" and to form the subject matter of ethnomethodology.

BRANDOM'S PROBLEM

Brandom asks what justifies explicit normative assertions, such as statements about the correctness or incorrectness of actions and claims, and says that the best explanation is this: ultimately, justification must rely on implicit norms, or "practices," meaning, for him, regularities of action that are normative. This is very simple social theory takes the following form: there are such things as implicit norms, or "practices," and they explain why the things that are taken to be normatively correct *are* taken to be correct. The meaning of *normative* is a complex issue that I will return to later, but it will suffice to say at this point that Brandom seems to be making a distinction within language—that is, between normative and nonnormative language—and between the expectations that are bases for the claims made within language, some of which are normative and some of which are not.[1] The expectation created by a promise, for example, is normative; some expectations, for example that the sun will rise on the morrow, are not. We may even have normative and nonnormative expectations about the same thing. I may correctly expect, empirically, that my deadbeat brother-in-law will not pay his debts to me; but I will also be correct if I claim that by failing to pay his debts to me he has wronged me. The latter is a normative expectation, and as Brandom says, it is an expectation about statuses, in this case the statuses of "in debt" and "out of debt."

Brandom identifies two constraints on answers to the question of the justification of explicit normative assertions like "My brother-in-law is in debt to me." The first is the "regress problem." The argument here is that norms, such as "Debts are created by promises to repay plus the giving of something," are not self-applying. The correct way to apply an explicit rule is a matter that is also "normative." Because there is an implicit notion of mistake and correctness, there are implicit rules governing the correctness of the application of a rule, and these are also normative in character. However, it would be absurd to suppose that implicit rules are governed in their application by other implicit rules, which are governed by other implicit rules, which are governed by other implicit rules, on into an infinite regress of rules for applying rules.

---

1. The issue of what is normative and what is not is itself a puzzle. Brandom quotes Frege, with approval, to the effect that Logic is a normative science (1994, 12), and goes on to make, as a central claim of the text, that inference is too—"that inferring should be understood in an impersonal context, as an aspect of an essentially *social* practice of communication" (158). It is relevant to my comments on inference in chapter 7 that I see no reason to define *inference* to exclude those inferences made by infants without language, autistics, and so on.

So the regress needs to stop. It cannot stop at the point of explicit rules, which are not self-applying and need to be applied in accordance with implicit rules, but it can stop at the point of implicit norms, or practices. The "must" in this case is a bit elusive. One might take the regress problem differently: to be simply a reductio ad absurdum of the notion of implicit rules. One might ask why they can be thought to be self-applying if explicit rules are not, or indeed whether it is sensible to talk about "rules" for whatever is not explicit. This possibility we may leave aside, for the moment.

The first constraint, the regress problem, has the following implication. Implicit norms must be a kind of stopping point for analysis rather than the sort of things that are themselves justified "normatively" by other rules (Brandom 1994, 26) or "explained" by deeper norms. Ordinarily in discussions of implicit norms there is some sort of appeal to the notion of their connection, in some sense, to the facts of community life or membership in a community. This connection, which is often rather hazy, is understood not so much as a justification of the rules or an explanation of them as a kind of characterization of their location or fundamental character. Brandom has a good deal to say about this, particularly in criticizing Saul Kripke (38), the source of the other major constraint, which Brandom calls the "gerrymandering problem."

The gerrymandering problem was made famous by Kripke in his book on the private language argument (1982). He took from Wittgenstein the point that any continuation of the mathematical series 2, 4, 6, 8 can be characterized as the following of *some* explicit mathematical rule. Thus, although we "naturally" continue the series 2, 4, 6, 8 with the rest of the even numbers, there is, and can be, no mathematical reason for doing so, for there is potentially a very large set of mathematical formulae which fit any set of numbers that could be claimed to "continue" the series, and thus be representations of the "implicit rule" to which a person was appealing when saying "continue the series." This means that mathematics rests on something outside of mathematics.

Brandom takes this problem to have implications for the issue of normativity. It rules out, he claims, the possibility that "continue this series" can be construed nonnormatively. Because such a large array of possible rules or possible sequences are theoretically consistent with the claim that they continue the series 2, 4, 6, 8, any account that attempts to treat this as a matter of a "regularity," meaning a purely causal phenomena, will fail, or in some way cheat by defining as inappropriate all of the series other than the "correct" series. The only way to pick out the correct sequence is to appeal to something normative rather than something merely causal.

The gerrymandering argument together with the regress argument establish that implicit norms are necessary to account for normative claims and that they are understandable only as norms, and not as regularities. Brandom's slogan for this is that these social practices are "normative all the way down"

(1994, 44). He quotes a saying of Fred Dretske that one can't bake a normative cake out of nonnormative ingredients: The point is that the ingredients of the cake must already be normative (41).

We can see what these two constraints together mean in terms of the practice of promising. By making a promise, we alter the normative relations between individuals, or what Brandom calls their statuses. A practice like promising is "normative all the way down" in the sense that the end point for an account of promising cannot be a causal fact or process of some kind that is "nonnormative." The idea of expectation in and of itself is nonnormative. We have various causal expectations about the world that may or may not be true and that we correct empirically. His point is that these expectations cannot suffice to explain how it is that making a promise amounts to a means by which something in the way of statuses is changed, because the change in status is a change in the *normative* expectation that we are permitted to have about someone who makes a promise rather than in any causal fact. Whether someone has made a real promise is not a matter of a predictive law that says if someone makes a promise he or she will fulfill it. Such a law would obviously be false, and my deadbeat brother-in-law would be its refutation. No refinement of this empirical law, it seems, would work either. The only true "law" that one might form about promising is a normative one that anyone who makes a promise is *bound* to fulfill it. This, of course, is also overly simple, because there are many conditions under which we could think that a person's promise was no longer binding. But Brandom's point is that all these exceptions are also in the form of normative expectations or riders involving "statuses" such as being unable to fulfill the promise for some reason, and these statuses are themselves normative in character. His account is designed to resolve a complex dilemma. He does not, as I have suggested, wish to accept that the regress argument is a reductio ad absurdum of the idea of implicit norms, as this would still leave him with the problem of explaining how anyone could justifiably say "correct" or "incorrect" or how anyone could have normative as opposed to causal explanations. He also does not wish to say that the regularities that make up social practices are merely empirical and nonnormative, but somehow become so because many people do the same thing. He quotes John McDowell's point: "If regularities in the verbal behavior of an isolated individual, described in norm-free terms, do not add up to meaning, it is quite obscure how it could somehow make all the difference if there were several individuals with matching regularities" (McDowell 1984, 350). So he is forced to accept implicit norms or practices—normative regularities—as an explanation.

The term *explanation* may seem to be misplaced here, and with it the notion that Brandom is just another social theorist whose theory can be assessed in familiar social theoretical terms. But the idea that it is misplaced rests on a confusion about what Brandom is doing. He is not *justifying* normative justification, he is *explaining* the phenomenon of normative justification. The problem that has the greatest similarities to this in the history of philosophy is the problem of explaining the phenomenon of legal validity, as Brandom himself notes. He quotes Samuel Pufendorf at length on this, and accepts something like Pufendorf's idea that

> as the original way of producing physical entities is creation, the way in which moral entities are produced can scarcely be better expressed than by the word imposition. For they do not arise out of the intrinsic nature of the physical properties of things, but they are superadded, at the will of intelligent entities, to things already existent and physically complete, and to their natural effects, and, indeed, come into existence only by the determination of their authors. . . . Hence the active force which lies in them does not consist in their ability directly to produce any physical motion or change in any thing, but only in this, that it is made clear to men along what line they should govern their liberty of action. (Pufendorf [1688] 1964, par. 4)

Brandom points out that this does not commit Pufendorf to any thesis about the physical nature of the process of "imposing." As he puts it, it is possible to agree with Hamlet that "there is nothing either good or bad, but thinking makes it so" (Brandom 1994, 49), and also to reject the idea that there must ultimately be some sort of physical explanation of the thinking that makes it so. To put the point in a somewhat different way, Brandom's task is sociological rather than normative. It is not an attempt to do what philosophers of law sometimes have thought they could do, namely to account for legality itself, but rather to account for legitimacy, that is, the phenomenon of taking an order as legally valid.

THE PARALLEL CASE OF LEGAL VALIDITY

As this comparison suggests, the same kinds of issues arise in connection with the law. What justifies a law? That it is legally enacted? And what justifies the law ordaining what counts as legal enactment? Eventually, as one questions the justifications, one must arrive at some sort of justification that must be outside the law proper, just as the justification for continuing 2, 4, 6, 8 with 10, 12, 14, 16 must be something outside mathematics. But with the law the problem is typically framed in the reverse of the notion of normativity all the way down. What is seen to be required is the distinctive fact that makes a body of regulations and predictable behavior genuinely "the law," something that is binding normatively upon us (cf. Olivecrona 1948). The special thing that makes a command or regulation legal, is however, elusive. One traditional answer was the will of the sovereign, understood as a kind of transformative element that takes mere rules and activities and makes them genuinely legal and binding.

There is no law that says the will of the sovereign is binding—it just is. So the will of the sovereign is part of the definition of law, but "will" is also its causal source.

Needless to say, a huge body of legal thinking in the nineteenth century went into this problem. Ultimately, the problem was finessed or abandoned by legal positivism, which simply rejected it and said that the law should be treated as a normative fact requiring no further justification or basis. As Carl Schmitt puts it, according to Kelsen:

> The state, meaning the legal order, is a system of ascriptions [Brandomlike norms!] to a last point of ascription and to a last basic norm. . . . For juristic consideration there are neither real nor fictitious persons [i.e., actual or theoretical sovereigns], only points of ascription. The state is the terminal point of ascription, the point at which the ascriptions, which constitute the essence of juristic consideration, "can stop." This "point" is simultaneously an "order that cannot be further derived." The decisive argument, the one that is repeated and advanced against every intellectual opponent, remains the same: The basis for the validity of a norm can only be a norm. (Schmitt [1922] 1985b, 19)

So what positivism in the legal context does is to cut off a certain kind of regression problem. And it does so in order to avoid the bad end toward which the regression problem, in this case the problem of the legal justification of legal enactment, leads.

The bad end is a historical one. Once a legal system is in place, its transformations can be examined with respect to their legality, and this may be done "normatively," entirely within the system of law. But establishing a legal system seems to require something more—a transformation from something prelegal or nonlegal to something legal, or at least to some moment of the origin of legal validity. Norms generally, one might think, also have to have origins, for they are diverse and mutable. So there ought to be some sort of solution to the problem of what gets norms going in the first place.

Brandom does not deny that the problem of origins is a legitimate explanatory concern. He says that "the issue of what it would be for norms to be implicit in practice ought to be kept distinct from the issue of how such practices might in fact plausibly arise" (1994, 658–59 n. 45). But even if the issues should be kept distinct, in the sense that different answers might be given to the latter issue without affecting the answers to the former, for Brandom's purposes there does need to be *some* plausible answer to the question. His arguments establish the explanatory necessity of "implicit norms," or practices. But *practices* is a theoretical term. Establishing the explanatory necessity of practices does not establish their possibility. If, however, one can establish the possibility of the existence of practices, the argument for their explanatory necessity turns possibility into necessity. Identifying a plausible explanation serves to establish possibility. But there are problems with the plausibility of the available explanations.

Kripke's explanation is that norms are based on "communal assessment," meaning, as Crispin Wright puts it elsewhere, they rest on "the authority of securable community assent" (Wright 1980, 220). Brandom objects to this line of argument on the quite solid ground that the notion of communal assent is a fiction and that "assenting, endorsing, accepting, and regarding as right are in the first instance things done by individuals" (1994, 38). Accepting this fiction is like accepting a fictional origin of the law or a fictional sovereign. It is not an explanation at all, but merely a stand-in for an explanation. Is there a plausible explanation? Or can something like Kripke's notion of communal assessment be made into an explanation by removing its fictional quality? With these questions we move into the realm of actual explanation and the problem of plausibility itself, rather than the problem of possibility. And here some new constraints emerge.

The ideal account would answer at least three basic questions about normativity: a question about the historical anthropology of normativity or, alternatively, about the emergence of particular moral notions; a question about the genealogy of morals or particular morals, about socialization; and about the problem of the historical diversity of morals. One may think of these three issues differently, namely as constraints on a general account of morality that a minimally adequate theory must meet. In either case, it is useful to survey the actual history of theories of morality to determine what the range of plausible solutions might be.

EXPLANATORY PROBLEMS
Getting to the Source of Normativity

Brandom discusses, or alludes to, several social theories of normativity, including those by Thomas Hobbes and Weber along with Pufendorf's theory of law. Each of these thinkers supports, in some fashion, the idea, as Brandom puts it, that

> our activity *institutes* norms, *imposes* normative significances on a natural world that is intrinsically without significance for the guidance or assessment of action. A normative significance is imposed on a nonnormative world, like a cloak thrown over its nakedness, by agents forming preferences, issuing orders, entering into agreements, praising and blaming, esteeming and assessing. (1994, 48)

It is difficult to see what it means, as a matter of social theory, to impose normative significance in this sense. What sort of action does this? But it is somewhat easier to see how one might do so in the case of law, and the case of law suggests some problem with these kinds of explanations.

A once famous figure, Rudolph von Ihering, provides a good place to start on the problem. His account is the one to which the much more influential formulations of Nietzsche ([1887] 1956), Durkheim ([1887] 1993), Tönnies (1961), and Weber ([1922] 1978) respond. Ihering begins with the problem of the binding character of law ([1877] 1913, 105–10, 189–92, 239). The theory he proposes works, to the extent that it does work, for law. It operates as follows. Legal commands are initially simply imposed by force—here "imposing" is an intelligible phenomenon. Some person or faction makes commands backed by force that are initially accepted simply and only because they are backed by force. But in time people come to recognize the benefits of operating under these commands, and Ihering suggests that this recognition is at once a recognition of the normative character of the commands and of their collective basis or significance. The moment of recognition is one in which something nonnormative, namely commands backed by force, transmutes into something normative, the law. Brandom accepts something like this account himself, when he comments that contractarian explanations of rights and obligations, as well as those that invoke positive law, "explain . . . these deontic statuses in terms of what agents are doing in instituting or constitutively recognizing such entitlements and commitments" (1994, 49). One may note that the diversity of legal orders falls out of this account quite naturally, since different commands are imposed by different leaders at different times.

Ihering's explanation of the "binding," or normative, character of the law is nevertheless elusive. The account explains people's interest in obeying the law and in there being a legal order rather than the validity of commands made by the legal ruler. But does it explain their recognizing them as normatively binding? Wouldn't they need a normative notion of the law in order to recognize something as an example of the law and hence binding? Is recognizing the benefits of an order the same as recognizing the order as binding? A parallel problem arises in connection with socialization. To explain an aversion to stealing, John Austin cites the fact that as a child a person is punished for stealing and associates stealing with pain. Austin thought that this association accounts for belief in the wrongness of stealing ([1832] 1995, 37, 50–52). Critics of Ihering's and Austin's explanations noted that an illegitimate inference is being made here from pain to the quite different kind of belief, a normative belief in the wrongness of stealing. The right inference would have been the painfulness of or the possible consequences of stealing, which would not be a "moral" response at all. The "burnt child shuns the fire" explanation accounts for the child's expectations, but it is entirely within the causal world. Normativity somehow needs to get inserted into the process of learning (or recognition) at some moment at which the purely causal is replaced by or altered or transmuted into the normative.

Tönnies provides a clever solution to the problem with Austin's explanation by identifying the voice of moral command with the voice of the parent. The child is in awe of the parent, responds to the commands of the parent, and habitualizes these commands. The commands of parents are themselves normative, so this solves the problem of the insertion of normativity into socialization by deriving it from the fact of parental command. The commands are then habitualized and, more important, habitualized as norms rather than merely as prudentially useful habits. Norms are thus acquired.

But on examination, Tönnies's account has the same problem as Austin's. When, later in life, we respond to the habitualized commands of our parents, we regard *some* of them as moral and binding upon other people, but others as merely the peculiarities of our parents. And we seem to make this distinction by reference to something other than commands of parents. Thus, the difference between moral commands and commands has to arise from another source. Tönnies has a solution to this problem: Norms derive from the commands of the will of society and are merely expressions of this will. When we listen to our conscience we are really listening to the will of society commanding us to behave in a particular way or to feel particular feelings. Of course, this answer rather closely resembles answers to the question of the validity of law, which refer to the will of the people or the will of the sovereign and suffer from the same problems.

Appealing to society in this way is perhaps not much better than appealing to a fiction. But Durkheim, who presents an even more radical solution to these problems, does seem to go one better. Durkheim's approach is similar to Tönnies's notion that within each of us there is a feeling of the social will in addition to our own individual will. For Durkheim there are actually two forms of consciousness within us, one collective, the other individual; and the phenomenology of our feelings is a product of the causal pushing and shoving of these forms of consciousness, each of which operates in a slightly different way. Durkheim's solution to the problem of normativity is to identify it, under the broader heading of constraint, with the causal pushing and shoving that arises out of the collective consciousness and is experienced by us phenomenologically, like our conscience, as internal to us. He solved the socialization problem in a way that also parallels Tönnies. The problem of moral education, for Durkheim, is a problem of building up the collective consciousness in a way that distinguishes the collective constraints from the mere constraints that one individual might exercise over another. The solution to Tönnies's problem is that the collective is moral, and the moral can have no origin other than the collective. There is no problem of separating the parental will from the social will, because the moral source is the social will, to which some of the commands of the parents conform.

Durkheim focuses on the child's experience in the classroom and describes the need for teachers to subordinate themselves to the rules and higher symbols of authority. Through observing the teacher subordinating him- or herself to authority and exercising his or her authority on behalf of and in accordance with this higher authority on the student, the student develops the collective heart of the consciousness and comes to see the binding character of the commands of society, which are initially mediated through symbolic representations like the flag. Durkheim has the idea that, parallel to the special moment in Tönnies in which the child in awe of the parent internalizes commands, it is in the moments of high collective emotion that the individual is especially susceptible to common feelings and common senses of subordination to something higher.

Durkheim's views are instructive in relation to Kripke's because they point to what a "normative all the way down" social theory would have to look like—if by "all the way down" we mean all the way down historically—and seek to explain the origins of communal assessments, their changes, and their diversity.[2] Durkheim provides an explanation of normativity by identifying it with collective constraint. But it is not clear that the idea of a collective consciousness is a plausible explanatory idea. And it raises the question of whether going all the way down historically in our quest for a plausible account of normativity makes sense. Durkheim and appeals to collective phenomena do not exhaust the possible forms of explanation of communal assessments, of course, and communal assessments may not need to be a part of the explanation of normativity. As we shall see, Brandom indeed has a different suggestion that does not appeal to any communal facts.

Explaining Nonnormativity

McLuhan says at one point that there is no such thing as a grammatical error in preliterate society, by which he means that the rules of grammar are the byproduct of practical exigencies of writing. I would not attempt to say whether this view is correct. However, it points to an interesting form of argument. Rules of grammar do not need to be "normative all the way down" in the historical sense, if we accept McLuhan's argument as at least logically possible. Prior to writing, there is no correct or incorrect grammar; there are merely utterances that are understood and utterances that are not understood. It may be that we can have an activity, perhaps even an extremely complex activity, which is not characterized in normative language at all, much less in the language of binding rules or "norms" proper. But it may subsequently come to be characterized in normative language, and in so doing become normative.

Something like this reasoning, I take it, is essential to both Nietzsche's and Weber's genealogies of morals. Both philosophers begin their accounts of

---

2. For a more elaborate discussion of Durkheim's actual theory on these subjects, especially on the role of collective effervescence and the fusion of minds in the creation of morals, see Turner (1993).

morality not with Ihering-like individuals who are thought of as already rational and faced only with the problem of whether to accept legal orders or norms as binding, but rather at a somewhat more primitive level of the herd, a group driven by primal, quasi-biological urges, of which one important urge is simply the urge to conform. There is a certain similarity between this primal stage and childhood in Tönnies and Durkheim, but for Nietzsche and Weber this stage is not, properly speaking, moral at all. The herd has no real consciousness, and certainly no moral consciousness. Nevertheless, there is a kind of collective reflex in that if anyone in the herd does anything unusual the rest of the herd recoils in a kind of fearful horror. For Nietzsche and also for Weber, early morality or the early development of society in the historical/anthropological sense has this character.

In Nietzsche's account, it is only at the very late stage, at which an individual breaks out of this fearful conformity and makes his own morals, that there is any real issue of morality at all. Once an individual steps out of the herd, the herd comes to define itself in moral terms in opposition to this individual. Consequently, strictly speaking, the origins of morality are in the actions of the exceptional individual and the morals he makes for himself, without which the herd would simply remain a herd. Actual moralities in the form of moral doctrines are, on this account, ideological articulations of the impulses and aims of this exceptional individual and, when it is stirred to respond, of the herd itself. The herd ideologizes its horror of exceptional individuals and forms morality through a process of resenting these individuals; and the exceptional individual articulates justification or accounting of his own project, which is characteristically also a project of commanding others, so that it requires a kind of theory—though obviously this can be a pretty minimal affair, such as the "theory" that the gods will be angered—legitimating the command.

Weber handles these problems somewhat differently. He begins with the same biologically driven conformist herd and argues that the biological urge to conform continues to drive much of human action, along with the force of habit. Rational action or action approximating rational action is only a small portion of human life, and actions themselves are characteristically mixed, being determined partly by rational considerations and partly by forces of emotion and habit. It is only at, so to speak, the highest levels of the articulation of moral theories that it makes sense to speak of morality, and "implicit norms," with the awareness that their very existence can only be habitualizations, perhaps married to emotion, of previously articulated moral theories of some sort. In a sense, this is the McLuhan argument applied to morality. Moral theories are not about preexisting implicit norms, but rather the beginning of norms and normativity as such.

This, of course, applies to the historical/anthropological moment of the origins of norms rather than to the problem of socialization, but one may imagine socialization being given a parallel treatment. Children are not born making elaborate distinctions among the will of parents, that which is causally effective, that which is universally commanded or obligatory, and so forth. The distinctions are obviously the product of developed explicit ideas or, in a minimal sense of the word, "theories" of one sort or another, and most of the relevant theories or beliefs are magical or religious in character. Ideas about natural justice or natural morality, and obviously Kantian ideas about obligation, are very late developments. We can identify two processes here. One is the process, meaning the McLuhan process, by which feelings and responses become theorized about in such a way as to make them "moral." Another is the process by which moral distinctions degenerate from the level of conscious belief to a level of habit together with a moral vocabulary of approval and disapproval in which the original "theory" is forgotten. Once it is forgotten it can be reflected upon in new ways. There is, in connection with these processes, no need to appeal to the notion of implicit norms as some sort of distinct order of fact, or to think of moral reflection as the process of making explicit and theorizing about these supposed implicit norms. In fact, as I have noted elsewhere, Weber goes out of his way to categorize actions and repeated actions, as well as repeated actions governed by or understood in terms of theories about their validity, in such a way that no category of action corresponding to "action governed by implicit norms" actually arises (Turner and Factor 1990). In the case of Nietzsche the problem is less clear, but what is apparent is that the stuff being reflected upon and articulated by moral theories is not some mass of implicit norms but rather a mass of common feelings of resentment, which are neither collective nor obligatory, but merely common to the individuals comprising the herd and responding herdlike to one another.

Something similar to this form of argument, but far more clever, is to be found in the writings of the philosopher of law Axel Hägerström. As I have noted before, Hägerström very effectively ridiculed theories of the law based on ideas of the will of the sovereign or the will of the people, thus paving the way for legal positivism, though in some respects legal positivism was quite alien to his understanding of the law. Rather than positing a *Grundnorm*, like Kelsen, which simply evades the question or blocks the question of causes and of legal validity, Hägerström constructs a kind of sociological history of the Roman law in which he makes the point, evident even in writers like Weber, that a great many of the legal formulae familiar to us from Roman legal practice are essentially magical in character (Olivecrona [1952] 1953, xiv).

This approach may be usefully compared with the line of attack Brandom employs with respect to performative utterances. In discussing this in chapter 4, I noted that the classic performative utterance is the priest who says, "I pronounce you man and wife," thus changing their statuses. Classifying this as a performative utterance is valuable for some philosophical purposes, no doubt, and one might construct a "philosophical theory" of performative utterances. But the obvious question raised by this particular performative utterance is why anyone takes it to have the magical effects of transforming the statuses of the relevant individuals and, more important, making them into a different kind of people bonded in a different kind of way. It is possible to speak of these changes purely in van Gennepian terms, as Brandom quite unconsciously does, and think of this as a ritual involving a changing of statuses (van Gennep 1960). The point Hägerström makes is that the issue is not so much the mere changing of statuses, and consequently of normative expectations, but rather the magical powers attributed to the priest that make him alone (or something with the same powers) capable of performing this magical transformation, as well as the participants' beliefs in the detailed specifics of the transformation they have gone through. Obviously, this transformation is more than a mere change in statuses, in legal powers in relation to one another. But even the notion of "legal power" in relation to another has a certain magical significance that is not accounted for in the bloodless notion of changing statuses, unless we understand status itself, as Weber would, to imply something essentially magical about the charisma and powers of the individuals in question.

My point in reiterating this is to show that something like the undifferentiated state that Nietzsche and Weber attribute to premoral society applies, or can be employed, in the case of the law. Reasoning like this obviously has its nineteenth-century roots in writers like Comte, who also begins with a kind of undifferentiated magical thinking in the case of science. This thinking gradually becomes differentiated, first through theological reasoning and later through science, yet retains, as in the case of the concept of causality, the remnants of the age of magical thinking: for example, the notion of causal powers or the notion of law, as in physics, as something more than mere description. For Comte, when physics reached the positive stage, all these prepositive notions would evaporate, and we would no longer feel the need for metaphysical notions such as "cause." Hägerström may be read as suggesting that in the law they never quite evaporate, or rather that they leave as a residue a "general social estimation" (something like a set of habitual expectations produced by the experience of living under law as a method of cooperation), which will persist "even if feelings originally produced by superstition should lose their power over men's minds" (Passmore 1961, 154). To put this point in terms of an example, consider promising. It is difficult to get an account of the origins of promising, but it is plausible to say that it arises from the kinds of institutions, and beliefs, that Marcel Mauss describes in *The Gift*. The idea that one must fulfill promises makes perfect sense if it is associated with a belief that in accepting something one accepts a spiritual attachment to the thing which must go home to its source through a return gift. That the ritual of promising survives the decline of the belief also is understandable, as the belief depends on other beliefs that are not about promising.

WITTGENSTEIN

Wittgenstein may be taken, as indeed Brandom takes him, to have a "norms all the way down" account of the learning of rules, and consequently a pervasive notion of the normativity of social life. One might also interpret Wittgenstein as claiming that norms in some sense inhere in (or are rooted in or based upon) facts about communities, and that expressions about what we do or say are expressions of a kind of community "we."[3] I think these are all bad interpretations; nevertheless, I do not intend to mount a full-scale assault on them here. However, I would like to sketch out an alternative answer to both the problem of the two moments of normativity and the problem of regression on the basis of some Wittgensteinian texts. What I have said about Weber and Nietzsche is especially relevant to this interpretation.

Let me begin with some material from Wittgenstein's lectures of the early thirties. Here he speaks of rules being based on "language habits" (Ambrose 1979). When he says this I take it that he means to distinguish between something that is not a matter of "rules" and something that is. This raises an appropriate question about the notion of norms going "all the way down." "All the way down" in the sense of the actual causal basis of rule following seems in these passages to mean all the way down to our language habits, which are the psychological facts forming the causal basis of rules. We may ask, Are the habits themselves normative? Some things that Wittgenstein says in these lectures, especially about training, suggest that these habits *are* already "normative." When we train someone in such a way that she or he acquires the language habits that are the basis or conditions of rules, we train her or him by saying things about whether something is right or wrong. Training, one might say, inherently involves rightness and wrongness and consequently normativity. So the moment of training is the moment of normativization in the socialization sense.

But there are other places in which Wittgenstein seems to come closer to McLuhan in thinking that the distinctions between normative and practical do not apply universally or are not universally meaningful. In the second paragraph of the *Philosophical Investigations,* in discussing the builders, for example, he describes a language game in which there is no vocabulary for right and wrong. Moreover, certain familiar linguistic distinctions do not have any application to the example as he has described it. This raises an interesting possibility, namely that the child's experience of learning a rule or learning

3. A useful discussion of these issues is to be found in Schatzki 1996, 65–68 and passim.

how to speak is not (in the same way that the language of builders is not) yet differentiated into the categories of normative and practical or causal. When one teaches a child to say "please" in order to have a request honored, the child simply repeats the term and learns, and learns empirically, what happens when the term is used. She or he learns that it increases the likelihood that requests will be honored, and may also be corrected when the term is misapplied, if indeed the child misapplies it.

The idea that this is the "right" thing to do is somewhat problematically related to its causal effectiveness. One could imagine discussing this with a more experienced user of the term, a child who noticed that it worked sometimes and not others, and explaining that saying "please" is a polite thing to do whether or not it works, or whether or not it works with a particular person. One wonders whether it is at this stage that one begins to differentiate between the causal practical sense of "please" and the normative sense, but one also notices that at this point one is giving explicit accounts—a "theory of politeness," so to speak, in which saying "please" is claimed to be "normative"—not something implicit.

The same question may be asked more generally about language. When we train a child in linguistic use, are we simply giving some sort of normative lesson (and perhaps do we think we are doing something normative because we know something historical/anthropological about language, namely that the rules of language are normative), or are we simply conveying a practical skill that is no different from other practical skills, such as tying a shoe, in which we teach a technique? One answer to these questions might be that in the initial formation of language habits, and many other things, these distinctions are not really applicable. Giving a child linguistic knowledge or forming a linguistic habit by ostensibly training a response to "bird," for example, is more or less like saying, "Call this thing and things like it 'bird,' and other people will understand what you are talking about." We can think of this knowledge as altogether causal; indeed, highly functioning people who have autism and people who have personality disorders that prevent them from acting morally or recognizing moral obligations also can learn to use this language to serve their purposes.

It is an interesting question as to whether a body of sociopaths, users but not normative followers of moral rules, could create moral rules or develop moral vocabulary in the historical/anthropological sense. But what they would create, if they created any rules, would be causal prudential rules that would be indistinguishable from what we call moral rules. It is an interesting question as to whether one could have a community of sociopaths and highly functioning autistics, but there is no question that such individuals often nicely mimic both rule following and moral behavior, which arguably they apprehend in a nonmoral fashion.

An objection might be raised at this point that a trick has been introduced into the argument. Language habits are not rules, for language habits as such do not involve the notion of mistake. As soon as the notion of mistake appears, one has normativity, and one is in an entirely different domain. Notions like mistake are inherently normative, and don't in any obvious way derive from a theory that has been habitualized and forgotten, leaving merely the residue of the moral vocabulary of right and wrong. So it is as though a condition for language use, namely language habits, has been substituted for the whole explanation of a norm, which must include a "normative element" in addition to the habit. One might also reason, as Brandom does, that this normative element is the thing that solves the problem of gerrymandering because it picks out the one possible habit that is the correct one. In short, someplace, some sort of tacit normative element has been slipped into this discussion, or else the moment of the emergence of the normative has been misdescribed in some way.

I think this objection has something to it, but not what it appears to have. Consider a mundane example. I am teaching my child to hammer a nail. I believe that there is a right and wrong way to do this, and I even have some criteria for distinguishing the two. I can say, for example, that some ways of hammering a nail leave hammer marks on the surface of the thing into which the nail is being hammered. If the nail is bent, the hammering job is incorrect. These are all external factual criteria that do not really dictate the "right way" to hammer a nail, which I believe to be executed in three successive strokes: one soft, one hard, and another soft. I train my child in my preferred method until the child can do it easily. A habit has been acquired, along with a vocabulary of right and wrong. It looks as if we can actually use the notion of gerrymandering here to distinguish between the causal and the normative part of this acquisition of a technique. The causal part pertains to the damage done to the surface or to the nail. But there are obviously many other nail-driving methods that fulfill these criteria than the particular one that I advocate and call correct. Now I, the trainer, am picking out one of the possible ways of doing this that I label correct. Unfortunately, in this case, I also have a theory about what is correct. I not only know the right way of pounding a nail when I see it, but can actually articulate some aspects of the process.

Suppose, however, that I am an inarticulate carpenter and I know both how to drive a nail and how to recognize that one is being driven correctly, so that I can say, "That was a mistake" or "That was right," and I apply these notions not to the result—the driven nail, which might have gone in nicely merely from a lucky blow—but to the technique. What would training consist of for the inarticulate carpenter? The trainee would merely get "correct" and "mistake" or "right" and "wrong" or a nod or shake of the head as responses to his attempts to drive the nail. Consequently, of all the habits that he might be forming at the beginning, one after another is extinguished gradually as the responses of "mistake" or "wrong" eliminate certain possible habits out of the total range of possible habits with which the trainee began. Now consider the following. Are nods and shakes of the head any different, from the trainee's point of view, than the appearance of a mark or a bent nail caused by a hammer swing? The difference is their source, obviously. But the effects are identical in that each of them forces the habit into a smaller possible range. In the end, the training produces performances within some acceptable range, no less for the bending of nails and the making of hammer marks than for the "rights" and "wrongs" uttered by the trainer. At some stage the trainee may come to recognize that he was getting the hang of it and also to recognize other people doing it correctly. The trainee may even come to reflect on this even to the extent of developing his own theory about these habits.

The narrowing of the scope, or the gerrymandering, is done as a matter of habit, and there is no essential difference from the point of view of psychological mechanisms, or for that matter of eliminating alternatives, that distinguishes between somebody saying "right" and "wrong" and somebody looking at the marks made by the hammer or the bent nails. This is important, because it suggests that normativity does not enter into language habits at some mystical point at which the term *mistake* first gets applied by someone; nor is there any mystical transubstantiation that occurs because in addition to the feedback one gets from the nail and the surface, one gets "right" and "wrong" from a trainer. For indeed, to this point in the discussion, nothing mystical happens at all. In a sense it is only when we make some sort of distinction between two kinds of right and wrong, the one that derives solely from the trainer and the one that derives from the physical world, do we have a hint of something distinctly "normative" And the distinctive thing turns out to be nothing other than the input of the trainer. But even this input is not normative in the differentiated sense. The trainer may not even be aware that there is any other way to hammer a nail without bending it or making a mark, and may think that his "right" and "wrong" are themselves solely in the domain of the causal or practical world; he may even be right about this. It seems like a factual question whether there are other ways of producing results with the hammer. One way we might go about answering this factual question would be to survey other carpenters or other communities of carpenters and see whether they possess any such techniques. If they do, then it is clear that what has been added is in some sense normative and connected to particular communities, as this case may be. In this case one could be normative without knowing it. And perhaps this is the only case of implicit norms that can be made to pass muster. But what is implicit here is not the activity or the standards of right and wrong but their normative character, which is misrecognized as something else or not noticed at all.

Consider a third case. The carpenter is completely inarticulate. He hammers, and produces goods, but cannot train anyone by saying, "That's right." Is it the case that no one can learn carpentry from this person? Is it the case that this person could not have learned carpentry from another person without that other person using normative language like "right"? Would there be any visible difference between carpentry done by a person who learned in this manner and one who learned "normatively"? Wittgenstein clearly wishes to respond by saying that it is possible. He discusses the possibility of a person picking up chess by observing chess players without learning the rules. The problem with this case is this: is the person's knowledge of chess normative knowledge? Does the fact that some people play by and know rules mean that everyone does so, only that some do so without realizing it?

The issue arises in connection with each example that we discussed. If the inarticulate carpenter says "yes" or "no," are these terms used normatively, or could they simply be expressions of preference and distaste, or comprehension and incomprehension, or satisfaction and fear? Learning to perform the activity is consistent with any of these. The only responses that are unambiguously normative as distinct from expressing something else are those in which terms explicitly classed as normative are explicitly given, and given an explicit justification in terms of something that is explicitly normative. And this means that whatever is implicit cannot be distinguished as normative.

Perhaps the largest source of support for the notion of implicit norms, once we get rid of the notion that only normativity solves the problem of gerrymandering, is the problem of what makes something normative, which we can now see as a certain aspect of the regression problem. Justifying something as normative seems to require normative justification, which according to the regression problem eventually must be implicit. Thus, the implicit thing must be normative. But if Weber, Nietzsche, and as I have argued, Wittgenstein, are right, there is a great deal of undifferentiated causal and "normative" activity that goes on; it may even be associated with various emotions without being clearly normative in the sense that a normative-causal distinction clearly applies to it. This is important to recognize because it is sometimes tempting to think that organized activity is not possible without normativity and that normativity requires some sort of universally applicable and radically separated notion of normativity. If it does not, the real issue is not the activity or even its social character, but rather the question of the nature of justifications for using terms like *mistake* and *wrong*. Here I think Nietzsche, Weber, and Hägerström are more plausible.

Brandom cites Weber's use of the term *Entzauberung* by way of explaining the notion that we impose normative significance on the world. He comments that "[o]ne of the defining characteristics of early science is its disenchantment of the world" (1994, 48). The process of disenchantment is one in which "The meanings and values that had previously been discerned in things are stripped off along with the supernatural and are understood as projections of human interests, concerns, and activities onto an essentially indifferent and insignificant matter" (ibid.). But Weber's *historical* point is quite different from this sentence, and closer to what Brandom says about early science. For Weber, the fact that matter is essentially indifferent and insignificant is a late discovery. We did not impose the meanings and values and supernatural on these things—we never separated supernatural from natural until very late in our intellectual development. The world came to us, so to speak, enchanted: We disenchanted it through explicitly theorizing about it. We do the differentiating between normative and factual on our grounds, in the course of improving our expectations about the world. There is no process of imposing norms on the world, such as Brandom supposes. But there is a process of reading normativity back into phenomena, such as the grunts of the carpenter or the acquisition of the practice of carpentry, which are not unambiguously normative, and this is the process in which Brandom is engaged.

If we return to the original question of this chapter, the question of whether one can make normative soup out of nonnormative bones, we can now see a number of possible answers. One answer would be that normative and nonnormative, causal and intentional, are distinctions that arise late both in the historical/anthropological development of social life and in the child's development. When they emerge, they emerge through the differentiating of something that is already there. In the case of historical/anthropological development, the initial thing is some sort of magical thinking that is neither normative nor causal but which is retained in some sense in these ultimately emerging categories. It is very difficult to eradicate from science quasi-magical notions such as a causal power or theological notions such as law, just as it is very difficult to eradicate charismatic elements from legal procedure and mystical theological elements from moral discourse. In each case the difficulty betrays the origins of the things that we have now elected to put into these categories. In this case the normative soup is not being made out of nonnormative bones so much as decomposed from something that is neither normative nor causal, such as magic, into something normative and something causal.

An alternative way of looking at this problem of making normative soup is a bit more reductionist. Consider the poets' saying that "stone walls do not a prison make." The cynics' response to this is "But throw in some guards and barbed wire, and you have something there." Something similar may be said with respect to norms and normative practice. We call something normative not because we think there is a normative element but because, taken together, the activity amounts to something we call normative. Calling something normative is a factual rather than a normative enterprise, much less a matter of imposing or instituting. It requires having grounds for doing so, and the grounds may be highly varied, and justify quite different kinds of normativity claims. To say that one must do something, or that something is the right way to do it because it is the way the "best people" do it, is to give a justification of this sort, and to assert a very specific kind of normativity, the normativity of etiquette books. These justifications or theories may not be very good theories, and in the end they may all rest on quasi-magical notions, such as the goodness of the "best people." But they are theories nevertheless.

BRANDOM'S ACCOUNT OF ORIGINS

Brandom's own suggestion of an answer to the problem of the origins of normativity is found in a footnote. His starting point is in the phenomenon of "acting correctly according to one's intentional states" (1994, 659 n. 49), and his problem is the question of how correctness in this sense, which requires "the distinction of perspective between producing performances and assessing them," (152) can arise in the first place. Brandom agrees with Davidson "in seeing intentional states and speech acts as fundamentally of co-eval conceptual status, neither being explicable except in an account that includes the other" (ibid.). Davidson's reasoning is that understanding speech acts requires the attribution of intentions to the actor, but only language users can attribute intentional states.[4] Put differently, assessing performances and having the perspective of assessment is a language-dependent phenomenon, but at the same time language use depends on attributing intentions. Normativity is thus co-eval with language.

Brandom observes that what Davidson "has given us is not so much an argument as the form of one," and Brandom seeks to remedy this (1994, 153). What I have done in this chapter is also to deal with the form of arguments about normativity rather than to provide actual explanations of norms. But even at this level some important things can be seen. One is that any account of rules behind the rules—implicit norms—has two major defects. The first is that making norms implicit does not make them self-applying. The second

4. A more complete quotation follows:

it is not evidently incoherent to imagine one organism shaping its own behavior by responding to its responses with positively and negatively reinforcing behavior. What makes such a suggestion odd is that one would think that the capacity to distinguish correct from incorrect performance that is exercised in the postulated responsive disposition to assess would also be available at the time the original performance is produced, so that no behavior-shaping ground is gained by the two stage procedure. But this need not be the case; the assessment might be addressed toward the performance as characterized by its consequences, discernable more readily in the event than the advent . . . the behavior-shaping in question is not here . . .deliberate, a matter of explicitly expressible intentions. . . . If the intra-organism reinforcement story is coherent, then regularity versions of the sanctions approach to implicit norms need be social only in the sense that they essentially involve the distinction of perspective between producing performances and assessing them. (Brandom 1994, 658–59 n. 45) is that any account that demands some sort of radical alteration in kind between nonnormative and normative requires an explanation that can account for a radical alteration in kind. As Brandom sees, it is unhelpful to appeal to the emergence of a perspective of assessment, or the emergence of speech acts, or of intentionality, because they all depend on one another, and because there is no equally radical prior alteration of similar magnitude that is independent of these things to which an explanation can appeal. So it is unlikely that there will be a plausible resolution of a problem constructed in this way. But *some* plausible argument must be constructed to give the necessity argument its explanatory force.

If an alternative account that avoids the problem of a radical alteration is possible, it is instantly better, if it is at all plausible. What I have tried to show here is that an account that is, to make a geological analogy, uniformitarian, that does not depend on supposing there to have been processes in the past that differ from those of the present, can handle the explanation of the taking of particular things as normative. The account is simply this: the fact that we can give explicit arguments, or minitheories, in justification of claims that something falls into the family of things that we call "normative" *is* the answer to the problem. The fact of something becoming normative is that these arguments are accepted (thought they may later be forgotten). Ihering was half right in his recognition theory of legal validity. It is not the recognition of good effects that makes the law binding, so much as the acceptance of *explicit* arguments to the effect that it is binding that makes it binding.

The arguments are not necessarily themselves normative, though they may appeal to "magical" or charismatic notions. One can say that these are "normative." But in the end, the classification of explicit theories, for example the concept of *mana,* into these categories is of little interest, for there is no mysterious fact of normativity, no normative ingredient, that the classification will enable us to filter out. "Normativity" is just our category for distinguishing theories of this sort from theories of another sort, factual ones. Brandom, of course, insists that explicit arguments, and theorizing about commitments of this sort, always depend on implicit norms of argument. He is caught in the trap described by Schmitt in relation to the law. But if what I have said about the pragmatic character of the child's use of *please* is correct, the point may be extended to argument as well. To establish that there is a moment at which the whole business of human conduct, such as using language to persuade, becomes normative requires us to read back features of our account of normativity into the conduct.[5]

5. I should note that a great deal of Brandom's actual discussion, especially in his conclusion, is congenial to the approach I have taken here, as when he discusses the moment at which we, in effect, discover that we have had assumptions and can become explicit about how ours differ from those of others:

Parsons and ethnomethodology, as I have suggested, rest on a similarly "read back" notion of the normative. In the case of Parsons, the problem of normativity arose from the problem of the explanation of action. He reasoned that every action had to have, by definition, an end, and that ends were ultimately either means to other ends or ends in themselves, and that all means to other ends had to lead to ends in themselves. Such ends were, by definition, normative, and all action thus had, by definition, a normative dimension. So the fact that actions could not all be accounted for by reference to explicit norms, such as the law, meant that they had necessarily to be explained by implicit ones. But this necessity follows not from any fact, but from the theory of action and definitions of means and ends with which Parsons begins. Ethnomethodology employs a different notion of necessity. It claims, like Brandom, that various social activities are impossible without the existence of implicit rules, which it purports to discover. But it cannot rid itself of the suspicion that these activities can be accounted for by a combination of explicit considerations and habits, and thus that the rules it "discovers" to operate have themselves also been read back into what is not normative or even rule governed.

Having been all along implicitly normative beings, at this stage of expressive development we can become explicit to ourselves *as* normative beings—aware both of the sense in which we are creatures of the norms and of the sense in which they are creatures of ours. (Brandom 1994, 641–42)

The difference between us is a difference over what we are doing when we reach this stage. I think we become aware that other people behave and reason differently (a process I discuss in Turner 1979, 1980) and construct theories about these differences, some of which help us to make sense of their behavior or reasoning. Brandom thinks that in doing this we are making something explicit—hence the title of his book. I think there is no "it" there to be made explicit. The "assumptions" we attribute to them are at most useful accessories to our ways of constructing and translating their actions into ours, not things in their head, or in the social ether. The only "it" that is not explicit is habits of mind (cf. Turner 1994).

SEVEN

TEACHING SUBTLETY OF THOUGHT /
The Lessons of "Contextualism"

The physicist P. M. S. Blackett was one of the founders of operations research, and made an enormous contribution to the British military effort during World War II. One of his success stories involved the use of ten Beaufighter aircraft to deal with Focke-Wolf 200 aircraft, which were taking a heavy toll on shipping west of Ireland. The practice before Blackett was to use the Beaufighters when all ten were serviceable, so that the entire sea lane of two hundred miles could be "swept clean" (Lovell 1975, 59). The reasoning was that if fewer than the total number of Beaufighters were used, some of the enemy aircraft would be missed. Blackett, using the concept of Poisson's Distribution, showed that the probability of "not sighting" was relatively small, and that, therefore, the Beaufighters should be flown whenever any were available.

This style of reasoning was applied to a great many topics. The idea was to subject existing dogmas and rules to critical analysis. Blackett said that "in nine cases out of ten, the rules or dogmas were found to be soundly based; in the tenth, sometimes, changed circumstances made the rules out of date" (Lovell 1975, 58). As in this case, the strategy was to take the rule and put it in mathematical form, so that one could see whether the practical implications "really" followed. In this case they did not—the problem was with mistaken intuitions about probabilities of relatively rare events, the events of "not sighting," that misled the air officers about the real consequences of the rule they were following.

In an odd way, critical thinking, as it is often taught, mirrors the kinds of successes and failures of operations research, and indeed, in a sense, operations research is a paradigm case of critical thinking. The basic strategy of operations research is to abstract a series of key inferential elements and clarify the logic (and in these cases, which happen to involve numbers, doing so involves mathematics) of the relations between these elements as they actually function and as they might ideally function if different results or outputs are desired. The case for operations research is very much the case for other sorts of critical thinking exercises, such as translating arguments into standard logical forms. The process of abstraction or translation in each case serves to "reveal assumptions."

There are failures, however. On the basis of another analysis Blackett proposed the diversion of 190 heavy bombers to duty attacking U-boats in the Bay of Biscay, where the U-boats docked. He was opposed by the air officer, Slessor, who wanted "aircraft of the right type, with the right sort of radar equipment and crews trained in the right way—and . . . quickly" (Lovell 1975, 63). In the records of the Anti-U-Boat Committee, after Blackett's presentation, the following ministerial aside is recorded: "c'est magnifique, mais n'est pas la guerre" (ibid.). Slessor had perhaps read his Clausewitz on the uses of friction in war, or knew intuitively that for this kind of work better training and equipment would get better results. In any event, the battle was won with seventy aircraft—significantly fewer than Blackett had proposed. Thus, the strategy *can* misfire, and when it does, as the case of Blackett's second suggestion, it is typically because the process of abstraction has left on the cutting room floor or ignored some detail or aspect of the problem that shouldn't have been scrapped—such as the practicalities of training and using inappropriate equipment. Critical thinking, as it is taught, generally involves abstracting in ways that might go wrong. It is not subtle, in the sense that it does not preserve all the complexity and richness of the thinking it supplants and "improves" on. But there is a form of analysis, "contextualism," associated especially with Quentin Skinner (1966, 1969, 1970, 1972, 1974, 1978; Tully and Skinner 1988), that does concern itself with conceptual subtlety, and that in some ways bears on the "going wrong" that occurs in the course of abstraction. It was originally motivated by a desire to counter the historical errors that arise in a particular kind of abstraction very similar to the kind taught in critical thinking courses, namely the kind of abstraction of arguments and positions that philosophers and authors of textbooks of political thought perform on classical political texts.

This form of abstraction discards the things that are deemed irrelevant to a contemporary, or, as the term of abuse goes, "presentist," account of a thinker. *Presentism* is a term that covers a multitude of not very well defined sins, but its main meaning is this: texts may be read in a variety of ways, and a text that is read as though it were a text written in the present and responding to present-day concerns and present-day distinctions is "presentist." Authors of these classic texts, as historical agents, of course did not intend to say these things, and indeed may not have been in a position, owing to the lack of the network of relevant concepts, to have even formed intentions of the kind necessary to hold the views that presentist readings attribute to them. Very often the classic text is primarily an attempt to persuade certain contemporaries, in pursuit of particular tactical ends. So the question of what they actually intended and what, in this "historical" sense, the text meant is a separate question from the question of what can be made out of the text in the way of a present-day argument, problem, or position.

CONTEXTUALISM

Without being very subtle about this, let me abstract the key ideas of contextualism, all of which I myself have disagreed with for various reasons (Turner 1983). The first idea is that in all historical periods, discourse occurs within the framework of conventions of discourse, conventions that limit what can be intelligibly said and understood. The second idea is that great texts of political theory characteristically rest on these conventions, as by definition they would have to, and also innovate by making unconventional conceptual moves, but of a particular kind—moves that appear innocuous, or at least entirely intelligible within a given tradition, but which nevertheless lead to drastically novel conclusions. Conceptual innovation that is understandable only in relation to these preexisting conventions is the subject of contextual analysis. It is often subtle, because the changes are necessarily subtle—they are necessarily so because these are texts, and this is the third key idea, meant to persuade rather than simply to innovate, and necessarily meant to persuade people schooled in a particular set of distinctions and ways of thought and expression. The great innovations, to put it simply, are actually *subtle* innovations. They are small changes in relation to existing conventions, small enough not to be unintelligible, with large consequences in which certain kinds of novel circumstances create suitable conditions for the occurrence of these subtle-in-origin but radical-in-consequence innovations.

So the meanings of texts of interest to contextual analysts are those of the author and the contemporaries of the author, that is, their historical meaning. The meanings that can be attributed to these texts by later thinkers are of no interest. They reflect the fact that old texts can be read according to new conventions, a fact of undoubted importance regarding such matters as the reception and reuse of classic texts but of no importance in accounting for the intended meanings of the authors of the classic texts themselves. This is a critical insight, for it brings the notion of anachronism into the world of thought, particularly the analysis of aspects of texts concerned with reasoning and with concepts in connection with their inferential roles.

A typical historical setting for an innovation of the kind focused on by these analyses is a novel political or moral situation to which the old conventional categories no longer apply very successfully. In this situation there is new scope for the kind of conceptual change in which distinctions that formerly made little practical difference may come to seem to make a great deal of difference, and the innovative thinker is characteristically in the position of revising and expanding conceptual differences to deal with the new situation. But the perspective of the authors and readers at the time is quite different from ours as later readers. We tend to misidentify what is distributive to the author, because we do not realize how much of the "argument" we have abstracted from the text was simply the conventional wisdom of the day.

There are two senses of the word *context* at work here, though they are not always distinguished and perhaps ought not to be, as I will hint in the second half of this chapter. The sense involved when categories no longer apply is a practical or "sociological" sense of the term. A quite typical example is found in Alasdair MacIntyre's *A Short History of Ethics* (1966), which is one of the founding texts of contextualism. In explaining what it was that made Stoicism and Epicurianism different from the ethical thinking of Socrates, even when it sounded similar, MacIntyre notes that

> [i]n Greek society the focus of the moral life was the city-state; in the Hellenistic kingdoms and the Roman empire the sharp antithesis between the individual and the state is inescapable. The question now is not In what forms of social life can justice express itself? or, What virtues have to be practiced to produce a communal life in which certain ends can be accepted and achieved? but, What must I do to be happy? or What goods can I achieve as a private person? The human situation is such that the individual finds his moral environment in his place in the universe rather than in any social or political framework. (1966, 100)

This is the human situation of the individual. But there is also, however, the conceptual situation, which MacIntyre goes on to explain:

> The individual who is situated in a well-organized and complex community, and who cannot but think of himself in terms of the life of that community, will have a rich stock of descriptions available to characterize himself, his wants, and his deprivations. The individual who asks, What do I desire, as a man, apart from all social ties, in the frame of the universe? is necessarily working with a meager stock of descriptions, with an impoverished view of his own nature, for he has had to strip away from himself all the attributes that belong to his social existence. (Ibid.)

The conceptual situation, the availability of a stock of distinctions, is related to the social one, but it is not the same. One can't very well have—in the sense of having access to and use of as part of lived experience—a rich stock of descriptions if one is living in a community, or rather state, in which the descriptions have no use, and are therefore not part of our lived experience. So the conceptual context, though it is not the same as the sociological one, is conditioned on the sociological one.

Thus MacIntyre argues that the characteristic concerns of Stoicism and Epicurianism make sense if one sees that these are really the Socratic concerns applied in a setting in which all that these concerns can mean is a matter of the individual's happiness. Doing anything about the social order or even having any sense of obligation to it is now meaningless, because nothing can be done about it.

These two senses of the term *context* are in this case quite close, because the concepts that are used, or the descriptions that are available, are closely connected to the sociological circumstances, the human situation, of the authors. But there are some other senses of the term *context* that are not so close, such as the sense which refers to literary conventions. This, however, shades into "conventional wisdom," and conventional wisdom in turn shades into what an author's near predecessors said. Each of these senses is relevant to the historians' task. Much of the time contextual analysis comes very close to simply identifying the proximate textual sources for great thinkers' ideas in the writings of lesser thinkers and showing how modest were the adaptations made by these thinkers.[1] A famous example of this is the historian Lawrence Dickey's description of the Protestantism of Old Wurttemberg and the ways in which it and the political history of the area reappear in Hegel's philosophy. From a "presentist" perspective, these writings resemble things in Aristotle; from the point of view of Hegel himself, they are part of recent history and present sensibilities (Dickey 1987, 135).

AN EXAMPLE: WEBER ON THE STATE

In what follows I would like to discuss a very brief and simple example of the kind of difference a contextual reading might make. The text is Weber's famous definition of the state: "A compulsory political association will be called a state insofar as its administrative staff successfully upholds the claim to the monopoly of the legitimate use of force" ([1922] 1978, 54). A reasonable guess at the contextual origin of this definition is that it is adapted from a text in jurisprudential theory which was influential when Weber was a law student. Weber himself cites the text, though not in connection with this definition. The probable source is Rudolph von Ihering, who says the following: "The state is

---

1. There are many examples of the application of this method, and indeed these ideas are enshrined though not always followed in the Cambridge *Ideas in Context* series.

the only competent as well as the sole owner of social coercive force—the right to coerce forms the *absolute monopoly* of the state" ([1877] 1913, 238). If we compare the two definitions the similarities are striking, but so is the small difference. Ihering uses the phrase "social coercive force" and Weber uses the phrase "legitimate force."

The historical background to Ihering's usage is actually rather intriguing. Ihering was thought to be the great German follower of Bentham's, but he was also known for a critique of utilitarianism with respect to its arguments for the prohibition of the act of selling oneself into slavery. Ihering's point was essentially that in selling our labor we routinely engage in miniature acts of selling ourselves into slavery, and it is impossible to give a theoretical account of the distinction between the miniature acts and selling oneself into slavery as such that is not obviously ad hoc.

Ihering's solution to this and other infirmities of utilitarianism was to argue that there was such a thing as a social interest in addition to and commensurate with individual interests. The supposed social interest was congenial to his German audience and also enabled him to do away with such problems as justifying the prohibition of slavery, which could now be claimed to be the fulfillment of the social interests. The state, too, in this definition, could be seen as the representative of the social interest, and the history of the state and the law could then be interpreted in terms of the successively greater fulfillment of a wider range of interests, including social interests. This reasoning led to Ihering's use of the phrase in this definition. The perspective is evolutionistic and teleological: the state fulfills interests, and advances by doing more of this and doing it better.

Weber simply tweaked the definition in a way that strips it of its teleological significance. There is no social interest in Weber's definition, only the monopoly on the legitimate use of force. In a sense the definition is a retrogression in that the notion of legitimacy, employed in this way, is even more mysterious than the relatively well-developed notion of interest and social interest employed by Ihering. It is apparently unhelpful in accounting for the evolution of legal systems. Indeed, what seems to be required is a theory of legitimation. Weber, of course, supplied such a theory in the form of a tripartite classification of types of legitimating bases, including traditional, charismatic, and rational legal beliefs about the legitimacy of a given authority. This classification is only quasi-historical and determinedly nonteleological and nonevolutionistic. Traditional bases for legitimacy mostly lie in the past; rational legal bases in the future, and charisma erupts now and then, but in its purest form is largely in the past, or that which occurs in association with one of the other forms of legitimacy.

It is often argued that interesting as these little snippets of fact might be for the intellectual historian, they essentially lack interest or value for the contemporary student of politics or political theory. What is of interest about Hobbes, to put it bluntly, is what thinkers like David Gauthier abstract out the great mishmash of Hobbesian arguments (Gauthier 1986). Understanding the subtleties of Hobbes's massaging of available ideas is of no use to the person who wishes to solve these modern problems. The big questions, so to speak, are untouched by the little distinctions with which contextualists concern themselves. The big questions, this seems to say, are the abstracted questions, and by definition the stuff that's left over after abstraction is irrelevant.

If one looks at the reception history of Weber's argument, one would find a great deal that appeared to bear out the thought that this historical snippet is of no importance except for historians. Nozick, for example, refers to "the tradition of Max Weber" and uses the phrase "having a monopoly on the use of force in a geographical area, a monopoly incompatible with the private enforcement of rights, as crucial to the existence of a state" (1974, 23). He ignores the whole business of legitimacy, because he thinks it just leads in a circle in which legitimacy is explained in terms of the attitudes and beliefs of subjects, and in which the notion of legitimacy is reintroduced "when it comes time to explain the precise content of the subjects' attitudes and beliefs," yielding "a legitimate government is one that most of its subjects view as legitimately ruling" (134). This doesn't help as a morally informative definition of the state, since one still wants to know whether the beliefs are justified.

Talcott Parsons, for example, simply reincorporated the notion of legitimacy back into the problematic from which Weber was liberating it: "The fact that an order is legitimate in the eyes of a large proportion of the community makes it *ipso facto* an element of the *Interessenlage* of any one individual, whether *he* himself holds it to be legitimate or not" (1937, 636). Parsons, no less than Gauthier, had his eye on what he took to be the main problem, namely the problem of how to obtain a social contract, or, as he puts it, solve the Hobbesian problem. So he made Weber into a solver of this problem.

But the subtlety of Weber's revision of Ihering is missed in both Nozick's and Parsons's accounts, and along with it the innovation with large consequences that Weber makes. Weber by defining the state in this way showed that there is no necessary connection between the state and "social utilities." The thing the state is, namely a successfully asserted claim to a monopoly of legitimate violence within a territory, is not "essentially" based on the concert of interests, or any other external fact. Interests, Weber later goes on to argue, may indeed be one motive for accepting a claim of legitimacy, but it is typically not the only motive and need not be a motive at all. The radical consequence is that the problem of the social contract simply disappears. What one needs to explain is the origin of legitimating beliefs. And whether this is an easier task or not, it is clearly a different task. In a sense, what is revealed by Weber's little definitional innovation is that the traditional problem of social contract theory is largely circular and hinges on the assumption that explaining the state is fundamentally a matter of explaining the role of the state in relation to interests, when this is at most an ancillary feature of this state. The very fact that we can very nicely define the state without reference to interest concepts shows that the statement of the problem is the problem. Similarly for the problem of justification. No fact about the state secures its justification, and by the same token, there is no general fact about states as such that serves the justification of the state as such. One needs to put the moral information into one's account of the state to get it out of it, because it isn't there in the sociological phenomenon of the state itself. Consequently, any morally informative definition of the state is really a concealed sort of special pleading, which is what he took Ihering's account of the state to be. Weber's point is that we can have a perfectly useful definition of the state without asking whether the beliefs are justified.

I don't mean to hold this discussion out as a model of subtle reasoning, for indeed it is not all that subtle. But it does represent a kind of thinking that ordinarily is not thought of as part of critical thinking. What contextualist historical analyses search for is not a history that consists of successive approximations to the solution of reconstructed and abstracted problems, such as the problem of the social contract. It looks instead to the way in which "problems" are problems within some set of givens, including tacit conventions. The approach relativizes problems and solutions to a richer "context" of conventions, literary models, and whatnot. It is this relativization that appears to doom contextual analysis to irrelevance. But the same strategy of relativizing to a richer context can be a tool of critical thinking as well, if we use it to identify the less obvious features of a doctrine, problem, or thesis that we can work with, that we can vary or replace—just as Weber replaced the term *social utility,* which is at the core of the problem of the social contract as it was conceived throughout social contract tradition. We don't really grasp how Weber has innovated until we see his definition against the contrasting background of the conventional wisdom. And this puts us in a position to assess the conventional wisdom, or at least talk about it.

The charge against contextualism is that it estranges the classical political thinkers from us by stressing the dependence of their meaning on local circumstances and motives, dead traditions of discourse, and dead conventions. What I have suggested here is that estranging ourselves in this self-conscious way allows us to see things that we can alter and replace. Distinctions that were, for them, distinctions without a difference may well be, for us, very useful distinctions indeed. And if contextualism does not provide a formula for discovering which distinctions do make a difference in our context, it nevertheless encourages us and in a way trains us to look for these distinctions, and in this way, to look past the abstracted forms of argument that make up such things as social contract theory that otherwise appear to be constitutive of the problem itself. We gain, in other words, a new ability to redefine what the problem is, and this is what frees us to deal with it in new ways.

CONTEXTUALISM AND LOGIC

Since much of what is taught as critical thinking is logic, it is not surprising that discussions about teaching run into fundamental questions about the nature of logic. In this case the issues arise pretty directly. Contextual analysis employs a good deal of logical vocabulary, though not in an especially technical way. Notions like "presupposition" are, of course, part of the "old" historicism that persists in the "new historicism," and the idea behind their use is that in a particular historical era there are, in fact, shared presuppositions. In a sense, the program of contextualism, by the use of these bridge concepts, fits neatly into the program of the teaching of critical thinking, especially that aspect suggesting that critical thinking requires identifying hidden assumptions.

But a certain conflict arises between the normative and "historical" uses of logic. If we teach that, in part at least, good reasoning is a matter of conformity with formal principles, or more simply a matter of formulation into valid formal schemes, it may appear to students that we are setting standards that a good many texts in the history of ideas cannot meet. Where this kind of hint is likely to cause trouble is where students naively think that they have detected fallacies or suppressed premises. There are, clearly, invalid arguments in these classical texts. The temptation to think that the normative standards of good thinking by which one attempts to abide are the appropriate standards for the rest of the thinkers in history is obviously a natural one; indeed, if critical thinking teaching is not about timeless standards of reason, it is a bit of a problem to know what exactly it is about. But reading historically also requires reading charitably. Many of Weber's readers thought, as Nozick intimates, that appeals to legitimacy were circular arguments, and from a certain point of view they are. But to learn something from Weber we need to understand ourselves and our desire to abstract Weber in a certain way by taking the validity of his reasoning for granted, and seeing what that implies about our own reasoning. This is, of course, what I have tried to do here: to problematize the problem situation of social contract theory. The standard tools of critical thinking, such as fallacy hunting and suppressed premise identifying, are unhelpful here: they would suggest that Weber has failed to solve a problem he was intent on undermining.

Another, simpler, example might clarify this. The idea that Plato reasons according to suppressed premises about the inferiority of barbarians that are racist and therefore that his comments on the subject are instances of defective reasoning, would be a quite natural conclusion from a critical thinking course. But it is quite a strange conclusion if our purpose is to analyze the actual reasoning of the texts. In a sense, it is helpful to say that Plato's reasoning can be reconstructed as a formally valid argument if we include some suppressed premises about barbarians which happen to be false, thereby establishing that Plato was not a bad reasoner but a racist. But this is also potentially misleading, especially when we start freely attributing the contents of these suppressed premises to the historical Plato or to the shared mentality of the Athenians.

Contextualism serves to provide a little bit of distance by using the term *convention,* and thus making the missing premises into analogues of literary conventions. This helps us avoid saying that Plato was a racist or Athenians were racists and allows us to focus not on the form of argument itself but on the question of what Plato was trying to do with the argument. It is here where the whole question of innovation becomes central. If Plato is read as trying to persuade people of something within the literary conventions of Athenian discourse, he might very well employ "racist" modes of inference that we would regard as based on suppressed false premises to make points which are not themselves racist. The same kinds of points may be made about Machiavelli, and indeed here is where the value of contextual analysis is most obviously apparent. Machiavelli employs various quite different literary forms, the "mirror of princes" in *The Prince* and the praise of classical authors in *The Discourses on Livy,* and says things that may be thought to conflict with one another, or to point to some sort of deeply evil underlying intent. But Machiavelli was writing for people who not only were familiar with these literary forms but treated them as more or less transparent and unproblematic. Consequently, in employing them he was simply avoiding the necessity of giving arguments for all kinds of things that in context not only didn't need to be established but indeed didn't matter: he is simply reasoning in the way that we reason with people whose beliefs we take to be false but who would be persuaded of the conclusions we would like them to be persuaded of if they reasoned in accordance with their false beliefs. There is nothing terribly mysterious about this kind of persuasion and indeed we do it all the time.

So despite the congeniality in general between contextualism and the kind of discussion about reasoning one finds in critical thinking, there is a somewhat different approach to the question of the character of what we may loosely call suppressed premises. The point of the reasoning for the contextualist and, more generally, the point of some particular political utterance, has little to do with the contents of the "presuppositions" that make it valid if these contents are "conventional." What makes Machiavelli and Plato good or bad or important or innovative is not the conventions they employ but the innovations they introduce with the new things they do with those conventions. This is quite explicitly understood as a historical matter, and asserting things about the intentions of a historical writer requires one to identify those intentions in light of the existing conventions at the time of the utterance. In a sense what contextualism does is extend the notion of anachronism to the world of thought. To fail to acknowledge the conventionality of a form of reasoning is to import anachronisms, and from this point of view claims about Plato's racism are simply anachronisms.

In a sense it is a nice exercise in critical thinking to make these distinctions between premises in a psychological sense, premises in a conventional sense that might be merely employed, premises that are assumed to be accepted by the person being persuaded, and so forth, for it is clearly an error to mix up these things. Nevertheless, there are some difficulties in doing this that reveal something about the project of teaching people how to infer and to evaluate inferences that deserve some reflection. One aspect of this problem is pointed to by the form of the terms themselves. *Hidden assumption, suppressed premises, literary conventions,* and the like all have a peculiar elusiveness. They are each analogical. There is no delicatessen from which a writer chooses "descriptions" from the available "stock"; this is an interpreter's notion. Similarly, as I have suggested, as regards the suppression and hiding of premises, they are not so much "hidden" as attributed by us, and for our interpretive purposes, during the minimally charitable interpretation necessary for us to make any sense out of what we read in these texts. Literary conventions sound like something much more solid. Romance novels, after all, are written according to an explicit formula. But the formulae that contextualists and literary theorists mean are only analogous to such explicit rules, and are thus themselves just analogies. There is a sense in which the main defect of the old historicism was its reliance on notions like "worldview." The vocabulary of contextualism, which is largely shared with "critical thinking," is perhaps equally dubious.

It is simple to grant that it is misleading to attribute racism as a personal intention to Plato or racism as a certain collective presupposition to the Greeks. We can stop at this and say that what we're doing when we interpret Plato is supplying the premises necessary for making his reasoning intelligible to us, without making any psychological claims. For us, something might not follow from the term *barbarian* that follows "naturally" for Plato or for fifth-century Athenians. Supplying the premise makes it follow for us. Once we make this separation between the psychological content of Plato's mind and our standards of inference, it becomes clear that all this talk about suppressed premises is actually part of the machinery of *translation*. The inferences are part and parcel of the concept "barbarian" for the Athenians rather than some complicated set of beliefs that are "tacitly adhered to" by these Athenians. Our only evidence of their beliefs is in the uses to which they put these concepts in making what we take to be inferences; and the only reality that these premises have is in our necessity to attribute them in order to make sense of the inferences that we think they actually made, or appear to have made, in texts involving these concepts.

But what sorts of things are these conventions? In a sense the conventions and their associated concepts are fairly autonomous facts or procedures with a certain life of their own. The fact that they can be translated into, or analyzed into, conventional logical form seems in some obscure way to secure this status as autonomous fact. The temptation is to think that the conventional logical form is in some sense the fundamental or primitive fact; and that lurking behind all this complicated literary machinery of such things as literary conventions being manipulated by or used by Machiavelli, are something like hidden or suppressed beliefs, which, linked with the standard logical operators, produce the outcomes that one actually observes in discourse. The complicated literary forms that Machiavelli relies on are a bit like the appearance of the Wizard of Oz. The actual wizard is hidden inside him doing conventional logical inferences in terms of claims that are not really accessible from the surface except through analysis. The analysis consists of translating the things that are accepted on the surface as "inference" into the formalism, and then augmenting the formalism with whatever beliefs and additional premises are necessary to make the inferences valid. This picture is certainly not completely foreign to Quine and Davidson, where we get the picture of an individual possessing a theory of the world in terms of which she interprets the claims and sayings of others, adjusting hidden premises here and there in order to make interpretations come out, and so forth. It is even more congenial to the idea of a common human "mentalese," which is a bit like the Wizard, supplying something analogous to the computer code in which all "applications," which appear differently to users, are written.

An alternative to this is to take the "surface" inferences as primitive, and to see the step of translating this into some formal locution as one in which the structure of inferences surrounding the concept linking the concepts, such as "barbarians," is made explicit. This style of thinking about the problem derives from Wilfrid Sellars and has been powerfully revived by Robert Brandom. As the title of his book *Making It Explicit* shows, Brandom is committed to something like the idea that there is an "it" to be made explicit, some structurelike thing to be analyzed.[2]

Brandom argues that if we employ a strategy of making inferences explicit by first making explicit those connectives whose inferential structure we can

2. This was discussed by Brandom (1994, 98–99), and earlier by Sellars (1963, 321–58), commenting on Wittgenstein. The issue about the "it" was formulated nicely for me by the political scientist Richard Ashcraft ten years ago, when he asked me a question about Karl Mannheim: If the frames within which historical thinkers interpreted the world are relative to their time, what about the claims about frames that we, as historically situated figures, make? Sellars argues that material inferences are real and primitive. Brandom argues in the same way. My argument, in contrast, follows the lines of my "Translating Ritual Beliefs" (1979).

make fully clear and rule governed, the connectives of logic, we can then proceed to make more and more things fully clear—though this may well be a process that is interminable. Logic for Brandom is both a means of making the inexplicit explicit, and a kind of model of explicitness about inferential structure that can be applied to all the actual material inferences people make using concepts which have particular powers. In a sense, what logic amounts to is a part of a game like chess—Sellars's analogy—in which the powers of all the pieces are clear, though in the case of the inferences that we're actually attempting to analyze the powers are not clear, and they need to be discovered and made clear. So the model is capturing all inferential moves that can be performed with a concept. This way of thinking about material inference comports even better with contextualism than the idea that logic provides us the normative standard of valid inference. It allows us to dispense with the whole business about the Wizard of Oz hiding in the machine using the logical operators and patching inferences together with a lot of complicated hidden presuppositions. From an explanatory or naturalistic point of view, there are plenty of good reasons for skepticism about the necessity for all this machinery.

But if we grant this view of inference, that is, if we take material inference to be primitive, and we grant this view of logic, namely that logic provides us with some refined concepts whose inferential role is completely explicit, then it is obviously something of a problem to explain what critical thinking as a subject of instruction can amount to. Inference on this view is the correct use of concepts, and there is no logical check on the inferential validity of uses of concepts or indeed any sort of external logical standard to which inferences may be held. We may discover that certain material inferences, such as those involving barbarians, get us into trouble, and our troubles force us to refine our concepts, or, what is the same thing, rearrange the powers that we give to these concepts so that we don't have those troubles. But that is largely a matter of discovering how things work out, and a pragmatic notion of inference.

The idea of getting into trouble, then making one's troubles more explicit and accessible to solution through conceptual revision, does sound a bit like the kind of "making explicit" that Brandom is talking about. And this activity, in turn, looks a lot like the kind of interpretive analysis that contextualists do when faced with a text whose surface meaning is problematic, when the problematic character is made unavoidable for us by the problem of discerning the intentions of the author. This is, of course, a famous aspect, perhaps the core, of the problem of interpreting Machiavelli. But it is no less a problem when we look at some later figure such as Weber. The problem of discerning a coherent intention of an author is in a sense insoluble as a purely textual matter, since texts taken by themselves allow for a quite incredible range of intentional attributions. What the contextualist does is to radically narrow this range by supplying conventions against which changes can be seen as intentional, and therefore limiting what it is that can be attributed as part of a distinctive intention of the author.

The kind of trouble that we can explain to people whom we are instructing in the art of critical thinking is, on the basis of our contextual knowledge, trouble that arises when the changes or difference between two formulations are subtle. One common case is when the conditions of applications are pretty much the same, or precisely the same, but the uses—that is, the inferential uses—differ. To take a very familiar example, the conditions for application of "rabbit" and "undetached rabbit" are identical. Their inferential uses are not identical. We could ask questions about the number of undetached rabbit parts in a whole rabbit, for example, and do things like count the number of undetached rabbit parts. The contextualists, as I have said, concentrate particularly heavily on these kinds of changes. MacIntyre's discussion of Stoicism, for example, has as its point the idea that moral concepts that worked a certain way—that is, in our terms, supported or allowed for certain kinds of inferences in one society, did not support those inferences in another, and therefore amounted to and evolved into entirely different kinds of moral systems. Machiavelli, on one interpretation, was making the point that in his time there was no difference between greatness and successful criminality, though obviously the two notions are connected to quite different concepts and support quite different inferences. I think one can do little more than to exhibit this kind of thinking and hope that students who learn to apply it in one setting can apply it in novel settings. But applying it requires a good command of a lot of concepts, which is to say of their uses or inferential powers. No method or course in critical thinking can teach that. The grasping of the distinctions is mostly a matter of local knowledge, of usages, and in a sense this is what contextualists' historical studies strive to obtain, and present to readers in the form of "conventions of discourse."

AGAINST THE "IT"

I said earlier that I had some objections to contextualism. Now it would perhaps be fair if I said what they were. They apply to Brandom as well. I have been hinting at a kind of risk involved in talking about "suppressed premises." To explain my concerns, let me tell shaggy dog story. I once had a department chair who was Chinese. When we would meet, there would be a lot of what in the radio business is called dead air, that is, long silences. This irritated me intensely, and typically when this gentleman did not respond to something I was saying I would fill the dead air by politely making more explicit whatever I was saying, or by elaborating on what I had just said, which it seemed to me, inferring from his silence, he had not quite grasped. I interpreted his silences, in short, as the silence of incomprehension. And I attempted to correct the problem of comprehension by telling him more. After several frustrating conversations of this sort, I read an airline magazine containing an article on business etiquette in the Far East. The article explained that among the Chinese silence meant that the auditor did not like what was being said and, consequently, was waiting until something was said that he or she wanted to respond to.

I think this is a model instrumental rule of translation. It tells someone having one kind of expectation to construe some sign, in this case silence, as having a different meaning. Whether this is a scientifically warranted interpretation or whether an anthropologist would have come up with this characterization does not really matter. It is a quite practical rule for dealing with a situation in which one simply needs to know what people are acting as if they mean. This rule is an "as if" rule in two senses. When a Chinese is silent it is "as if" he is telling me he doesn't like what he hears, and it is an "as if" rule in the sense that it does not depend on the sort of claim that the Chinese actually have "in their heads" something corresponding to this rule. It is enough to know that they behave "as if" they were following this rule, and that one can interpret what they are saying by keeping this "as if" rule in mind, and not get into trouble.

I think it is reasonable to say the Chinese have to learn something in order to "play" in accordance with this little language game of silence. Pretty obviously, they do not learn the rule that *I* use, which is a translation rule. Indeed, there may be no particular reason to think the Chinese "learn a rule" at all, though this is a question of a different kind. There is no particular reason that everyone would have to have the exact same interpretive hypothesis in order to understand one another, if *understand* means to get by in interacting with other people. I don't think one needs to be terribly fancy here. The Chinese learn something that makes them behave in a tolerably predictable way in connection with these silences, and, given this behavior, it is possible to formulate this "as if" rule in such a way that one can more or less successfully deal with the Chinese. But there is no "it" to be made explicit. There is a job of translation, which is governed by our imperatives or my imperatives in explaining them to you, and all this machinery such as talk about presuppositions is misleading, at least potentially, if we think of it as out there, as having independent reality and structure, and as being a domain to be described.

Where does this leave logic? Let me quote from Wood and Serres' standard text on diplomatic protocol on the reasons for the use of French as the language of diplomacy: "that it has qualities of clarity, precision and firmness not found in English, the latter being too often elliptic and its construction and vocabulary lacking conciseness, thus resulting in a looser version of the same text" (1970, 178 par. 712). Whether this is true or not, it seems true to somebody, so there is for someone a kind of pragmatic value of translating at least diplomatic exchanges and treaties into French. Presumably one can detect the unclarities in one's own formulations by translating them into French. Logic still has this utility even if one accepts my view that there's no "it" to be made explicit, and goes on to say that logic, no more than French, is a uniquely valid detector of unclarity.[3] If we dispense with the idea that Latin or French or logic is the standard against which other formulations are judged and found wanting and concentrate on the differences that are revealed, we have a kind of mirror on our own material inferences and concepts that is nonarbitrary but, like the mirror of Dorian Gray, reveals something about them.

Of course, Brandom also has the idea that our knowledge of the complete rules governing the inferences of the logical connectives is a goal toward which analysis aspires, while conceding that we are not likely to reach it in many of the philosophically interesting cases. If we compare this with the Quinean view that, for the most part, philosophy happens in the course of translating into a formal idiom rather than in reasoning within it, we get the hint that many of these "translation" questions are not univocally decidable. If this is so, perhaps there is no point to engaging in an infinite task and more of a point to the tactical use of translation into and out of whatever idiom serves our purposes—the larger purposes previously thought to be served by making "assumptions" explicit—without committing ourselves either to the univocal superiority of kind of comparison, or to the existence, in some netherworld, of an "it" to be made explicit. Subtlety, in this way of looking at the problem, is a matter of recognizing our failure to adequately translate, and then of employing distinctions and elaborating our concepts to overcome at least some of these inadequacies.

WHAT CAN BE TAUGHT ABOUT PROBLEMS OF ABSTRACTION?

In teaching students to read texts contextually, we teach them something about thinking subtly that they may themselves deploy. Perhaps a good deal of this teaching can be done in fairly unsubtle way by showing students that formulations they thought of as identical, or virtually identical, support different kinds of inferences. If the examples are from a domain that is familiar to them, we can rely on the knowledge of how concepts work that they already possess, without immersing them in Renaissance texts and the study of Renaissance literary conventions.

I began this chapter by talking about the kinds of abstraction that is done

---

3. Consider a story Golo Mann told about Rickert: "Er zitierte dann einen Satz Heideggers und fragte: 'Kann man das ins Lateinische übersetzen? Was man nicht ins Lateinische kann, das existiert für mich nicht!'" (1986, 289) Heidegger would of course have expected it to fail, because Latin, in his view, was not a language in which one can philosophize.

in operations research, and how it sometimes goes wrong. Contextualism as a kind of historical enterprise is an exposé of one kind of abstraction that goes wrong when one interprets texts. The abstracting that noncontextual interpreters do when they extract the argument of Hobbes or the argument of Machiavelli is not so different from what Blackett did in abstracting the principles of military operations. They manufacture an alternative object on which to operate. Sometimes reasoning in terms of this alternative object is pragmatically better; sometimes it is not. It usually is clearer, at least for us, and perhaps having certain kinds of clarity about inferential structure is, in particular circumstances, an important desideratum. But sometimes we need to be able to make distinctions and recognize distinctions between concepts that are embedded in uses other than the particular task at hand for which the abstraction has been produced. This is, one may say, the negative lesson of contextualism, and it is worth teaching.

Is there a simple teachable *positive* lesson that could reasonably be made into a unit of a critical thinking course deriving from all this? Perhaps. Another lesson of contextualism is that a distinction may be without a difference in one context but make a significant difference in another, so that the inferences one would make in one context quite reasonably would be quite unreasonable in another. A simple example of this is found in MacIntyre's discussion of the uses of Greek ethics in the large-scale political world of the Romans. Where ordinary individuals had little power, and no one had civic power, questions like "Can a good man be harmed?" take on a quite different significance, and to hold this view consistently requires one to go much further than Socrates did in the direction of elevating the self and distinguishing the self from the community over which individuals have no control. In analyzing the political utterances of present-day writers, their morals, or for that matter their epistemology, this is perhaps a lesson that is good to keep in mind. The consequences of an assertion, and the way in which it can go wrong, depend very much on the setting in which it is used and on the other inferences that in that setting are connected to it. One is well advised to inquire into the setting and ask whether the inferences work in the same way in a new setting.

Writers like MacIntyre tend to employ the term *intelligible* in cases of changed circumstances, and suggest that doctrine X or Y is no longer intelligible or fully intelligible in a changed setting. The paradigm case of this is his early article on religion, in which he argued that "understanding Christianity is incompatible with believing in it, not because Christianity is vulnerable to skeptical objections, but because its peculiar invulnerability belongs to it as a form of belief which has lost the social context which once made it comprehensible. It is now too late to be mediaeval and it is too empty and too easy to be Kierkegaardian. Thus skeptic and believer do not share a common grasp of the relevant concepts any more than anthropologist and Azande do" (1970,

76–77). This makes "a common grasp" of the relevant concepts into an all or nothing affair.

One of the virtues of Brandom's treatment of the inferential character of concepts, and his stress on the distinction between conditions of application and conditions of use, is that we are permitted to understand specifically which particular material inferential powers of a concept become problematic in a new setting. The usual problem is that the new use, or the use in a different context, is *not* "unintelligible," but rather *is* intelligible, but its use leads to the wrong conclusions, conclusions whose wrongness one cannot grasp by simply looking at the formal structure of arguments and looking out for informal fallacies.

This returns us to the place at which this article began, to Blackett. If Blackett's calculations about the number of fighters necessary to secure the Bay of Biscay from submarines was wrong, as indeed it was, there would have been no way for him to have known this. If the strategy had failed, of course, he could have gone back and redone the calculations until he got the results that he wanted and needed. But if he had simply failed to grasp one of the relevant distinctions, such as the role of friction in war, and the difficulty of training, no amount of revision would have allowed him to discover his omission, at least if he was restricted to the mathematical manipulation of his original scheme of abstraction. The problem arose when he discarded those things in the course of abstracting.

Perhaps the analogous mistake in critical thinking is an uncommon one. Perhaps people recognize without instruction that they are employing distinctions that no longer work in the way that they expect them to because the setting in which they are applied has changed and thus changed their implications. But I suspect otherwise: that this is the most common of mistakes, and indeed not really a mistake but a product of our inevitable blindness as we stumble through the world with concepts whose material inferential uses derive from past settings, which we apply *faute de mieux* in new settings. Teaching people not to make this "mistake" is of course an impossibility. But showing them what sort of problem it is, and equipping them to recognize it when it arises, is not impossible. And doing so is as inevitable a part of "critical thinking" as the problem is itself an appropriate part of thinking.

There are two main subfamilies of the concept of practice, one of which arises in connection with the theory-practice distinction, the other in connection with explanations of distinctive, stable forms of activity, which are said to rest on "different practices." There are perhaps other forms of the concept of practice, however. What I shall argue here is that Andrew Pickering's use of the concept of practice in *The Mangle of Practice* (1995) is in neither subfamily, but is nevertheless appropriately placed in the practice family, and illuminates some important family characteristics. My device for bringing out the features of Pickering's argument will be to compare it with Michael Polanyi's notion of tacit knowledge, which is the grandfather of all "practice" accounts of science.

Concepts of practice have a hook on us because of two basic arguments, which in some contexts amount to the same argument. They are arguments involving necessity and irreducibility, arguments that claim that some notion of practice is necessary to account for some facts or phenomena, and the argument that practice, conceptualized in this way, is irreducible to something other than practice, such as explicit theories or habits. The peculiarity of the concept of practice lies in the supposed ineffability or unapprehensibility of the thing to which the term refers. Practices are held to be a condition of understanding that cannot itself be understood in fully explicit terms. "We know more than we can say," as Polanyi's slogan puts it.

Polanyi's notion of tacit knowledge fits both notions of practice I have mentioned here. Tacit knowledge is a *basis of an activity* which is in some sense separate from the activity itself, and on which the activity thus may be said to depend. It also fits with the idea of practice as *an activity which is larger than that which theory can comprehend.* In the case of an activity, such as producing a particular kind of scientific observation, the notion of practice in the sense of the theory-practice distinction figures as a way of describing this larger whole. As a basis, the term describes *what it is that practitioners of a technique possess* that enables them to perform, but which is not and perhaps cannot be formulated in a cookbook description of the technique. It is a part of the remainder that theory cannot articulate or subsume. The difference between the two conceptions of practice, roughly, is that the notion of practice in the "larger whole" sense usually has a kind of teleological significance; in the "basis" sense it is a causal or conceptual condition.

I have said all these boring things primarily to get a map of the concept and its uses, but it is obviously easier to think of these things in terms of examples. The standard examples of practices in the "basis" sense are activities that cannot be performed properly according to the explicit theories or cookbooks of the activities and, in the "larger whole" sense, purposeful activities such as lawyering or doctoring that cannot be fully reduced to the explicit theory of the activity.

RELATIVIZING PRACTICE CONCEPTS TO EXPLANATORY PURPOSES

Even at this very crude level, one can see that what is left as a remainder depends on the explicit theories in whose terms one is trying to explicate practice, and the purposes for which these theories are constructed (and therefore the standards for which they are adequate). It also depends on the activity and how it is conceived. In connection with artificial intelligence applications, for example, a basic problem might be to see if one can construct a program that can read a legal contract and assess its validity or point to deficiencies within the contract. One question that this kind of exercise raises is whether one has to know a good deal about what a contract is before feeding it into the machine. Does the operator have to put in near-contracts to get meaningful output? What is the contrast space within which the program can make distinctions? The temptation is to characterize the task in such a way that it can be solved by artificial intelligence methods. Similarly, the objects of "practice" explanations are usually not well defined, and there is a similar temptation to adjust the object of explanation to the available means of explanation. A second kind of consideration is what counts as adequacy. Is the concern of the program to produce almost equivalent results to what some practitioner would do or to perfectly mimic the *ideal* practitioner? In the case of practice explanations what counts as adequacy is typically even less clear.

The problem that practice explanations solve is thus somewhat artificial.

One is not really concerned with comparing the explicit theory or program with the activity itself, so much as with a particular account of the activity. I leave aside the "in principle" aspects of this problem, and the implication that the entire question to which practice accounts are an answer may be essentially a fake or a misapprehension, but I will return to it briefly at the end. My point, however, is that the appearance of a difference that requires an appeal to practice is itself a construction, and is based on reasoning that is usually not made terribly clear in the first place. This in turn suggests that, despite similarities in form, divergent accounts of practice are really about different problems. In discussing Pickering (Pickering 1995), what I hope to do is to say something about how his notion of practice compares with others with respect to the problems of insufficiency and irreducibility. He gives very nice examples, and a fair discussion would deal with these examples. What I propose to do is a little less fair. I propose to discuss a very small number of "metatheoretical" comments that Pickering makes about what he is doing, from which I will try to construct his version of the problem of practice, specifically from the point of view of the question of what insufficiencies it serves to overcome. In other words, I am going to assume that Pickering's argument is like all other practice arguments in having this particular structure. I will also assume that we can see in the pattern of his comments some sort of collection of usages that fill the gap that he constructs for us, and that his account of practices consists of these usages.

THEORIES OF PRACTICE: STANDARD FORMS

For the most part, theories of practice follow a fairly simple pattern of describing or positing tacit analogues to explicit things. If explicit norms can account for something, for example, *implicit* norms (with somewhat different properties but with similar powers) can fill the gap. This is not the only model of practice, but it is hard to do much more than appeal to analogues of the sorts of things that we are familiar with describing and characterizing. Pickering's discussion of the mangle of practice is far too complex, but also perhaps too vague, to capture in a very simple model, such as the model I have given here of artificial intelligence programs reading contracts. In that model, one has some explicit rules of law that need to be supplemented in various ways by other, tacit rules, which need to be made explicit to produce a machine that performs a certain specified task, producing particular correct discriminations, on certain specified material.

In the case of science, practice accounts have typically been concerned with a gap between what can be contained in a formal structure and what scientific knowledge actually consists of in practice. Polanyi formulates the problem of the limitations of formal structure in this way:

There are an infinite number of mathematical formulae which will cover any series of numerical observations. Any additional future observations can still be accounted for by an infinite number of formulae. (1964, 9)

For Polanyi, what this means is that no mathematical reduction of scientific theory can be equated to scientific knowledge, and that what is needed to close the gap between the two is a tacit coefficient which consists of a tacit analogue to explicit knowledge. In this case, Polanyi thinks, the tacit stuff must have a particular content, "an intuitive conception of the general nature of things" (1964, 10).

Polanyi's explanatory model works like this: We have one general phenomenon that can be described in one way, namely scientific knowledge, which has certain properties, in this case a whole array of behavioral and psychological properties that require a kind of community structure. We compare this with the explicit formalism of the scientific theory and, lo and behold, there is a difference between the two. We then account for the difference by filling in with the intuitive conception of the nature of things, which a scientific community shares. But Polanyi did not stop with this: He populated the tacit dimension with a variety of concepts and distinctions, such as the subsidiary-focal distinction, which he used to fill the gap between observational data and what the knower sees.

If we ask how Pickering's gap-filling device, the mangle of practice, works, we can do what we can do for Polanyi, namely construct a kind of function from the explicit concept to the analogical, mangle, version of the same thing. In several of these cases the concept of the mangle corresponds to more than one explicit concept. The innovation in Pickering, at least in relation to the sociological science studies tradition, is that he attempts to provide within the framework of the concept of the mangle an analogue to the process of hypothesizing and testing that is the central focus of most philosophical accounts of science. Instead of prediction and predictive failure we get accommodation and resistance, and the extent or application of these concepts is altered to include, not (as in Polanyi) some sort of tacit realm, but rather the process within which a given individual research program develops. The larger set of difficulties and facilitating or resisting objects is made a part of this process. The difference from Polanyi is that Pickering provides a new explanatory object with which to compare the nonpractice parts of science or the defective theory of science, namely the course of an individual's research. He makes sure that this cannot be construed teleologically by insisting that the object is understood in "real time," meaning, among other things, that each step of development must be explained in terms of what is available to the scientist at a given moment.

DANCING IN REAL TIME

The notion of "real time" serves a variety of purposes for Pickering. It is an important differentiating notion, since it is a constraint on accounts of practice and of science generally, one that he believes other accounts fail to live up to. The constraint also serves him by identifying the object of comparison so that a particular gap, necessitating a particular concept of practice, can be identified. Pickering is right to emphasize that insisting on real time as a criterion does radically alter the job that a concept of practice is supposed to, and needs to, perform, since goals as well as skills evolve and are replaced in the course of real time. So this is an important idea, perhaps more important than the actual content of his account of practice. But it is also a bit obscure. Although Pickering's account certainly does not preclude the consideration of the researcher's own larger strategic purposes and goals, these strangely seem to drop out of the discussion, in sharp contrast with the dominant, indeed overwhelming, roles they play in both philosophical accounts of scientific method and such texts as Weinberg's *Dreams of a Final Theory* (1992). The image one gets from Pickering's account is a bit like the image of water taking the path of least resistance or greatest accommodation, that is, the direction in which extensions are channeled by accommodations and resistances, and seemingly nothing else. This is an interesting image, and underlines the valid point that scientists are largely blind to the successive steps that the successes of previous extensions will permit.

Nevertheless, it does seem plausible that scientists are guided by a great many and perhaps highly constraining general strategic considerations or general pictures within which they can see their activities and channel their efforts. They may also even be constrained by habits of mind of various kinds. Consider what Conant describes as general pictures and Holton later describes famously as *themata*, Toulmin describes as "ideals of natural order," and the like. These can be fit into the framework of real time analysis, in the sense that if they are in the heads of people at some particular moment, they are part of the intentions of those people and of their audience. And one could plausibly treat them as things that resist and accommodate particular extensions. But I question whether, by so doing, one effectively undermines the image of blind extension in a way that makes it essentially devoid of interest. If these things count as resistances, extending blindly within them looks a lot like thinking strategically.

THE PATH OF LEAST RESISTANCE

Yet unquestionably the adjustment of temporal scale to real time produces some novel results, especially in relation to what Pickering rightly describes as

one of the most neglected aspects of both sociological and philosophical accounts of science: namely the dependence of developments in science on technical developments in apparatus. The devices and equipment that scientists
use not only serve as fixed building blocks to constrain what data the scientist
can collect, but are themselves developed, sometimes by the scientist, to produce particular results. They often work, or fail to work, in ways that have little
to do with the validity of the scientist's theories or the formal ideas the scientist is trying to develop or test. This is especially true in particle physics, so
that a good autobiographical account of work in this area, such as Luis Alvarez's (1987), is focused on the business of getting machines to work, getting
money for more machines, deciding what kinds of machines to make, having
trouble, or, alternatively, getting lucky and getting machines to produce unex-
pected things that can be made into "results," and so forth. This kind of narrative about science makes science look a lot like the activity of inventors living at a stage in which a fairly wide variety of technical options are available,
and in which the consequences of technical choices are for the most part not
terribly well known, such as the early stages in the development of the auto-
mobile. Facts about finance, for example, as Pickering points out elsewhere,
come to play large roles in the decisions and directions in which ideas are developed, and these decisions are nicely adapted to the broader notion of accommodation and resistance.

Accommodation and resistance, then, are much more than just testing.
The notion includes things like success and failure in getting money and success and failure in getting a machine to do what one would like it to do, and in
a phenomenological sense fits very nicely with the actual experiences of scientists trying to get experiments to run and trying to figure out what to do next
that would work. Certainly this is something that is not driven by any sort of
simple (or complex, for that matter) formula and involves a great deal more
than ideas or the kinds of accommodations one might make with peers or audiences that is the focus of social constructionist accounts. In this respect
there is little to criticize in this account, and it is an important corrective to
overrationalized and overcognitivized images of the development of science.

To say this is not yet to appeal to the concept of the mangle itself, and this
raises a question. Does the notion of the mangle do any work that the notion
of contingency, together with the notions of accommodation and resistance,
has not already done? In what follows, I will suggest that it does not, and this
in turn raises the question of whether the gap Pickering tries to bridge with
the concept of the mangle might be too large to be bridged by *any* single concept if that concept is to be terribly informative. In respect of informativeness,
I think, there is a quite dramatic contrast in style between Pickering and
Polanyi. Polanyi tried very hard to identify a very rich set of analogues to the
various things that he claimed fell in the category of tacit knowledge, and was

especially concerned to link his claims about what went on in scientific discovery with more general psychological claims, for example about perception. This meant that Polanyi's account could be given support by psychological findings, and to some extent could even be said to yield testable implications of various kinds. So Polanyi's account is really a large collection of analogical devices, each of which was fairly securely rooted in either some well-understood explicit domain or some well-established experimental domain in psychology. This certainly lent a great deal of weight to the structure that Polanyi labored to produce, though it was still essentially analogical.

In Pickering's account of the mangle, the irreducibility argument is well developed. It is clear that no other account can deal with the contingent world of accommodations and resistances he describes. The concept of the mangle itself is relatively weightless. It explains so much that it is unclear that it explains anything. In a broad sense, notions like accommodation and resistance are pretty hard to get around. But like Schopenhauer's insight that the world is that which resists what we will, the mangle doesn't lead either very far or in a determinate direction.

Polanyi's version of this account did lead in some fairly explicit epistemological directions, notably of elevating the scientific community to the status of arbiter of scientific truth, because of the collective properties of tacit knowledge and the necessarily shared character of some aspects of tacit knowledge. Polanyi wished to trace scientific fact to the crucial element, the thing that made it fact, which for him was certification by collective scientific opinion. If we look for something similar in Pickering, however, I think we won't find it, or anything remotely like it. But Pickering does use language that seems to point to some such claim, and it is thus a puzzle as to what he does mean. My hypothesis is this: when he says "the mangle determines what scientists believe," he is not identifying something analogous to the activity of the community. He is saying no more than that collectively ratified scientific belief can only be made up of scientific facts that are a product of contingently governed processes. Contingency, understood in connection with accommodation and resistance, does the explanatory work here, not the mangle; or to put it another way, contingency together with accommodation and resistance are all there is to the mangle.

The role of contingency is an important point, but it is not a point that anyone really denies. Notoriously, Reichenbach dismissed Polanyi's work on the grounds that whatever happened in the context of discovery was essentially irrelevant to what happened in the context of justification. Polanyi had a perfectly good answer to this and, like Harry Collins *avant la lêttre*, said that there was a tacit coefficient in the activity of replication as well as the activity of discovery (1964, 94–96). But in the end this is a rather weak reply, in that the contingencies of discovery that relate to individuals seem to be essentially blotted out by the massive fact of the collective ratification of these discoveries, which seems less contingent.

Pickering's alternative might be construed to be this: there is no crucial thing that makes a fact scientifically true, or what is the same thing, determines scientists' beliefs; but rather science is a whole cyborglike collection of things that accommodate and resist one another in various ways. We should think of collective scientific acceptance as analogous to the case in which molecules in huge complex chemical structures are bound in networks by the forces of accommodation and resistance. We could say this. But I think it is hard to see what problem is solved by talking about the mangles and cyborgs that wasn't already solved by appealing to the contingencies, the specific technical conditions, the facts about scientific opinion, and the like, that make up the resistances and accommodations themselves.

My unease can be summed up by another analogy, a bad one, but one that indicates what would need to be done to give a convincing account of what determines scientific belief. Consider the possibility that scientific beliefs are essentially the product of a great deal of redundancy, so that the flaws or contingencies in each of the processes that produce scientific beliefs are of no particular moment. The situation may be much like the situation in information theory governing telephone communications: Imperfect telephone lines mean that the microstructure of information transmitted through them is always incomplete and these incompletenesses are entirely contingent, unpredictable, irreducible, and ineliminable, and grow larger with the smaller slices of time one makes. Nevertheless, because so many messages include portions of the same things contained in previous messages, the content at the other end of the line is complete. Thus, the contingencies of transmission are overridden by the redundancies in the message. What this model "explains" is the qualitative difference between established scientific belief and the kinds of result that are products of various contingencies and haven't yet become "established." It is a bad model, because "more evidence is accumulated" is a bad explanation of why beliefs are accepted. But it is a bad response to an important question.

I take that at least part of the reason that many critics of social studies of science discount the emphasis on contingency is precisely that in some sense it doesn't matter in the end. This is at least an issue that needs a substantial response. Whether the necessary response can be constructed from the notion of the mangle is one that I will leave to Pickering. But I will say that I do not see any way of getting to the notion of the determination of scientific belief in this more traditional sense from Pickering's starting point without substantial supplementation. Obviously, to say this is to move the goalposts. But as I suggested, this account like any account of practice depends on selecting fairly artificial goalposts in the first place.

nine /
THE SIGNIFICANCE OF SHILS /

Edward Shils, who died in 1995, was a widely recognized figure in social theory. He received many honors, among them the Balzan award, a Nobel-like prize for fields without Nobels; and the Jefferson Lectureship, perhaps the highest form of recognition in the humanities in the United States. Truly transatlantic, he divided his time between Cambridge and Chicago. He left a strong mark on the intellectual life of Britain, where he played the major role in introducing both Weber and American-style empirical sociology during the postwar years. The journal he founded and edited, *Minerva* (1996), published a memorial issue that included tributes from students and associates, especially in England, and a memorial appeared in the proceedings of the American Philosophical Society (Eisenstadt 1997). His work was the subject of a *festschrift* to which many of the most prominent figures of the social sciences contributed (Ben-David and Clark 1977), and of another edited volume, based

This article was presented in a different form at the Theory Section of the American Sociological Association minisymposium on the Vocation of Social Theory in Toronto, 1997. It was revised while I was a fellow at the Swedish Collegium for Advanced Studies in the Social Sciences, whose support is gratefully acknowledged. I am also pleased to acknowledge the advice of three anonymous reviewers for *Sociological Theory*, one of whom suggested that, given my references to what Shils said, I explain my personal relationship to him. I was in contact with him with some frequency after 1982, when I was a member of his NEH Seminar on the Sociology of Intellectuals and attended a seminar on Weber and Tocqueville. We usually met when we were both in Chicago, every year or two, and on a few other occasions. We always spoke about science, but the discussions digressed in many directions, notably toward the history of social thought, universities, and sociology. Shils did not regard me as a disciple, and, in the course of his that I attended while in the seminar, he would ironically note my disagreements with his interpretations of Weber.

on a 1985 Symposium, on his notion of center and periphery (Greenfeld and Martin 1988). A volume of his work appears in the University of Chicago Press Heritage of Sociology series (Shils 1982). His students, such as S. N. Eisenstadt and Joseph Ben-David, became world-class scholars in their own right. Toward the end of his life he was an active member of the Castelgandolfo Colloquia and an officer of its sponsor, the Institut für die Wissenschaften vom Menschen, which brought him into personal and mutually respectful contact with the pope. Memorial services were given for him both in Chicago and Cambridge, and a memorial symposium was held in Vienna.

Many of Shils's writings have been influential, and several are minor classics. "The Cohesion and Disintegration of the *Wehrmacht* in World War II," written with Morris Janowitz, is the classic account of military unit solidarity and the role of ideology in relation to it. His paper on "The Meaning of the Coronation," with Michael Young (1956), in which the idea of the charismatic character of central institutions appears in its developed form, has often been reprinted. Works more familiar to present fashion, notably Clifford Geertz's *Negara: The Theatre State in Nineteenth-Century Bali* (1980), are its direct descendants. The series of papers that followed "Center and Periphery" established this as a sociological concept, and as his most used concept. His short book, *The Torment of Secrecy*, written in the McCarthy era, is still read and was recently reissued (1996). It stands out as an example of Shils's ability to penetrate beneath the level of ideological dispute to recognize the intrinsic problems of social life that political conflicts embody, in this case the problems of trust that arise in connection with science, bureaucratic secrecy, democracy, and "populism," and the difficulty of resolving them from within the framework of liberal democracy. *Tradition* was published in 1981. His translation of Weber's methodological writings, now fifty years old, is still standard. New collections have appeared of his writings on higher education (1997b, 1997a). It is perhaps an important sign that his long-standing concern with civility, a topic whose importance is now clear, was the focus of at least one obituary (Boyd 1998) and one of the collections of his papers, beautifully edited by his student Steven Grosby, that have appeared after his death (1997d).

To speak of Shils as a lost figure would thus be somewhat peculiar. But there are good reasons for doing so, especially in connection with American sociology and more broadly with social theory. Shils never received the kind of recognition that his contemporaries Robert K. Merton and Talcott Parsons did, and in particular was never recognized for his "theory of society," though in fact Shils was one of the few writers on social theory in this century whose primary concern was the nature of society, and one of the much smaller number to say anything distinctive on the subject.

The reasons Shils never was taken up as a leading "social theorist" are various. One is that he never presented this "theory" in final form; indeed, for reasons that will become clear later, there is a category problem with Shils's thought that does not arise for Parsons and Merton, who are straightforwardly "sociological" thinkers. Another reason is that his thought appears not to hang together. The list of concerns and topics given above, for example, seems incoherent, and the list is not complete. Yet this incoherence is perhaps illusory: as it is sometimes said of Veblen, he thought systematically, that is, in terms of the overarching relations between his themes, but did not write systematic works. The topics fit closely with his main theoretical concerns, and through this, with one another, and each of his apparently unrelated interests led him to modify his general picture of society.

Yet another reason is this: his concerns were insufficiently recognizable to the kind of thinking that came to dominate social theory after the seventies, and all too recognizable as part of a fifties obsession with consensus, shared values, and the rest of the now unfashionable Parsonsian problematic. This, I will show, was a profound misperception. While still in his early forties, Shils collaborated with Talcott Parsons on *Toward a General Theory of Action* (1951), consequently sticking in the consciousness of many sociologists as a junior partner to Parsons. But Shils was never as narrow as this relationship might have suggested, and in any case he soon moved on with respect to the central concerns he shared with Parsons, and moved in a direction that has proven to be more durable and significant than the failed effort of the early fifties to create a scientific theoretical sociology around a scheme of definitions. Nevertheless the association lingered, and there were indeed many commonalities between Parsons's concerns and his own. Shils never publicly repudiated Parsons, and respected him personally. The discrediting of Parsons in the early seventies, justified or unjustified, tainted the concerns they had in common.

The misreading is understandable. Shils was read in terms of the familiar, the Parsonsian, and the other dimensions of his thinking were ignored. One moral to this chapter will be that what obscured his thought for American sociologists and social theorists is closely connected to the deficiencies of American social theory, and especially of sociological theory. The problem may be put in the following way: if anyone rose above the usual deficiencies of American sociological theory—its monolingualism, limited general literacy, ignorance of history and philosophy, obsession with local disciplinary status hierarchies, faddishness, political naivete, intellectual subservience to European thinkers, reductive thinking in terms of brand-name "perspectives," and its self-abasing craving for respect from quantitative sociologists—it was Shils. Yet precisely in the respects in which he rose above all this, it seems, his work ceased to be recognized as relevant, in large part because the context of his thought was simply unknown to his American readers. There is a sense, of course, that if he had been a European he would have been taken more seriously by American audiences, but this is not the same as being taken seriously on the original terms of reference of his thought.[1]

It is not the intention of this chapter to rectify all of the misunderstandings of Shils, or even to provide an overview of his thought, and indeed I will say little about the texts themselves, almost all of which are readily accessible. The chapter is an attempt to understand the larger intellectual context of Shils's thought. He read, as Thomas Kuhn said of him, everything (1979, vii). It would be hopeless to "derive" the thought of such an omnivorous reader from a set of textual "influences." But I will attempt to indicate, through the genealogy of several particular but crucial themes in Shils's thought, *how* he read, and how what he read was absorbed in his own thought, or used like the grain of sand in an oyster, as a kind of continual irritant to produce a valuable response, and how this improvement or transformation by slow accretion interacted with other, contemporary developments, such as the great political issues of the moment, which he in turn placed into a larger framework. This form of theorizing, or style of work, deserves to be understood on its own terms and, indeed, emulated. But before it can be emulated, it must be made visible. Relatively little of what Shils wrote was commentary, but the way he worked resembled writers such as Leo Strauss, who primarily expressed their own thought through commentary. And to understand each of them, one must know what they are commenting on.

The payoff for this effort is surprising. Shils's theoretical concerns can be located within twentieth-century thought in a way that we can see their historical kinship with the concerns of Habermas and Foucault, the twin gods of present-day social theory. Understood in the right context, the context of European social and political thought, Shils is the representative—and perhaps the sole representative, with the possible exception of Ernest Gellner—of a fully developed social theoretical defense of liberal democracy, a defense that is comparable with the critiques of liberal democracy found in Foucault and Habermas. But grasping Shils's significance without understanding the context is impossible. And to do this we must begin with the dissolution of marxism in the twenties, when the paths that lead to Shils and to Habermas and Foucault diverge.

DE MAN AND THE CRISIS OF SOCIALISM

Shils made many autobiographical comments about his reading and his responses to texts, both in conversation and in print (1982, 1997c). He often

1. I am reminded of the comment by the great historian of the Maghrib, Abdallah Laroui, who remarks in the introduction to the English translation of his great work, that "American scholars . . . tend to overestimate everything written in French, and this is true of not just an isolated few" (1977, 4). And not just, one might add, in French.

mentioned the books that had greatly influenced him, among them works that have now passed into the recesses of the collective memory of sociology, some of them works that were never part of the canon of sociology. One of these books was Hendrik de Man's *The Psychology of Socialism* (1928, cf. Shils 1972, vii), about class and ideology. De Man, one of the most prominent socialist thinkers of the time, is best remembered today for his nephew, Paul, the late deconstructionist and self-proclaimed "cheerful nihilist," and for his own political journey from the Left to the extreme right, or rather from the left-wing thirties notion of planning to the barely distinguishable fascist notion of planning, and from this, in one brief but defining episode, to collaboration with the Nazis (which led to his trial for collaboration and a sentence of death in absentia). De Man justified this step by suggesting that if there were to be a state strong enough to carry out planning on behalf of the working class, the state first had to be strengthened, and only fascism provided a means by which this could be done (Dodge 1979, 326–27; Pels 1991, 1998a; Sternhell 1994).

Shils's attachment to the de Man book, which he reiterated many years after he first read it, is deeply revealing, for a number of reasons. One is that the book itself was written for a European audience, in the political context that was formative for the major contributions to European social theory. It was a work of what Kolakowski calls the dissolution of marxism, another product of which is the more influential work of the Frankfurt School and Georg Lukács. It addresses the same puzzle that motivated the Frankfurt School, namely the question of why the proletariat had failed to live up to the revolutionary expectations that marxist theory had placed on it, but answered it earlier and differently. With it, we can locate Shils in the space of this discussion, which is in many respects the core conversation of twentieth-century social theory. The second reason is this: in this book we see several of the characteristic Shilsian themes stated both very explicitly and, moreover, together in the same overarching argument. It would be an error, of course, to try to derive his career from his response to one now-forgotten text. But the text is particularly revealing of what separated him from American academic sociology and from thinkers of a different kind, like Parsons, for whom this question never arose, except in the confused and politically jejune form of the convergence thesis.

De Man wrote as a socialist who rejects, as empirically and psychologically erroneous, the marxian doctrine of class consciousness, particularly the doctrine of true interests, and its various implications. De Man's book provides a psychological interpretation of the kinds of processes of worker social attachment later made famous by E. P. Thompson's *The Making of the English Working Class* (1966), though he draws different morals. De Man's basic argument is against the commonplace of marxism—and indeed of the present "political" critique of hegemonic power—that ideas about one's "interests" are often matters of false consciousness. In its classical form, this is the thesis that the true interests of the working class are concealed from workers by social attachments, patriotism, and traditional religion. De Man makes the opposite point: that worker solidarity is dependent on a prior moral sensibility, including a sense of justice, a sense of decency, and so forth, that is essentially the product of the Western (Christian) tradition, but is so deeply ingrained as to be almost instinctual.

> The individual human being who, as a working man or woman, reacts on the environment of contemporary industrial capitalism, is the product of a long precapitalist past. The motives which make him (or her) a socialist are not created by the present; they are rooted in that distant past. The time honored customs of social life have traced deep furrows in his instinctive and affective disposition, and these furrows indicate the course of the valuations and the volitions by which he reacts to present circumstance. His present life can only influence this course in so far as it creates new habits of affective valuation, and furnishes new customary directions for the will. ([1928] 1974, 39)

Socialist doctrine thus elaborates on a moral and social foundation that is already established.[2]

De Man's *Ideologiekritik* of marxism is based on a Schelerian-Nietzschean idea about the emotional substructure of theories like marxism, which are seen as sublimated expressions of more fundamental impulses of *ressentiment*. Socialist theories are an intellectualization of an "affective complex" that arises from the conflict between a particular deeply furrowed moral inheritance and present circumstances. The basic disposition of the European masses, for de Man, was "characterized by a certain fixation of the sense of moral values, a fixation which can only be understood with reference to the social experiences of the days of feudalism and the craft guilds, to Christian ethics, and to the ethical principles of democracy" ([1928] 1974, 39). The condition of the masses was such that these dispositions were unfulfilled, leaving workers with a feeling of being exploited, of impaired independence, but nevertheless with a hope of a happier future. Workers' explicit beliefs in equality, the right to the full product of labor, and so forth were psychologically compensatory ideologies. Each element of the belief system of socialism corresponded to an affective complex caused by a reaction to the conditions produced by the interaction between the environment and the basic moral disposition (45–47). In short, there was a conflict between ingrained moral ideas or intuitions and present realities, which distressed people and led them to adopt compensatory beliefs.

2. De Man points out that even the symbolism and iconography of socialism taps into these more fundamental psychological sources: almost all of the symbolism of the socialist working-class movement is of Christian origin. There is nothing strange in that. If symbols are to touch our affects, they must be linked with our customary associations ([1928] 1974, 134).

Like many other socialist thinkers, de Man argued that the marxist interpretation of the state as the executive committee of the bourgeoisie was simply
mistaken, and that anyone familiar with state operations, and with the minus-
cule and largely parochially self-interested role of the bourgeoisie in politics,
could see that the marxist analysis was untrue. The state is not only largely
self-directed, it is dominated by intellectuals, and intellectuals are thoroughly
bound up with the state. Intellectuals are produced by the state, in its universities, and the state employs intellectuals. The real significance of the French
Revolution, he suggests, was that it established the close relationship between
the intellectuals and the state.

De Man saw the problem of intellectuals—and for him this was a reflexive
problem, for he described himself as "a voluntarily declassed university graduate serving the labor movement in a salaried employment"—as a serious
anomaly in marxist theory ([1928] 1974, 230).[3] What in marxist theory explained the attraction of marxism for intellectuals? There was another aspect
to this puzzle. De Man was acutely sensitive to the differences between the
marxism of intellectuals and that of the working class. "I have learned by personal experience how much an intellectual feels expatriated in this environment," he says, and he catalogued the ways he attempted to become "an au-
thentic proletarian" (ibid.). Here is where he discovered "that most of my
comrades . . . were at bottom far more bourgeois in their ways of living and
thinking than I was myself" (231). The passions of the intellectual on the Left
were not the passions of the working class.

So what was the nature of the "socialism of intellectuals"? What was the attraction? He argues that some forms of the fascination of intellectuals with
marxism had psychological sources. The basic psychology of the declassed intellectual, the bohemian, was the resentment of the "unrecognized genius."
Bohemianism was soon outgrown as universities absorbed intellectuals into
the state apparatus. But the sense of alienation between the intellectuals and
the bourgeoisie persisted. Why? De Man approaches the problem of the incli-
nation of intellectuals to socialism through the content of the kinds of socialist ideas favored by intellectuals, and notes that it is guild socialism that most
attracts them—the idea, central to the Fabians and Tawney, that in the future
"the acquisitive motive of the capitalist and the worker will be replaced by a
new motive, that of service to the community" ([1928] 1974, 223). He suggests
that this represents "a desire to make all members of the community into intellectuals," an idea paradigmatically expressed in the notion that "industrial
work should become a 'profession'" (ibid.), or in Germany that it should be
motivated by a sense of public service, like a civil servant (224). At bottom,
de Man notes, these formulations are simply an expression of the *intellectuals'*

3. As did Gramsci (cf. 1996, 184–93), Mannheim, and a great many others.

own will to power, a will to "use their functions of domination in order to grasp the totality of power" (222). The misrecognition was entirely theirs, and it was misrecognition of their own motives.

The text had the core elements of what were to be Shils's great themes. There was, in the first place, the problem of the intellectual, particularly the intellectual with a desire to be "political," and in the second, the idea of tradition, of fundamental moral impulses that were deeper than ideas, and which informed and provided the impulses behind even those who were attacking the established order. Implicitly, there is the contrast between ideology and tradition, and the problem of ideology itself, of its relation to ordinary morality, and its psychological roots. But these themes were developed by Shils in a context that needs to be recovered.

THE EMERGENCE OF SHILS'S BASIC PICTURE OF SOCIETY

Shils did not immediately identify these themes as issues. This was characteristic: ideas that Shils came across and noted often did not mature for decades, and when they did they reemerged in forms that reflected his own attempts to think systematically about the nature of society. These attempts were made in a field of intellectual forces that can be crudely distinguished into four distinct groups. One was the phenomenon of the dissolution of the marxist tradition and the continuing political importance of the Left, especially for intellectuals. Shils did not abandon this topic, and for reasons that will become apparent shortly, it was to take on a large significance for him. The second was empirical sociology, which he practiced with a strong Parkian accent. During the war he participated in the analysis of the morale of *Wehrmacht* units, and had observed (as he, of course, was intellectually well prepared by the American sociological tradition to observe) the difference between primary bonds and the kinds of attachments to central things exemplified by the attachments of a few soldiers to Nazism. In the early fifties he was involved with the study of New Nations, and especially with Indian intellectuals, whom he had encountered first as students at the London School of Economics. The third was "sociological theory," reflected in his collaboration and friendship with Parsons, but also in his intense engagement with Weber and especially with the concept of charisma, a concept that is largely absent in Parsons, but which Shils extended creatively. The fourth was surely the most important: the emergence of a British liberal response to communism and fascism that gave an account of culture, science, values, religion, and politics that countered the attacks of fascists and communists with respect to each of these subjects. It is the least understood of the influences on Shils, but it is the one through which all the others became meaningful. It was also the source of perhaps his deepest intellectual relationship, with Michael Polanyi (see Swartz 1998; Turner 1996b). The arguments he derived from these sources set him apart from the American sociological tradition, and indeed from sociology itself.

Shils was no stranger to the dispute over the basis and nature of liberal democracy, and taught a course called Freedom and Order (later Soc Sci 3) before the war, at a time when a vivid debate raged on the University of Chicago campus between defenders of a natural law conception of moral truth and a "scientific" relativism (Purcell 1973). But Shils approached the issues in a way that is understandable only from outside the American context, in terms of a discussion that evolved in England during the war, and to which Shils was exposed firsthand during his wartime service and afterwards, when he taught at the London School of Economics.[4]

One aspect of this discussion has recently been much discussed in connection with Isaiah Berlin, who recently died (see Ignatieff 1998), and his doctrine of the plurality of values. Berlin was in some ways an unrepresentative figure of a group that had no truly representative figure and indeed was not a group so much as a current of thought within which were a large number of personal relationships. But it was a deep current, and the commonalities between its concerns were strong. Among its major contributors were Michael Oakeshott, T. S. Eliot, Michael Polanyi; at a degree removed, Friedrich Hayek, Karl Popper, and more distantly yet Berlin;[5] as well as some thinkers who are now less well known, such as J. P. Mayer and the Catholic Christopher Dawson, both of whom were associated with Eliot, who was Mayer's editor at Faber and became a personal friend. Mannheim's wartime writings are also touched by these concerns, and evolved through contact with some of these figures; several of them used Mannheim as a foil for their own arguments.

The commonalities were these: they rejected the ideological cast of mind, and sought to identify and defend something valuable at the basis of liberal democracy that could not be understood in the marxian way as an ideology. They did not so much find this thing—which they most frequently called tradition—as find arguments for its ineffability, its irreducibility to explicit doctrines or creeds; for the inadequacy of such notions as norms and values, or for that matter principles, as a means of characterizing it; and for the peculiar

4. "The Concept of the Political," Schmitt's famous text, was cited by Shils as early as 1958 and as late as 1992, as I will show in what follows. This raises the question of when Shils encountered Schmitt's thought first. A partial answer was given to me by Wilhelm Hennis, who told me that when, as a young student, he met Shils in 1950–51, Shils was very interested in Schmitt and grilled him about the subject, as did Leo Strauss.

5. J. P. Mayer, whose book on Weber is an exemplary work in this current (1956), went on to serve for many years as the editor of Tocqueville, where he extended the argument. It is to many discussions with Mayer that I owe my knowledge of wartime London and its intellectual life. There is no good published overview of the subject, though it is a very rich topic. It is briefly discussed in Turner and Factor (1984, 154–61).

qualities of tacitness and commitment that it possessed. Moreover, they found traditions, cultures, and the like in places previously not thought of in these terms, such as factories and the laboratories of research science. Rationalism, reductivism, and the closure characteristic of ideological systems were the errors they sought to avoid: explaining the rise of ideology was for them a problem of explaining a pathology. But the term *ideology* was treated with great care. It was the term of their enemies, and suspect in many of its uses.

Michael Polanyi, who wrote *Science, Faith, and Society* shortly after the war, tended to think of traditions primarily as traditions of learning embodied in institutions that assured their transmission, such as the law, the church, and science (1964). Polanyi also argued that tradition in this sense (far from being, as the Enlightenment had it, mere prejudice that reason could and should supplant) was essential to the higher activities of the mind itself, including science. This was based on an argument about the irreducibility of science to formulae or rules, in the fashion of positivism, or at least in the fashion of A. J. Ayer. Michael Oakeshott's essay "Rationalism in Politics" ([1947] 1962) made an analogous case for the irreducibility of political activity to rules or explicit principles. In 1949, Karl Popper published "Towards a Rational Theory of Tradition" ([1949] 1968), in which tradition was seen to be subject to rational evolution and thus justified by the notion of rational evolution.[6] T. S. Eliot's *The Idea of a Christian Society* ([1940] 1968) was written before the war, and published during it, in 1940; *Notes towards the Definition of Culture* ([1949] 1968) came out shortly afterwards, in 1948, of which more will be said shortly.

These texts worked with a distinction between tradition and ideology, though these were not always the terms employed—that is, similar to de Man's—but developed the idea of tradition in a different direction. The contrast between tradition and ideology became a matter of the difference between ideologies understood as doctrines purporting to be "rational" and traditions understood as the tacit bases of practice, in politics, science, the law, and in other areas of life. Oakeshott's essay is today the best known of these texts. Indeed, it is widely regarded as the greatest political essay of the twentieth century. It is the quintessential metapolitical text, concerned with the nature of politics and the errors that arise from its misunderstanding, and with the political implications of these errors. As Maurice Cowling later summarized it, it "emphasized that human behavior is a matter of art, not nature; that human conduct is rational when it exhibits intelligence appropriate to the idiom of the activity it is concerned with; and that concrete activity—knowl-

6. The text itself discusses Oakeshott ([1949] 1962, 121). The book in which Popper reprinted it was dedicated to F. A. Hayek, who became an enthusiast for Acton and Burke, as did Mayer. For a discussion of Hayek's relation to Polanyi, see Mirowski (1998). Popper and Polanyi had a brief flirtation and quick falling out. This hardly exhausts the connections, but is meant simply to give a flavor of the times.

edge of how to act—is 'practical' or 'traditional' knowledge" (1980, 272). Politics, of course, is a concrete activity. But it also dealt with values, though not in this language. Oakeshott's comment is revealing: "Moral ideals are a sediment; they have significance only so long as they are suspended in a religious or social tradition" ([1947] 1962, 36).

There is little in the way of an explicit theory of society in most of these writings, in part because their strategy is to point to features of political or social life, and especially of knowledge, that, properly understood, undermine the claims of ideologists and technicians of the human realm, reductive philosophers, and the like. They defended liberalism by denying that liberal politics was simply another formulaic doctrine, that it was a cookbook, like socialism or fascism, and then by denying that politics could be adequately conducted by following cookbooks. They were especially dismissive of the idea that *democracy,* the term that Dewey had made central to the American discussion (while becoming progressively more vague as to what it meant), was a sufficient ideal: Eliot notes that "the term . . . does not contain enough positive content to stand alone against the forces you dislike—it can easily be transformed by them" ([1940] 1968, 50). He wrote that the value of Aristotle's *Politics* derived not from its universality but from the fact that it was "founded on a perception of the unconscious aims of Athenian democracy at its best" and adds that "what I mean by political philosophy is not even the unconscious formulation of the ideal aims of a people, but the substratum of collective temperament, ways of behavior and unconscious values which provide the material for the formulation" (14). Oakeshott, similarly, in a discussion of the Chicago economist Henry Simons, comments that "[h]e is a libertarian, not because he begins with an abstract definition of liberty, but because he has actually enjoyed a way of living (and seen others enjoy it) . . . and found it to be good" ([1949] 1962, 39–40). The distinctions they urged were metapolitical, in the sense that they supported no particular political practice, but did distinguish invidiously between conceptions of politics.[7]

Why were these arguments so gripping, and what did they have to do with liberalism? The simple historical answer is that they were all directed against the idea that politics could be transformed, as the Saint-Simonian tag has it, into administration, or into "planning," but if this was their only significance they would be ignored today.[8] The key to their enduring significance is to be found in the fact that they have much the same practical conclusion as the very

7. The contemporary political theorist John Dunn states this in terms of the contrast between practical and theoretical reason, to the same effect (1990, 127–28).

8. The veterans of the sixties and the idea of participatory democracy would be shocked at the ease with which the figures of the Left in this period slipped into the idea that the rule of experts was a good thing and would be better than democracy (e.g., J. D. Bernal), and that culture and values could be planned (e.g., Mannheim), also and necessarily, by experts.

different, indeed opposed, Straussian argument for the possibility of normative political truth, which I will take up shortly. The claim that politics is a practical activity implies that it is not a theoretical activity, and that therefore there is no such thing as (theoretical) political truth as distinct from practical wisdom. To put this in a more recent locution, it is to say that there can be no such thing as political correctness, no extrapolitical principle that sets the standards for political activity, that defines its goals, or is greater than and trumps the claims of ordinary politics. Politics is more like the pursuit of truth than its application. And a politics that imagines itself to engage in the application of truth typically ends in the application of force. But liberal politics, that is, the politics of government by discussion, requires civility, and much of Eliot's attention in his writings of the forties was devoted to the argument, as Maurice Cowling summarizes the texts, "that 'civility in general' needed a 'total culture' which could not exist 'without a religion'" (1980, 123).

The background to this discussion is specifically English. Cowling's *Religion and Public Doctrine in Modern England* provides an elaborate genealogy of one strand of the underlying net of ideas, the problem of the political meaning of Anglicanism, and it is this strand that is perhaps the most alien both to the American discussion of the same questions, and to present thinking about liberal democracy. The American discussion of the problem of liberal democracy during the thirties had focused on such issues as the Natural Law basis of rights (see Purcell 1973) and the nature and meaning of "democracy" as an ideal, and in the forties on the problem of the intellectual legitimacy of a constitutional order based on the philosophies of figures like Locke, which were discredited both by historicism and by scientistic social science, which rejected the appeal to human nature and more generally the idea that norms could be grounded on facts. In the fifties, under the influence of Strauss (1953), this line of thinking evolved into the negative argument that nothing in the claims of historicism or scientism sufficed to disallow the possibility of normative truth about human nature, and therefore about the best political order; this in turn meant that the claims of the liberal political order to be in accordance with nature, laid down in figures like Locke and the American Founders, could be not simply dismissed.[9]

The American discussion was bounded by the issue of the validity and grounding of the Constitution. The First Amendment is a paradigmatic piece of liberal political engineering. By stating that Congress shall make no laws with respect to the establishment of religion, it answers the question of religion's place in public life: the state declares neutrality, and ties its hands in the face of matters of religion. In so doing, it defines the public sphere, the sphere

9. The Straussians did not embrace liberalism except, so to speak, tactically, as the best presently possible regime; and its philosophic sources were taken seriously—not on their own terms, that is, as true, but in light of this tactical consideration.

of political discussion—negatively, to be sure—by excluding issues that would disrupt the processes of persuasion and debate that enabled political issues to be resolved. This tactic is central to, even definitive of, liberalism. It creates a situation in which reasoned persuasion is possible by limiting the state to those activities which can be made subject to reasoned discussion. But there is another way to handle the problem of religion, and that is to allow the state to establish a church, and to regulate (or to encourage the self-regulation of) the political activities of the church, leaving it a defined sphere of the religious in which the state ties its hands and does not interfere. This was the English solution, which left the head of state at the head of the church and the national church interwoven with national life, but often in tension with the actual politics of the state. And this was the model that interested Shils most.

One might well ask what conceivable relevance any of this had to sociology, or to Shils. To see this one must turn to Eliot's *Notes towards the Definition of Culture*. The picture of society and culture that emerges in this text is marked by its origins in the problem of church and state, and the Anglican solution to this problem, but Eliot generalizes it. He traces the problem of religion and culture to primitive society, and the problem of class and culture to the Renaissance. A culture consists of the activities and interests of a people, or, as Eliot puts it, in a phrase that could have been lifted from Polanyi or any of these other writers, "culture can never be wholly conscious—there is always more to it than we are wholly conscious of" ([1949] 1968, 170). It is Derby Day, beetroot in vinegar, and the music of Elgar (104).[10] But it is more than this, as well: "we have to face the strange idea that what is part of culture is also a part of our *lived* religion," so "that from one point of view religion is culture, from another point of view culture is religion" (105). But the two concepts cannot be collapsed into each other, and the religious character of culture is not simply a matter of Christian belief, even in England: "the actual religion of no European people has ever been purely Christian, or purely anything else. There are always bits and traces of more primitive faiths, more or less absorbed . . . there are always perversions, as when patriotism, which pertains to natural religion . . . becomes exaggerated into a caricature of itself" (ibid.). Yet these widely distributed religious bits and traces are not entirely unordered in the Christian world: "anyone with a sense of center and periphery must admit that the western tradition has been Latin, and Latin means Rome" (148).

A "sense of center and periphery" is part of the inchoate feeling that is the true ground of culture. But culture, sensitivity to culture, and consciousness of culture, is distributed unevenly. In a phrase that could have been cribbed from a textbook of sociology, Eliot says that "[a]s a society develops towards functional complexity and differentiation, we may expect the emergence of

10. See Oakeshott's list of examples of traditions: "the common Law of England, the so-called British Constitution, the Christian Religion, modern physics, the game of cricket, shipbuilding" (1962, 128 n).

several cultural levels: in short, the culture of the class or group will present itself" ([1949] 1968, 97). But the relationship between class and culture is complex, more complex than Mannheim imagined. In the first place the meaning of the term *culture* changes in its application at different levels (134). Contributors to high culture may be members of an artistic elite without being upper class, and the upper classes may not be highly cultured in the sense of being particularly conscious of the culture. But "if we agree that the primary vehicle for transmission of culture is the family, and if we agree that in a more highly civilized society there must be different levels of culture, then it follows that to ensure the transmission of the culture of these different levels there must be groups of families persisting from generation to generation, each in the same way of life" (121–22).

For Eliot, there are and should be different cultures, and people should have various attachments, to the local or peripheral as well as to that which is more universal or central ([1949] 1968, 125). These attachments might include class attachments, but also cut across the category of class. That there are tensions among people's various attachments is inevitable, and also a good thing—uniformity would be the end of culture (131). Moreover, as the example of Antigone shows, there are basic conflicts of values in any society beyond the most primitive, and this too is a good thing for culture.

To acknowledge the deep identity of religion and culture is not to deny the existence of surface tension between the two. In 1940 Eliot had said that this tension is central to the idea of a Christian society ([1940] 1968, 44). In *Definition*, he reiterated and broadened these points by "insisting on the importance of various and conflicting loyalties" ([1949] 1968, 133) and on the point that this is a good thing precisely because "numerous cross-divisions favor peace within a nation, by dispersing and confusing animosities" (125). He also reiterated his insistence on the importance of the tension between religion and culture. The point is critical: when one finishes peeling the onion of social life, what one finds is not a core of something solid, like values, but rather a deep and irresoluble tension between two things that are bound to each other.

Eliot of course has in mind his own society and more generally "Christian society," the "idea" of which he considered in the 1940 book. The root idea is that the kingdom of God and worldly kingdoms are, on the one hand, bound to each other, and on the other, never reconcilable. Christian society is always unrealized, yet its Christian character is fundamental to what is realized. The external tension between the religious and the cultural in Eliot has a parallel in Weber's concept of charisma, which appears, flits, in and out of history, in and out of institutional practices, and in unstable combination with such things as discipline, educational practice, law, business rationality, and the like. At the broad historical level, an odd relationship of underlying tension and support between charisma and its partners holds. The tension is not precisely parallel to Eliot's, but if Eliot's is generalized to all societies, and Weber's emphasis is shifted from the charismatic individual to the charismatic aura of institutions, symbols, and the like, one has the core material for Shils's account of society. One needs to substitute this extended notion of charisma for Eliot's notion of the "religious" aspect or character of "culture," including institutions. In a sense, this is a short step, because Eliot had already extended the notion of the religious to reach what he himself called a "strange" result; and Weber had already extended a specific Christian doctrine of charisma to account for a wide variety of religious phenomena, and religious aspects of phenomena that would not ordinarily be understood as religious.

Shils did not hide these sources. In the preface to *Tradition*, which began as the T. S. Eliot Memorial Lectures at the University of Kent in 1974, Shils wrote that he "welcomed the opportunity [to give the lectures] because I thought it would enable me to compose my mind about this bewildering subject and also to acknowledge my debt to T. S. Eliot, whose writings had done so much to arouse and nourish my mind on tradition" and that he wished that "the spirits of Max Weber and T. S. Eliot look with charity on this effort to work out some of the implications of their unfathomably deep thought on tradition" (1981, vii–viii). The conjunction of the two names is telling, for it is the reconciliation of the one to the other that is at the core of Shils's thought.[11] In putting these ideas of Eliot and Weber together, Shils preserved their common idea that at the core of society (or in Weber's case, history) was a fundamental tension between its charismatic core and its actual forms, which nevertheless depend in part on their charismatic character. The tar baby of the unrealizable charismatic core of institutions can never be shaken off, nor entirely satisfied.

It is a picture of society that is at odds with Parsons. The tensions Shils speaks of, following Eliot, do not disappear, or tend to disappear, but are permanent. They are held in check by conflicting attachments, as Eliot also said, each of which having their own charismatic element. In contrast, values add up to a value system, at least for the Parsonian: "All societies have a more or less coherent set of central values and the more specific norms that express them in myriad particular behavioral situations" (Barber 1998, 57).[12] Charismatic elements do not necessarily add up in this way. Eliot saw that they live as bits and fragments, some pagan, some Christian, in the same society.[13]

---

11. Shils dated the beginning of his thinking on the issue of tradition, in which the notion of center and periphery figures importantly, to seminars that began in 1956 (1981, vi).

12. It is worth noticing the difference between the editors' preface to *Center*, which uses the language of "central value system" and makes it the principal meaning of Shils's term *center* (Greenfeld and Martin 1988, ix), and Shils's own concluding comment that "I was never satisfied with the argument that society is integrated by 'common values' or by 'shared values'" (264). Shils occasionally used this language, but for the most part he had something else in mind.

13. I recall that Shils once described the tombs of saints one finds scattered around the countryside in some Islamic countries as little concentrations of charisma.

Moreover, this is not an account of society in which anything, such as the continuation of the civility necessary for liberal society, is produced by equilibrating mechanisms and the like.

Shils identified many other sources for the idea of the essentially religious character of solidarity of social bonds. Rudolf Otto's "idea of the holy" (1924) also attracted him.[14] One can even find a rudimentary form of one part of the argument in de Man, who quoted a remark made by Guyau, Durkheim's source for the term *anomie*: "Religion is a universal sociomorphism; the religious sentiment is a feeling of the dependence of will-forces which man projects into the universe," with the observation that "[t]his much is certain, that every sense of social relationship tends to expand into a sense of cosmical relationship, in this way, that the motives which are seen to be at work in social destiny are introduced into the interpretation of the universe" ([1928] 1974, 425). This is the argument that social relations become sacralized, which appears in Shils in various forms, such as the fact that charismatic qualities are attributed to the center (1982, xvii). Eliot, as we have seen, goes beyond this by stressing the tensions this involves. Shils went beyond de Man in interpreting the character of common social symbols and their related moral ideas as religious, a strategy that was raised to its pinnacle in his essay with Michael Young on the "Meaning of the Coronation" (1956).

INTELLECTUALS AND CIVILITY

Intellectuals fit into this model of society in a special place. Eliot had seen that intellectuals were themselves greatly oriented to the center things, and that high culture was self-conscious culture. Shils, using the insight of de Man, saw that if intellectuals "rejected" their own societies they did so on the basis of a utopian standard of values which was itself derived from their own societies. They were, in a word, antinomian. They demanded that society live up to the impossible standards implicit in that society's highest idea of itself, or rather in a partial and overemphasized aspect of it that is believed to be insufficiently regarded (1972, 25). One sees here a reflection of the present idea that subalterns and the oppressed have distinctive knowledges. But Shils's point, based on his own extensive experience with Indian and African intellectuals as well as left-wing ideologists, was that even here we find a sensitivity to the center. Intellectuals' rejection of the societies in which they lived was not so much rejection as unrequited love deriving from the deepest and most

14. One might expect to find Durkheim as a source, but Shils claimed never to have appreciated Durkheim. The difference between Otto and Durkheim enables us to see why Shils preferred the concept of charisma, despite the fact that its main "individual" meaning was inappropriate to his purposes. For Otto, the numinous was self-subsistent or self-originating, like charisma, rather than reducible to its social origins, as was Durkheim's notion of the sacred (see Pickering 1994).

central moral impulses of the society, in a word, its sacred part: "However passionate" the reaction of an ideology against a culture, "it cannot entirely divest itself of important elements of that culture" (ibid.).

If we understand this in light of the problem of ideology and tradition that was so important in the forties British setting, and bring this together with the problem analyzed by de Man, we can see where and why Shils diverged from the kind of response to ideology found in Oakeshott, Berlin, Eliot, Popper, and the rest. The approach is characteristic of his thinking as a whole. For Shils, ideology was not error, but a deeply rooted though transient historical phenomena to be explained sociologically. The roots are in the basic tension between the sacred or charismatic aspect of institutions and social life and their actual operations. Shils added to this a bit of philosophical anthropology: the idea that people naturally seek to construct a "cognitive and moral map of the universe" (29). It may be noted that this need is located in individuals, though of course they ordinarily accept maps that are, so to speak, ready-made for them and are thus shared. Shils saw ideology, which is a systematic structure of thought, as the product of an "intensification" of this need for a map (ibid.).

Ideology is concerned with the sacred, a transcendent entity such as an ideal, and is thus inherently in conflict with ordinary liberal politics: "Ordinary politics are the Kingdom of Darkness; ideological politics are the struggle of light against darkness" (1972, 28). Yet ideologies have political consequences for ordinary politics, and occasionally invade and transform politics. Shils's older contemporaries of Continental origin typically understood the fatal course of central European history as a direct consequence of the failure of "ordinary politics" to contain these invasions, and accepted the inevitability of the collapse of liberal discussion into ideological struggle. Mannheim, whom Shils translated and had close contact with in London during the war, wrote, "If you come over from the continent one of the things that strikes you most is that over here it seems to be part of the accepted ways of life to leave unsaid many things which elsewhere would be plainly stated . . . differences of opinions are rarely fought out in full, and hardly ever traced back to their final source" (1943, 66). Mannheim thought this kind of civility was doomed.

The reasoning behind this assessment had already been fully articulated by Carl Schmitt. Schmitt argued that "the *ratio* of parliamentarism rests . . . in a process of confrontation of differences and opinions, from which the real political will results. The essence of parliamentarism is therefore public deliberation of argument and counterargument, public debate and public discussion, and parley" ([1923] 1985a, 34–35, italics in original).

Truth played a special role in relation to this process. Truth "becomes a mere function of the eternal competition of opinions. In contrast to truth [in the proper sense] it means renouncing a definite result. It is concerned with relative truth rather than absolute truth" ([1923] 1985a, 46). But "the development of modern mass democracy has made argumentative public discussion an empty formality" (6). "Today it is no longer a question of persuading one's opponent of the truth or justice of an opinion but rather of winning a majority in order to govern with it" (7).

Schmitt famously saw this as evidence of the contradiction in the core of the idea of "liberal democracy" between its "liberal" and its "democratic" elements. The possibility of rational deliberation belonged to the less democratic liberal past only, and to societies that were sufficiently homogenous so that rational discourse was still possible. The present, however, belonged to parties, and particularly to totalitarian or ideological parties, which by their very nature refused to "renounce a definite result," believed themselves to possess truth, and thus made public deliberation into a sham, since they participated in it only to express this truth, and were not themselves open to persuasion. When one of these parties seized power by winning a majority, it would end the sham of parliamentarism, whose peculiar attitude to truth it rejected in favor of a totalizing *Weltanschauung*. The fact that the Weimar Republic ended in this way was a powerful argument for the essential truth of this line of reasoning, and it is hardly surprising that it was deeply ingrained in the political thinking of the emigrés. Yet Schmitt was wrong. In the Anglo-Saxon countries, liberal politics did not collapse, and in the postwar period, liberal democracy became the normal form of government in Europe. Why?

In 1958 Shils published "Ideology and Civility" (1997d). The paper contains a direct reference to Schmitt's *The Concept of the Political* (28), specifically to the pages in which Schmitt explicates the basis of the concept of the political, and in which he attacks liberalism for having "attempted to transform the enemy . . . into a debating adversary" ([1927] 1996, 28). Schmitt reappears at the beginning of Shils's last essay on civility ([1958] 1997d, 63). The central feature of liberalism, according to Schmitt, is the creation of zones or spheres that are neutralized or depoliticized—the market, the religious, the legal, the scientific, and the cultural. Liberal politics, politics as discussion, depends on these neutralizations or depoliticizations and the respect for the limits of the politics and the limited role of the state that they imply. The problem of liberal *democracy* is that the "democratic" part of the combination is incompatible with these neutralizations. The majority will sooner or later decide that the line should be moved, that the formerly personal, or cultural, or economic, is political, and inevitably move in the direction of a totalizing state for which there are no boundaries to the political. "Totalitarianism" is the achievement of such a state.

Shils used slightly different terms to talk about exactly the same problem. For Shils, the domain of the liberal politics of debate is called "civility." Civility excludes certain things from debate, in that it neutralizes or depoliticizes them. Liberalism requires a recognition of exclusions, of the limits of politics. Discussion is impossible without these limits. The passions of religion and ideology preclude persuasion. The enemies of civility and therefore liberalism do not recognize the legitimacy of these limits. For Shils, the limits are a matter of at least a rough but possibly also quite fragile consensus. Shils was fascinated by, but never wrote on, the problem of the emergence of religious tolerance in England in the seventeenth and eighteenth centuries. This was a crucial step in the creation of the kind of rough consensus about the limits of political discussion and action in which civility consists.

The consensus originated, historically, in the liberal regimes of notables in the eighteenth century, and has gradually been extended. This extension, the inclusion of more and more people into the liberal discussion, is the great process of Western politics. Shils compared this to Tocqueville's secret force of equality (1988, 272). But he conceived of it in a somewhat different way, one might say spiritually, as the closing of the spiritual gap between center and periphery that formerly existed and had been embodied in the differences between the aristocratic sense of ownership of the society and the popular sense. He took the Putney Green debate to exemplify the difference between the old and the new, and he quoted Rainborough, who said that "the poorest he who is in England has a life to live as the greatest he," and Ireton, who replied, "no person hath a right to [share in the disposing of the affairs of the kingdom] that hath not a permanent fixed interest in this kingdom," that is, wealth in land or trade (in Aylmer 1975, 100). The growth of civility meant the closing of the gap between the two, and this meant the inclusion of the many in the discussions of the few, but more or less on the terms and within the limits of the rough "depoliticizing" or "zone of neutrality" consensus that had originated among the few. This process of the extension of civility is Shils's answer to the problem posed by the failure of Schmitt's prediction.

Schmitt had identified what he took to be the inevitable solvent of this liberal depoliticizing or neutralizing consensus. He considered the kind of political antagonism that "degrades the enemy into moral and other categories and is forced to make of him a monster that must not only be defeated but also utterly destroyed" ([1927] 1976, 36). In international politics, this is an enemy for whom merely containing within their own borders is not enough. Domestic politics has its own analogues to this degradation of the enemy into moral categories. It is this degradation—into the idea that one's political rivals are evil—that makes government by discussion an impossibility.

As Shils observed, this degradation of opponents into the category of enemy was characteristic of ideological thinking about politics (1997d, 28). And in the fifties his account of ideology became Schmittian, in the following sense: he recognized that the "political" issue with ideology was a matter of the boundary of the political, that ideological thinking was a denial of the boundary, and that something had to keep the boundaries secured, and that this something could not be a counterideology, for this would reduce politics to ideological struggle by definition. The answer was that civility was a "tradition" or rather was bound up in traditions that were the basis for the boundaries. He denied that the descent into ideological thinking was inevitable, and that the civility of Western democracies was a sham, a neutralization that was a political weapon, as Schmitt argued. Indeed, he pronounced the extension of civility to be a qualified success: not to be taken for granted, but no longer seriously threatened by ideological parties in the West, as it had been in the Weimar Republic.

THE END OF IDEOLOGY

Shils's conclusion about the passing of the threat of ideology was shared by other thinkers, notably Raymond Aron, who recounted its farcical life history in a *festschrift* for Shils. Shils and Aron used phrases very close to "the end of ideology" within months of each other in 1955, and were later joined in this by Daniel Bell. The issue, as both Shils and Aron saw it, was with the kind of ideological parties that Schmitt had in mind. Their point, in Schmittian terms, was that Schmitt's prediction of the collapse of liberalism in the face of ideological politics had been disconfirmed. On the marxist side, *ideology* had a different, non-Schmittian, meaning.

Two debates, equally bitter, ensued. The demotic debate, inspired by Bell's book, which used the phrase in the title, was inspired by the revival of "ideological" discussion in the sixties throughout the West. It was conducted for the most part in the terms of a marxism that was unaffected by Schmitt, in which the state was still the executive committee of the bourgeoisie, liberal democracy was its legitimating ideology, and opposition meant attacking this ideology. Reducing all political alternatives to "ideologies" was the basic move in this argument; the fact of "ideological conflict," it was circularly argued, was the living refutation of the thesis of the end of ideology. The main consequence of this debate in sociology was collateral damage: the fact of "ideological" conflict undermined the Parsonian image of society as rooted in shared values, and this ended Parsons's influence.

The other debate was different, and was conducted indirectly. The controversy occurred between sides that had taken the Schmittian argument on board, and moved beyond it. It did not hinge on terminology, even on the terminology of "ideology." Both sides understood the Schmittian point that in a political struggle all political terms and antitheses can become political weapons and that terminological quibbles thus are a distraction ([1927] 1996, 31). The similarities between this other debate and the demotic debate result from some commonalities in language, notably with respect to the term *ideol-*

ogy. But the language is used ironically and self-consciously in the second debate.

We may begin, to shorten a complex history, with the observation that the Frankfurt School had absorbed and incorporated the thought of Schmitt, just as Shils had, though it obviously developed it in different ways and for different purposes.[15] To put the point very brutally, when the first Frankfurt School argued that totalitarianism was the last stage of capitalism they already accepted the basic Schmittian recognition that that "capitalism," property, and the like are political rather than economic facts: a state in which "What is property?" is a political question is no longer a classic capitalist state, and the categories of marxist analysis apply only in light of the politicization of the formerly private sphere of economic life. Hitler achieved this, and the welfare state continued it. When they reached this point they became, so to speak, Left Schmittians. The Schmittian conception of politics was a substitute for the marxian notion of the state as the executive committee of the bourgeoisie, which the Frankfurt School had long abandoned.

Herbert Marcuse's famous essay, "Repressive Tolerance," is a late, but especially clear, document of this absorption. It simply repeats Schmitt's argument, unknown to Marcuse's popular audience at the time, but well known to other participants in this second debate, that the "pretense of an apolitical purity" or "designating an adversary as political and oneself as non-political (i.e., scientific, just, objective, neutral, etc.) is in actuality an unusually intensive way of pursuing politics" (Schmitt [1927] 1996, 21). For Marcuse, "tolerance," the political virtue of liberal regimes that is encompassed by what Shils calls "civility," once was "liberating," but "what is proclaimed and practiced as tolerance today, is in many of its most effective manifestations serving the cause of oppression" (1969, 81). As Schmitt had said, terms like *objectivity* "are incomprehensible if one does not know exactly who is to be affected, combated, refuted, or negated by such a term" ([1927] 1996, 31). This gives "Critical Theory" a task after having given up hope in the revolutionary potential of the proletariat—the task of exposing the political meaning of such terms, on the assumption that they can be comprehended if one knows exactly who is "affected" by them. *Tolerance* was merely one of these terms.

The task of post–Schmittian Critical Theory was to determine the nature of the political struggle, that is, the beneficiaries of the liberal regime, of government by discussion. This was a difficult thing to discern, and it became

15. I have not included a historical discussion of the relations between Schmitt and the Frankfurt School, though it is a fascinating story. The short story is this: the Schmittian sources were hidden and even denied for many years as a result of the association of Schmitt with the Nazis. In the last two decades they have been widely acknowledged. The full significance of Schmitt for twentieth-century social theory has only recently been seriously discussed. The best source on this is Pels (1998b), a brilliant and innovative text in its own right.

more difficult in the postwar period. The proletariat were now the rather visible winners in social capitalism. They had entered the tent of civility, and their leaders championed it. To stop at this would have been to concede Shils's point about the end of ideology, whatever language one chose. The sheer reduction of all terms, such as *scientific,* to their political meaning, led to apparent absurdities, as in Marcuse's attempt to treat science as ideology, an argument that Habermas critiqued (1970). But Schmitt's thinking was always concerned with exclusion, the exclusion of questions from politics, and this provided a basis for going forward.

Habermas's contribution to critical theory consists in his attempt to do so, and it is an attempt that is deeply marked by these Schmittian ideas. The problem with liberalism, for Habermas, is that it is insufficiently discursive, that it limits discourse in such a way as to exclude the questioning of the basic presuppositions, such as the notions of science, law, justice, objectivity, and so forth, which are used to exclude topics from political discussion. Liberalism depends on interdictions, and these interdictions have a political meaning; the ability to enforce these interdictions, the ability to refuse to answer questions, is the essence of power itself. The ideal speech situation is one in which there are no exclusions, no interdictions of questions. And this supplies us with a standard of criticism against which actual liberal regimes, with their limited discussions which exclude, affect, and negate, can be judged, and their political meaning made comprehensible.

There is a deep Shilsian response to this, and it is to be found in the concept of tradition. Habermas assumes that it is possible to surface—his term is *thematize*—the presuppositions of an activity or the elements of a shared lifeworld and subject them to discursive interrogation (1984, 82). Shils followed the reasoning of Polanyi's discussion of science as a tradition constituted by a tacit dimension that contained nondiscursively accessible contents. One of Shils's favorite sayings of Polanyi was that "science is an apostolic succession," meaning that great scientists conveyed the capacity to do great science not by writing articles, but by shared work in a laboratory. The hands of the bishop, in science, are the hands of the hands-on work of discovery. For Shils, it is impossible to be free of tradition in this sense in science, which is the most explicit and "rational" of all activities (see Shils 1981, 107–20).

The civility necessary for liberal democracy is necessarily traditional. It needs a "largely unreflective acceptance of these rules of the game of a free society" (Shils 1997d, 110). To say that civility is a matter of tradition is not to say that it is not bound up with beliefs and ideas, but it is to say that these are not the essence of the tradition, and it is also to say that the practice is what makes civility a matter of tradition. Shils's version of the idea of civility, however, was at variance in various ways with the tradition of talking about tradition that he absorbed in London in the forties, and it is important to notice these variances to see what Shils meant. Many of the thinkers in the British discussion did not believe that liberal democracy was for everyone. Mayer quoted Taine's view that "underneath charters, written laws . . . there are the ideas, the customs . . . in short a ramified network of deepseated and invisible roots beneath the visible trunk and foliage. . . . Plant the tree [of liberal democracy] without roots . . . it will fall at the first gust" (Mayer 1943, 78). Oakeshott was dismissive about the idea that the Germans had a political tradition at all. They tended to find its local roots and reason as Taine had, that liberalism was a wine that did not travel.

The idea of the traditionality of civility in Shils differs from this localized one. Civility is on the one hand highly particularized, with an identifiable series of self-understandings and a continuous sequence of transmission that varies from political tradition to political tradition, as manners vary; but is also a highly generic notion, for civility operates, analogously to Tocqueville's "equality," throughout advanced societies, and with similar consequences. The generic aspect was democratization or inclusion, as I have already noted: Shils thought there was a centuries-long process of the diminution of the distances between centers and periphery in that "the movement toward equality of deference, the reduction of differences in mode of life—both remaining quite large—and the spread of education and of civil and social rights are parts of this approximation of center and periphery" (1988, 257). The expansion of civility in the sense of more localized traditions supporting a rough consensus of the limits of the political needs to be understood in relation to this—as Shils liked to say, in terms of a circularity of effects (255).

The main effect of civility is that it "inhibits the extension of politics and the politicization of other spheres, e.g. the economic, the ecclesiastical, the academic and the domestic" (Shils 1997d, 95). The long process of inclusion signified by the phrase "the diminution of the distance between center and periphery" is made possible by the existence of a distinct political sphere, and other distinct spheres. The existence of distinct spheres makes inclusion possible by limiting what is included, though leaving these limitations open to criticism by those who wished to modify it, so long as the discussions were themselves governed by the rules of the game, particularly a mutual respect for the common good. By not importing into politics cultural differences, religious differences, and the like, it becomes possible for more people to participate in the limited zone of the political. The fact that these distinct spheres are themselves governed by religious and other traditions reduces the burden on the political, the burden of acting where consensus is impossible to obtain: the work of religion can be done in the church, not in the public sphere. The existence of limits on the political sphere allows the traditions of each sphere to continue and flourish. Civility is protected by the massive reality of these traditions, sustained by the primary group relations in which they are trans-

mitted or "reproduced." Both the negative and the positive side of civility depend on traditions. The negative side is the rough consensus (or, better, sense)
of what is excluded from the political. The positive side is the concern for the
common good that makes the discussions of civil politics into something other
than mere negotiations of interest (Shils 1997d, 111). These are the conditions
for the openness to persuasion that government by discussion requires, and
that Schmitt believed to have already passed from history.

SHILS, FOUCAULT, AND HABERMAS

"What should we understand by liberalism? . . . I tried to analyze 'liberalism'
not as a theory or an ideology . . . but rather, as a practice, which is to say, as a
"way of doing things" oriented toward objectives and regulating itself by
means of a sustained reflection." The words could be Shils's own. But they are
Foucault's (1997, 73–74). Shils was, very straightforwardly, what is now called
a practice theorist. *Tradition* is his term for *practice*. It means for him what it
meant for Polanyi, as contrasted to what it meant for Weber, which was a belief in the authority of the past. Polanyi accepted a kind of relativism or plu-
ralism about truth that was very radical: he was a philosophical antifounda-
tionalist of a sophisticated kind, who saw all knowledge as a matter of practice
carried in ungroundable traditions. By understanding Shils as a practice theorist, we can understand the way in which he represents a genuine alternative
to Habermas and Foucault.

The three stand in a triangular relationship. Foucault, too, is a practice theorist. There is no sense in which the kinds of *epistemes* or power-knowledge
complexes that appear in Foucault can be reduced to "values" or "presuppositions." They are nondiscursive foundations of discourse that may be exhib-
ited in various ways, but are not themselves discursively available in the form
of assumptions to be "thematized" and interrogated. In this Foucault is at one
with Shils, and in opposition to Habermas. But Shils, like Habermas, considers the construction of civil dialogue a project that requires our continued
reflective engagement.

All three are post–Schmittian thinkers. They accept the ultimately political character of the boundaries that constitute the limits of what Shils calls
"civility," meaning the distinctions that bound political discussion. They
come to different conclusions. Foucault captures the basis for the opposition
in what is only a slightly different context:

> Max Weber posed the question: If one wants to behave rationally and regulate
> one's action according to true principles, what part of one's self should one re-
> nounce? What is the ascetic price of reason? To what kinds of asceticism should
> one submit? I posed the opposite question: How have certain kinds of interdic-

tions required the price of certain kinds of knowledge about oneself? What must one know about oneself in order to be willing to renounce anything? (1997, 224)

Civility for Shils is a renunciation for the sake of a particular kind of rational political discussion; a form of discipline with limits or boundaries, requiring self-restraint, and "a general disposition to respect the whole" (1997d, 111). It may be asked here as well, What has been lost?

Each of these thinkers is a Schmittian in agreeing that what is lost is the truth, the absolute as opposed to the relative truth, as Schmitt puts it. For Habermas, this is destructive of human potential. Interdictions, for example in the name of scientific objectivity in environmental disputes, are exercises of power, and the elimination of interdictions is the path to genuine knowledge of the political good and the truth generally. Foucault and Shils see no "reason" that is genuinely autonomous from tradition or embodied practices, and consequently dismiss this. But they part company with respect to fundamental attitudes toward the liberal order. Foucault wished to preserve the possibility of protest without providing or believing in an alternative, much less engage in discussions of policy. For him, liberal practice, of which the machinery of repression and administration of the modern state is a major part, is inescapable, and liberalism is in no need of defense.

Shils, who said that "even the best traditions are not perfect and even these have costs which have to be paid in terms of other valuable traditions," accepted that liberalism and the present order have a price (1981, 323). But he also viewed it as fragile, and if no longer threatened by ideological parties, threatened by their cultural legacy in the form of the intrusion into ordinary politics of the radical attitudes of those for whom "there is ideological passion without a single authoritative ideology," a passion whose "ideological content is widely and vaguely dispersed around a hollow core of negation of existing authority" (1997d, 8). Foucault he would have put among these enemies of liberalism. Habermas posed for him a threat of a more traditionally ideological kind (ibid.).

Why did Shils think civility was fragile and under threat? In the fifties he was very much alive to the other kinds of threats to civility that still lurked, the most significant of which he called populism. Populism, like ideological politics, was inclined to degrade political opponents into moral opponents, into traitors, as in McCarthyism, without rising to the level of political organization or intellectual coherence of genuine ideologies. It is not too much to say that *populism* for Shils was a code word that means what Schmitt meant by *democracy*. But Shils grasped that these movements, American "nativism" and the like, were too weak to seriously damage civility. Yet by the eighties, he had come to see what he called collectivistic liberalism, the liberalism of political correctness and preferences, as a similar threat for its casual importation of the

THE SIGNIFICANCE OF SHILS ╱ 193

moralism of more straightforwardly "ideological" radical critics of society into daily politics. This threat is not as overt as McCarthyism, but is rather a danger of liberalism "obliterating itself through an unseen modification of its postulates" (1997d, 127).

A certain distasteful fustiness inevitably attaches to the language of threat and danger, and the discussion of threats and dangers with respect to such abstractions as civility and rational discourse is peculiarly distasteful. The Schmittian prophecy failed the first time. Why believe it will succeed now? Yet Schmitt may have gotten the prophecy wrong but the analysis right. And to the extent that we are all Schmittians now—all Schmittians at least in the respect that we take words like *objectivity* to have a political meaning, in which someone is excluded, negated, or affected—we are obliged to ask Shils's question of whether rational persuasion is possible if we do not bracket and more or less unreflectively adopt (subject to piecemeal reconsideration) the limits that these terms signify; and his follow-up question, of whether as analysts we have come to contribute to civil dialogue or are contributing to the replacement of discussion with struggle.

When a historian of France and French intellectuals describes the period between the end of the Great War and 1970 as one in which cultural polarization in politics ensured that serious discussion of national problems was jeered with the consequence that national illusions were preserved; that the policies that politicians "advocated—when they had something to advocate—were partisan in the narrowest sense, which is to say that they drew only upon the traditions and interests of a narrow segment of the community and made no serious effort to appeal beyond that segment"; and that intellectuals contributed greatly to this situation by their misinformed but theoretically elaborate "oppositional" stances (Judt 1998, 12), it becomes apparent that the problems of civility that exercised Schmitt and Shils are not merely the imaginings of hysterics. It should also be sobering that for France and Germany, Schmitt was right, that civility did fail, and that Foucault and Habermas are the legitimate heirs in their respective countries of intellectual traditions that contributed to the contempt for civil discourse that helped ensure its failure.

BIBLIOGRAPHY

Allport, Gordon. [1935] 1967. Attitudes. In *A handbook of social psychology*, edited by Carl Murchison. Worcester, Mass.: Clark University Press. Reprint, New York: Russell & Russell.

Alvarez, Luis. 1987. *Alvarez: Adventures of a physicist*. New York: Basic Books.

Ambrose, Alice, ed. 1979. *Wittgenstein's lectures: Cambridge, 1932–1935, from the notes of Alice Ambrose and Margaret Macdonald*. Chicago: University of Chicago Press.

Austin, John. [1832] 1995. *The province of jurisprudence determined*. London: John Murray. Reprint, Union, N.J.: The Lawbook Exchange, Ltd.

Aylmer, G. E., ed. 1975. *The levellers in the English revolution*. Ithaca, N.Y.: Cornell University Press.

Azjen, I., and M. Fishbein. 1980. *Understanding attitudes and predicting social behavior*. Englewood Cliffs, N.J.: Prentice-Hall.

Baldwin, James Mark. [1895] 1968. *Mental development in the child and the race*. New York: Macmillan. Reprint of 3d ed., Darby, Pa.: Darby Books; Fairfield, N.J.: A. M. Kelley.

Bambach, Charles R. 1995. *Heidegger, Dilthey, and the crisis of historicism*. Ithaca, N.Y.: Cornell University Press.

Barber, Bernard. 1998. *Intellectual pursuits: Toward an understanding of culture*. Lanham, Md.: Rowan & Littlefield Publishers.

Bellow, Saul. 1959. *Henderson the rain king*. New York: Viking Press.

Ben-David, Joseph, and Terry Nichols Clark, eds. 1977. *Culture and its creators: Essays in honor of Edward Shils*. Chicago: University of Chicago Press.

Berger, Peter L., and Thomas Luckmann. 1967. *The social construction of reality: A treatise in the sociology of knowledge*. Garden City, N.Y.: Anchor Books.

Boyd, Richard. 1998. Civility and social science: The contribution of Edward Shils. *Social Science Quarterly* 79:242–49.

Brandom, Robert. 1994. *Making it explicit: Reasoning, representing, & discursive commitment.* Cambridge, Mass.: Harvard University Press.

Burckhardt, Jacob. 1975. *The civilization of the Renaissance in Italy.* Vol. 2. New York: Harper & Row.

Campbell, Donald. 1988. *Methodology and epistemology for social science: Selected papers.* Edited by E. S. Overman. Chicago: University of Chicago Press.

Churchland, Paul. 2000. To transform the phenomena: Feyerabend, proliferation, and recurrent neural networks. In *The worst enemy of science?: Essays in memory of Paul Feyerabend,* edited by John Preston, Gonzalo Munévar, and David Lamb. New York: Oxford University Press.

Collins, Patricia Hill. 1997. Comment on Hekman's "Truth and method: Feminist standpoint theory revisited." *Signs* 22:375–81.

Conant, James B. 1951. *On understanding science: An historical approach.* New York: New American Library.

Cook, Gary A. 1993. *George Herbert Mead: The making of a social pragmatist.* Urbana: University of Illinois Press.

Cowling, Maurice. 1980. *Religion and public doctrine in modern England.* Vol. 1. Cambridge: Cambridge University Press.

Darwin, Charles. 1988. *The expression of emotions in man and animals.* New York: Oxford University Press.

Davidson, Donald. 1977. The method of truth in metaphysics. *Midwest Studies in Philosophy* 2:244–54.

Derrida, Jacques. 1972. Structure, sign, and play in the discourse of the human sciences. In *The structuralist controversy: The languages of criticism and the sciences of man,* edited by R. Macksey and E. Donato. Baltimore: Johns Hopkins University Press.

Dickey, Lawrence. 1987. *Hegel: Religion, economics, and the politics of spirit, 1770–1807.* Cambridge: Cambridge University Press.

Diderot, Denis. [1762] 1964. Supplement to Bougainville's voyage. In *Rameau's nephew and other works.* Reprint, Indianapolis: Bobbs-Merrill Co., Inc.

Dilthey, Wilhelm. 1960. *Gesammelte Schriften,* 8:38. Stuttgart: B. G. Teubner Verlagsgesellschaft. Translated and cited in Charles R. Bambach, *Heidegger, Dilthey, and the crisis of historicism* (Ithaca, N.Y.: Cornell University Press, 1995), 166.

Dodge, Peter. 1979. *A documentary study of Hendrik de Man, socialist critic of marxism.* Princeton, N.J.: Princeton University Press.

Dreyfus, Hubert, and Stuart Dreyfus. 1988. Making a mind versus modeling the brain: Artificial intelligence back at a branch point. *Daedalus* 117:15–43.

Dummett, Michael A. E. 1978. *Truth and other enigmas.* Cambridge, Mass.: Harvard University Press.

Dunn, John. 1990. *Interpreting political responsibility.* Princeton, N.J.: Princeton University Press.

Durkheim, Émile. [1887] 1993. *Ethics and the sociology of morals.* Translated by Robert T. Hall. Buffalo, N.Y.: Prometheus Books. Originally published in France under the title *Science positive de la morale en Allemagne* (1887).

Einzig, P. 1966. *Primitive money: In its ethnological, historical, and economic aspects.* 2d ed. New York: Pergamon Press.

Eisenstadt, S. N. 1997. Edward Shils (1 July 1910–23 January 1995). *Proceedings of the American Philosophical Society* 141:366–73.

Ekman, P. 1993. Facial expression of emotion. *American Psychologist* 48:384–92.

Elgin, Catherine Z. 1996. *Considered judgement*. Princeton, N.J.: Princeton University Press.

Eliot, T. S. [1940] 1968. *Christianity and culture: The idea of a Christian society and notes towards the definition of culture*. New York: Harcourt Brace Publishers, 1940, 1949. Reprint, New York: Harcourt Brace Publishers.

Ellis, Hayden. 1998. Face values. *The Times Higher Education Supplement*, 15 May.

Ellwood, Charles A. 1925. *The psychology of human society: An introduction to sociological theory*. New York: D. Appleton and Company.

———. 1938. *The story of social philosophy*. New York: Prentice-Hall, Inc.

———. 1944. *A history of social philosophy*. New York: Prentice-Hall, Inc.

Elster, Jon. 1983. *Sour grapes: Studies in the subversion of rationality*. Cambridge: Cambridge University Press.

Epstein, Joseph. 1999. *Narcissus leaves the pool: Familiar essays*. Boston: Houghton Mifflin.

Fingarette, Herbert. 1972. *Confucius: The secular as sacred*. New York: Harper & Row.

Fleck, Ludwik. 1979. *Genesis and development of a scientific fact*. Edited by Thaddeus Trenn and Robert K. Merton and translated by Fred Bradley and Thaddeus Trenn, with a foreword by Thomas Kuhn. Chicago: University of Chicago Press. Originally published under the title *Entstehung und Entwicklung einer wissenschaftlichen Tatsache; Einführung in die Lehre vom Denkstil und Denkkollectiv* (Basel: B. Schwabe, 1935).

Foucault, Michel. 1997. *Ethics: Subjectivity and truth*. New York: New Press.

Gauthier, David. 1986. *Morals by agreement*. Oxford: Clarendon Press.

Geertz, Clifford. 1973. *The interpretation of cultures*. New York: Basic Books.

———. 1980. *Negara: The theatre state in nineteenth-century Bali*. Princeton, N.J.: Princeton University Press.

———. 1986. The uses of diversity. *Michigan Quarterly Review* 25:105–23.

Gennep, Arnold van. 1960. *Rites of passage*. Translated by Monika B. Vezidom and Gabrielle L. Caffe. Chicago: University of Chicago Press.

Goldman, A. F. 1995. Empathy, mind, and morals. In *Mental simulation*, ed. Tony Stone and Martin Davies. Oxford: Blackwell.

Gramsci, Antonio. 1996. The intellectuals (from Prison notebooks). In *The continental philosophy reader*, edited by Richard Kearney and Mara Rainwater. London: Routledge.

Greenfeld, Liah, and Michel Martin. 1988. The idea of the "Center": An introduction. In *Center: Ideas and institutions*, edited by Liah Greenfeld and Michel Martin. Chicago: University of Chicago Press.

Gross, Neil. 1998. Review of *The social theory of practices*, by Stephen P. Turner. *Theory and Society* 27:117–27.

Habermas, Jurgen. 1970. *Toward a rational society: Student protest, science and politics*. Translated by Jeremy Shapiro. Boston: Beacon Press. Originally published under the title *L'università nella democrazia* (Bari, Italy: De Donato, 1968).

———. 1984. *The theory of communicative action*. Translated by Thomas McCarthy. Vol. 1. Boston: Beacon Press. Originally published under the title *Theorie des kommunikativen Handelns* (Frankfurt am Main: Suhrkamp, 1981).

Hacking, Ian. 1990. *The taming of chance*. Cambridge: Cambridge University Press.

———. 1991. The making and molding of child abuse. *Critical Inquiry* 17:253–88.

Hägerström, Axel. 1953. *Inquiries into the nature of law and morals.* Edited by Karl Olivecrona and translated by C. D. Broad. Uppsala: Almqvist & Wiksells.

———. 1964. *Philosophy and religion.* London: George Allen and Unwin.

Hansen, Chad. 1998. The Zhuangzi (Chuang Tzu): "In the social world: Is anything left of Lao-Zhuang Daoism?" <www.hku.hk/philodept/ch/>.

Hobhouse, L. T. [1924] 1966. *Social development: Its nature and conditions,* 12. London: George Allen & Unwin, Ltd. Quoted in Charles A. Ellwood, *The psychology of human society: An introduction to sociological theory* (New York: D. Appleton and Company, 1925), 18.

Huff, Douglas, and Stephen Turner. 1981. Rationalizations and the application of causal explanations of human action. *American Philosophical Quarterly* 18:213–20.

Ignatieff, Michael. 1998. *Isaiah Berlin: A life.* New York: Henry Holt.

Ihering, Rudolph von. [1877] 1913. *Law as a means to an end.* 4th ed. Vol. 1. Translated by I. Husik. New York: Macmillan. Originally published under the title *Der Zweck im recht* (Leipzig: Breitkopf & Härtel, 1877).

Jog, Mandar S., et al. 1999. Building neural representations of habits. *Science* 286, no. 26 (November): 1745–49.

Judt, Tony. 1998. *The burden of responsibility: Blum, Camus, Aron, and the French twentieth century.* Chicago: University of Chicago Press.

Kantorowicz, Ernest H. 1957. *The king's two bodies: A study in mediaeval political theology.* Princeton, N.J.: Princeton University Press.

Kessler, Hubert. 1941. Basic factors in the growth of mind and self: Analysis and reconstruction of G. H. Mead's theory. Ph.D. diss., University of Illinois.

Kovesi, Julius. 1971. *Moral notions.* London: Routledge & Kegan Paul.

Kripke, Saul A. 1982. *Wittgenstein on rules and private language: An elementary exposition.* Cambridge, Mass.: Harvard University Press.

Kuhn, Thomas. [1962] 1996. *The structure of scientific revolutions.* 3d ed. Chicago: University of Chicago Press. Reprint, Chicago: University of Chicago Press.

———. 1979. Foreword to *Genesis and development of a scientific fact,* by Ludwik Fleck; edited by Thaddeus Trenn and Robert K. Merton and translated by Fred Bradley and Thaddeus Trenn. Chicago: University of Chicago Press.

Laroui, Abdallah. 1977. *The history of the Magrib: An interpretive essay.* Translated by Ralph Manheim. Princeton, N.J.: Princeton University Press.

Laudan, Larry. 1981. *Science and hypothesis.* Dordrecht: Reidel.

———. 1984. *Science and values: An essay on the aims of science and their role in scientific debate.* Berkeley and Los Angeles: University of California Press.

Louch, A. R. 1966. *Explanation and human action.* Berkeley and Los Angeles: University of California Press.

Lovell, Bernard. 1975. Patrick Maynard Stuart Blackett. Baron Blackett of Chelsea 1897–1974. *Biographical Memoirs of Fellows of the Royal Society* 2:11–115.

McDowell, John H. 1984. Wittgenstein on following a rule, 350. *Synthese* 58:325–63. Quoted in Robert Brandom, *Making it explicit: Reasoning, representing, & discursive commitment* (Cambridge, Mass.: Harvard University Press, 1994), 659 n. 46.

McGuire, W. J. 1969. The nature of attitudes and attitude change. In *The handbook of social psychology,* 2d ed., vol. 3, edited by G. Lindzey and E. Aronson. Reading, Mass.: Addison-Wesley.

MacIntyre, Alasdair. 1966. *A short history of ethics.* New York: Macmillan.

————. 1970. Is understanding religion compatible with believing? In *Rationality*, edited by Bryan R. Wilson. Oxford: Basil Blackwell.

Man, Hendrik de. [1928] 1974. *The psychology of socialism*. Translated by Eden and Cedar Paul. New York: Henry Holt and Company. Reprint, New York: Arno Press.

Mann, Golo. 1986. *Erinnerungen und Gedanken: Eine Jugend in Deutschland*. Frankfurt: S. Fischer Verlag GmbH.

Mannheim, Karl. 1943. *Diagnosis of our time: Wartime essays of a sociologist*. London: Routledge & Kegan Paul.

Marcuse, Herbert. 1969. Repressive tolerance. In *A critique of pure tolerance*, by Robert Paul Woolf, Barrington Moore Jr., and Herbert Marcuse. Boston: Beacon Press, 1965. Reprint, Boston: Beacon Press.

Mauss, Marcel. [1925] 1967. *The gift: Forms and functions of exchange in archaic societies*. Translated by Ian Cunnison. New York: W. W. Norton & Co., Inc. Originally published in *L'Année Sociologique*, n.s. 1 (1925):30, 186.

Mayer, J. P. 1943. *Political thought in France from the revolution to the Fifth Republic*. London: Routledge & Kegan Paul.

————. 1956. *Max Weber and German politics*. London: Faber and Faber, 1944. Reprint, London: Faber and Faber.

Mead, Margaret. 1928. *Coming of age in Samoa: A psychological study of primitive youth for Western civilisation*. New York: W. Morrow & Company.

Mirowski, Philip. 1998. Economics, science, and knowledge: Polanyi vs. Hayek. *Tradition & Discovery* 25:29–42.

Needham, Robert. 1972. *Belief, language and experience*. Chicago: University of Chicago Press.

Nietzsche, Friedrich. [1887] 1956. *The birth of tragedy and The genealogy of morals*. Translated by Francis Golffing. Reprint, New York: Doubleday.

Nozick, Robert. 1974. *Anarchy, state, and utopia*. New York: Basic Books.

Oakeshott, Michael. [1947] 1962. Rationalism in politics. *Cambridge Journal* 1:81–98, 145–57. Reprinted in *Rationalism in politics and other essays* (London: Methuen).

————. [1949] 1962. The political economy of freedom. *Cambridge Journal* 2:212–29. Reprinted in *Rationalism in politics and other essays* (London: Methuen).

————. 1962. *Rationalism in politics and other essays*. London: Methuen.

Olivecrona, Karl. 1948. Is a sociological explanation of law possible? *Theoria* 14:167–207.

————. [1952] 1953. Editor's preface. In Alex Hägerström, *Inquiries into the nature of Law and morals*, translated by C. D. Broad, x–xxvii. Uppsala: Almqvist & Wiksells.

————. 1971. *Law as fact*. 2d ed. Copenhagen: Munksgaard, 1939. Reprint, London: Stevens.

Orlans, Harold. 1996. Edward Shils' beliefs about society and sociology. *Minerva* 34:23–37.

Otto, Rudolf. 1924. *The idea of the holy: An inquiry into the non-rational factor in the idea of the divine and its relation to the rational*. Translated by John W. Harvey. London: Oxford University Press.

Parsons, Talcott. 1937. *The structure of social action*. New York: McGraw-Hill Book Company, Inc.

————. 1951. *The social system*. New York: The Free Press.

Parsons, Talcott, and Edward A. Shils, eds. 1951. *Toward a general theory of action.* New York: Harper & Row, Publishers.

Passmore, John. 1961. Hägerström's philosophy of law. *Philosophy* 36:143–160.

Pels, Dick. 1991. Treason of the intellectuals: Paul de Man and Hendrik de Man. *Theory Culture and Society* 8:21–56.

———. 1998a. The proletarian as stranger. *History of the Human Sciences* 11:49–72.

———. 1998b. *Property and power in social theory.* London: Routledge.

Pickering, Andrew. 1995. *The mangle of practice.* Chicago: University of Chicago Press.

Pickering, W. S. F. 1994. Locating the sacred: Durkheim, Otto and some contemporary issues. Occasional Paper 12, British Association for the Study of Religions, Department of Theology and Religious Studies, University of Leeds.

Polanyi, Michael. 1964. *Science, faith and society.* Chicago: University of Chicago Press, 1946. Reprint, Chicago: University of Chicago Press, Phoenix Books.

Popper, Karl [1949] 1968. Towards a rational theory of tradition. *The Rationalist Annual:* 36–55. Reprinted in *Conjectures and refutations: The growth of scientific knowledge.* New York: Basic Books.

Pufendorf, Samuel. [1688] 1964. *On the law of nature and of nations.* Translated by C. H. Oldfather and W. A. Oldfather. New York: Oceana Publications.

Purcell, Edward A. Jr. 1973. *The crisis of democratic theory: Scientific naturalism and the problem of value.* Lexington: The University Press of Kentucky.

Rhees, Rush. [1954] 1970. Can there be a private language? *Proceedings of the Aristotelian Society* supp. vol. 28. Reprinted in Rhees, *Discussions of Wittegenstein.* New York: Schocken Books.

Rorty, Richard. 1991. On ethnocentrism: A reply to Clifford Geertz. In *Objectivism, Relativism and Truth.* Vol. 1. Cambridge: Cambridge University Press.

———. 1997. Thomas Kuhn, rocks, and the laws of physics. *Common Knowledge* 6:6–16.

Schatzki, Theodore R. 1996. *Social practices: A Wittgensteinian approach to human activity and the social.* Cambridge: Cambridge University Press.

Schmitt, Carl. [1923] 1985a. *The crisis of parliamentary democracy.* Translated by Ellen Kennedy. Cambridge, Mass.: MIT Press. Originally published under the title *Die geistesgeschichtliche Lage des heutigen Parlamentarismus* (Munich: Duncker and Humblot, 1923).

———. [1922] 1985b. *Political theology: Four chapters on the concept of sovereignty.* Translated by George Schwab. Cambridge, Mass.: MIT Press. Originally published under the title *Politische Theologie* (Munich: Duncker and Humblot, 1922).

———. [1927] 1996. *The concept of the political.* Translated by George Schwab. Chicago: University of Chicago Press. Originally published under the title Der Begriff des Politischen. *Archiv für Sozialwissenschaft und Sozialpolitik* (1927).

Searle, John R. 1969. *Speech acts: An essay in the philosophy of language.* Cambridge: Cambridge University Press.

———. 1983. *Intentionality: An essay in the philosophy of mind.* Cambridge: Cambridge University Press.

———. 1990. Collective intentionality and action. In *Intentions in Communication,* edited by Phillip R. Cohen, Jerry Morgan, and Martha E. Pollack. Cambridge, Mass.: MIT Press.

———. 1992. *The rediscovery of mind.* Cambridge, Mass.: MIT Press.

———. 1995. *The construction of social reality.* New York: The Free Press.

Sellars, Wilfrid. 1963. *Science, perception and reality.* New York: Humanities Press.

Shils, Edward. 1972. *The intellectuals and the powers and other essays.* Chicago: University of Chicago Press.

———. 1980. *The calling of sociology and other essays on the pursuit of learning.* Chicago: University of Chicago Press.

———. 1981. *Tradition.* Chicago: University of Chicago Press.

———. 1982. *The constitution of society.* Chicago: University of Chicago Press.

———. 1988. Center and periphery: An idea and its career, 1935–1987. In *Center: Ideas and Institutions,* edited by Liah Greenfeld and Michel Martin, 250–82. Chicago: University of Chicago Press.

———. 1996. *The torment of secrecy: The background and consequences of American security policies.* Chicago: Ivan R. Dee, Inc., 1956. Reprint, Chicago: Ivan R. Dee, Inc.

———. 1997a. *The calling of education:* The academic ethic *and other essays on higher education.* Edited by Steven Grosby. Chicago: University of Chicago Press.

———. 1997b. *The order of learning: Essays on the contemporary university.* New Brunswick, N.J.: Transaction Publishers.

———. 1997c. *Portraits: A gallery of intellectuals.* Chicago: University of Chicago Press.

———. [1958] 1997d. *The virtue of civility: Selected essays on liberalism, tradition, and civil society.* Edited by Steven Grosby. Indianapolis: Liberty Fund, Inc.

Shils, Edward, and Michael Young. [1956] 1975. The meaning of the coronation. *Sociological Review,* n.s. 1:63–81. Reprinted in Shils, *Center and periphery: Essays in macrosociology.* Chicago: University of Chicago Press.

Skinner, Quentin. 1966. The limits of historical explanations. *Philosophy* 14:199–215.

———. 1969. Meaning and understanding in the history of ideas. *History and Theory* 8:3–53.

———. 1970. Conventions and the understanding of speech acts. *Philosophy* 20:118–38.

———. 1972. Motives, intentions, and the interpretation of texts. *New Literary History* 3:393–408.

———. 1974. Some problems in the analysis of political thought and action. *Political Theory* 2:277–303.

———. 1978. *The foundations of modern political thought.* Vols. 1 and 2. Cambridge: Cambridge University Press.

Smith, Barry. 1997. The connectionist mind: A study of Hayekian psychology. In *Hayek: Economist and social philosopher: A retrospect,* edited by S. F. Frowen, 9–29. London: MacMillan.

Smith, Dorothy. 1996. Comment on Hekman's truth and method: Feminist standpoint theory revisited. *Signs* 22:392–98.

Smith, Eliot R. 1998. Mental representations and memory. In *The handbook of social psychology,* 4th ed., edited by Daniel T. Gilbert, Susan T. Fiske, and Gardner Lindsey. Boston: McGraw Hill.

Smith, Peter K. 1996. Language and the evolution of mind reading. In *Theories of theories of mind,* edited by Peter Carruthers and Peter Smith. Cambridge: Cambridge University Press.

Smolensky, Paul, Géraldine Legendre, and Yoshiro Miyata. 1993. Integrating connectionist and symbolic computation for the theory of language. *Current Science* 64:381–91.

Stern, David. 2000. Practices, practical holism, and background practices. In *Heidegger, coping, and cognitive science: Essays in honor of Hubert Dreyfus*, edited by Mark Wrathall and Jeff Malpas. Cambridge, Mass.: MIT Press.

Sternhell, Zeev, with Mario Sznajder and Maia Asheri. 1994. *The birth of fascist ideology: From cultural rebellion to political evolution*. Translated by David Maisel. Princeton, N.J.: Princeton University Press.

Strauss, Leo. 1953. *Natural right and history*. Chicago: University of Chicago Press.

Swartz, Louis H. 1998. Michael Polanyi and the sociology of a free society. *The American Sociologist* 29:59–70.

Thomas, William I., and Florian Znaniecki. 1918–20. *The Polish peasant in Europe and America: Monograph of an immigrant group*. Boston: The Gorham Press (Richard G. Badger).

Thompson, E. P. 1966. *The making of the English working class*. New York: Vintage.

Tönnies, Ferdinand. 1961. *Custom: An essay on social codes*. Translated by A. Farrell Borenstein. Glencoe, Ill.: Free Press.

Tully, James, and Quentin Skinner. 1988. *Quentin Skinner and his critics*. Princeton, N.J.: Princeton University Press.

Turner, Stephen P. 1979. Translating ritual beliefs. *Philosophy of the Social Sciences* 9:415–23.

———. 1980. *Sociological explanation as translation*. Cambridge: Cambridge University Press.

———. 1983. "Contextualism" and the interpretation of classical sociological texts. *Knowledge and Society: Studies in the Sociology of Culture Past and Present* 4:273–91.

———. 1994. *The social theory of practices: Tradition, tacit knowledge and presuppositions*. Chicago: University of Chicago Press.

———. 1996a. *Minerva* 34:1 memorial issue for Edward Shils.

———. 1996b. Obituary for Edward Shils. *Tradition & Discovery* 22:5–10.

Turner, Stephen P., and Regis A. Factor. 1984. *Max Weber and the dispute over reason and value: A study in philosophy, ethics, and politics*. London: Routledge & Kegan Paul.

———. 1990. Weber and the end of tradition. *Midwest Studies in Philosophy XV*. Notre Dame, Ind.: University of Notre Dame Press.

———. 1994. *Max Weber: The lawyer as social thinker*. London: Routledge.

Turner, Stephen P., ed. 1993. *Émile Durkheim: Sociologist and moralist*. London and New York: Routledge.

Wearne, Bruce C. 1989. *The theory and scholarship of Talcott Parsons to 1951: A critical commentary*. New York: Cambridge University Press.

Weber, Max. 1949. *The methodology of the social sciences*. New York: Free Press.

———. 1952. *Ancient Judaism*. Translated and edited by Hans H. Gerth and Don Martindale. Glencoe, Ill.: The Free Press.

———. [1922] 1978. *Economy and society: an outline of interpretive sociology*. Vol. 1. Edited by Guenther Roth and Claus Wittich and translated by Ephraim Fischoff et al. Reprint, Berkeley and Los Angeles: University of California Press. Originally published under the title *Wirtschaft und Gesellschaft* (Tübingen: J. C. B. Mohr [P. Siebeck], 1922).

Weinberg, Steven. 1992. *Dreams of a final theory*. New York: Pantheon.

———. 1996. Sokol's hoax. *The New York Review of Books* 8 (August):11–15.

White, J. B. 1973. *Legal imagination: Studies in the nature of legal thought and expression.* Boston: Little, Brown.

Wierzbicka, Anna. 1998. Angst. *Culture & Psychology* 4:161–88.

Winch, Peter. 1958. *The idea of a social science.* London: Routledge.

Wittgenstein, Ludwig. 1958. *Philosophical investigations.* 3d ed. Translated by G. E. M. Anscombe. New York: Macmillan Publishing Company, 1953. Reprint, New York: Macmillan Publishing Company.

Wood, John R., and Jean Serres. 1970. *Diplomatic ceremonial and protocol: Principles, procedures & practices.* New York: Columbia University Press.

Wright, Crispin. 1980. *Wittgenstein on the foundations of mathematics,* 220. Cambridge, Mass.: Harvard University Press. Quoted in Robert Brandom, *Making it explicit: Reasoning, representing, & discursive commitment* (Cambridge, Mass.: Harvard University Press, 1994), 38.

INDEX

Kant, Immanuel, 26, 120, 131
Kelsen, Hans, 84, 125, 131
Kessler, Hubert, 62n. 3
Kierkegaard, Søren, 158
Kolakowski, Leszek, 172
Kripke, Saul, 9, 122, 126, 129
Kuhn, Thomas, 95, 96, 97, 98, 107, 171; hot
    relativism and, 108, 111; on revolutionary
    change, 115; *Structure of Scientific Revolu-
    tions*, 96. *See also* paradigm

language, 17, 18, 64, 67, 67 n, 68, 69, 133; dif-
    ference and, 70, 70n. 8, 83; habits of, 133,
    135; learning, 58, 66; normative, 121, 129,
    139, 140; normative, practical, causal,
    134; practices and, 24; rules in, 2, 18, 25,
    36, 60 n, 135, 156; theory-theory and, 70,
    70n. 8, 72, 73. *See also* Background; lin-
    guistic model
Laroui, Abdallah, 171
Latour, Bruno, 112, 113
Laudan, Larry: *Science and Values*, 101 n
law, 44, 45, 46, 54, 127, 132, 140; binding
    character of, 127, 130, 140; iteration and,
    42, 43, 45; magical, 85–87, 103, 140; nor-
    mativity and, 53, 84, 140; path depend-
    ent, 104; theological, 138; validity of, 124,
    128; will of the sovereign and, 124–25.
    See also change; enactment; *Grundnorm;*
    Hägerström, Axel; Ihering, Rudolph von;
    legality; legitimacy
learning, 23, 26, 27, 29, 30; rules and, 80,
    133–34
legality, 53, 84, 104–5, 124, 125
legal positivism, 84, 125, 131
legal rituals. *See* ritual(s)
Legendre, Géraldine, 25, 26, 27, 28
legitimacy, 53, 124, 147, 148. *See also* force
Lévi-Strauss, Claude, 109
liberal democracy, 169, 179, 185, 187, 189,
    190; American, 178, 179. *See also* Shils,
    Edward
liberalism, 8 n, 106 n, 110, 180, 188, 189, 190,
    191; British, 175, 178; civility and, 190,
    192–93; ideology and, 176, 184, 187; lim-
    ited zone of the political in, 185, 186,
    190
life world, 14, 15
linguistic model, 37, 42, 49. *See also* Back-
    ground
Locke, John, 21, 179
logic(s), 20, 121 n, 143, 150, 154, 156–57

London School of Economics, 175, 176
Louch, A. R., 8 n
Lukács, Georg, 172

Machiavelli, Nicolo, 151, 153, 154, 155, 158;
    Discourses on Livy, 151; *The Prince*, 151
MacIntyre, Alasdair: contextualism of, 145,
    146, 155, 158; *A Short History of Ethics*,
    145
magic. *See* law; moral theories
"Making and Molding of Child Abuse"
    (Hacking), 113
making explicit, 131, 153, 154, 157
Making It Explicit (Brandom), 120, 153
Making of the English Working Class (E. P.
    Thompson), 172
Malinowski, Bronislaw, 107
Man, Hendrik de, 171, 172, 174, 177, 184; on
    marxism and western Christian tradition,
    173, 173 n, 183; *Psychology of Socialism*,
    172
Man, Paul de, 172
mangle of practice, 162, 163, 165, 166, 167
Mangle of Practice, The (Pickering), 160, 162,
    163
Mann, Golo, 157 n
Mannheim, Karl, 153 n, 174 n, 176, 178n. 8,
    181, 184
Marcuse, Herbert, 188, 189; "Repressive Tol-
    erance," 188
Marx, Karl, 110
marxism, 171, 172, 173–74, 175, 187, 188
mastery, 27, 28, 29, 30, 31, 32, 33
material inference. *See* inference
Mauss, Marcel, 80, 132; *The Gift*, 132
Mayer, J. P., 21, 176, 176n. 5, 177 n, 190
McCarthyism, 169, 192, 193
McDowell, John, 123
McGuire, W. J., 5
McLuhan, Marshall, 129, 130, 131, 133
Mead, G. H., 21, 22, 62n. 3, 66; imitation ac-
    count of, 60, 62, 62n. 2, 63, 64n. 4; on
    roles, 64, 65–66
Mead, Margaret, 3, 82, 84, 87, 88, 92, 101;
    Coming of Age in Samoa, 82
"Meaning of the Coronation" (Shils, Young),
    169, 183
mental contents, 2, 3, 5, 14–17, 18, 20, 37, 71
mental states, 59, 60
Merton, Robert K., 169, 170
Minerva (Shils), 168
"mistake" or "wrong." *See* habit; rule(s)